INCOME INVESTING TODAY

INCOME INVESTING TODAY

Safety and High Income through Diversification

RICHARD LEHMANN

BICENTENNIAL
1807
WILEY
2007
BICENTENNIAL

John Wiley & Sons, Inc.

Published by John Wiley & Sons, Inc., Hoboken, New Jersey.
Published simultaneously in Canada.

Wiley Bicentennial Logo: Richard J. Pacifico

For general information on our other products and services or for technical support, please contact our Customer Care Department within the United States at (800) 762-2974, outside the United States at (317) 572-3993 or fax (317) 572-4002.

Wiley also publishes its books in a variety of electronic formats. Some content that appears in print may not be available in electronic formats. For more information about Wiley products, visit our Web site at www.wiley.com.

Library of Congress Cataloging-in-Publication Data:

Lehmann, Richard, 1942–
   Income investing today : safety & high income through diversification / Richard Lehmann.
      p. cm.
   Includes bibliographical references.
      ISBN 978-0-470-12860-2 (cloth) JUL   2007
   1. Fixed-income securities.   2. Portfolio management.   I. Title.

HG4650.L445 2007
332.63'2044—dc22
                                                              2006038204

Printed in the United States of America

10 9 8 7 6 5 4 3 2 1

*To my wife, Sarah, for her encouragement,
and to George Weinfurtner and Aaron Himes,
for their editorial support.*

CONTENTS

Foreword   *xiii*

Preface   *xv*

Introduction   *xvii*

1
The Why and How of Fixed Income   *1*

Why Consider Fixed Income   *1*

    Growth versus Income (Stocks versus Bonds)   *1*

    What Kind of Investor Are You?   *4*

Investment Strategies   *5*

    Asset Allocation   *5*

    The Right Allocation for You   *6*

    Diversification   *7*

    Retirement Planning   *11*

    What's Exciting about 6 Percent Returns?   *14*

What You Need to Know about Risk and Uncertainty   *17*

    Subjective Risks   *18*

    Objective Risks   *19*

    Uncertainty   *20*

    Understanding Interest Rates: General Features   *21*

    Compound Interest   *31*

    When Interest Rates Rise   *32*

    Comparative Yields Explained   *34*

    What to Pay: Fair Value Pricing   *38*

    When to Sell   *40*

    Using Leverage and Margin   *43*

    Credit Ratings   *43*

Below-Investment-Grade Ratings   *46*
How to Read the Ratings   *49*
Credit Ratings Drift: An Ongoing Problem   *51*
The Federal Reserve Bank   *52*
Security Dealers and Brokers   *56*

2
Information Sources and How to Use Them   *59*

Investment Advice via the Media   *59*
Prospectuses   *60*
Misuse of the English Language   *64*
Getting Railroaded by China   *66*
When to Worry about the Accounting   *69*
Financial Statements   *71*
Balance Sheet   *73*
Income Statement   *75*
Statement of Cash Flows   *76*
Shareholders' Equity Statement   *77*
Defining Earnings   *78*
More Important than the Numbers   *79*
Summary   *80*

3
Bonds   *81*

Basic Features   *81*
U.S. Treasuries   *83*
Corporate Bonds   *88*
Equipment Trust Certificates   *90*
Direct Access Notes   *90*
Junk Bonds   *92*
Step-up and Pay-in-Kind Bonds   *93*
Zero-Coupon Bonds   *94*
Put Bonds   *95*
Insured Municipal Bonds   *96*
Lower Rated Muni Bonds   *99*

Conduit Bonds   *100*
Taxable Munis   *100*
Unrated Munis   *101*
Buying Municipal Bonds   *103*
Municipal Bond Defaults   *104*
Miscellaneous Topics   *105*
The Bond Indenture and Trustee   *105*
Call Provisions   *106*
Put Provisions   *109*
Money Market Accounts and Funds   *110*
Certificates of Deposit   *111*
Duration   *111*
Questions to Ask When Buying a Corporate Bond   *113*
Questions to Ask When Buying a Muni   *114*

4
Preferreds and Hybrids   *117*

General Features   *117*
Hybrids: Bonds/Indirect Bonds   *118*
Preferred Equity Traded (PET) Bonds   *118*
Trust Preferreds   *119*
Third-Party Trust Preferreds   *120*
Foreign Preferreds   *121*
Partnerships   *121*
Perpetual Preferred Stock   *122*
Buying Preferreds   *122*

5
Convertibles and Adjustable-Rate Debt   *127*

Convertible Bonds   *127*
Convertible Preferreds   *129*
Adjustable-Rate Debt   *132*

6
Income Stocks *135*

Overview	*135*
Canadian Energy and Royalty Trusts	*136*
Other Canadian Trusts	*138*
Real Estate Investment Trusts (REITS)	*139*
Other Common Stocks	*140*

7
Mutual Funds *143*

Overview	*143*
Bond Funds	*145*
Junk Bond Funds	*147*
Municipal Bond Funds	*148*
International Bond Funds	*149*
Exchange-Traded Funds (ETFs)	*149*
Closed-End Funds (CEFs)	*152*
Closed-End Bond Funds	*153*
Closed-End Preferred Funds	*154*
Buy-Write Funds	*155*

8
Securities and Other Investments to Avoid *157*

Unit Investment Trusts (UITs)	*157*
Derivatives	*158*
SEQUINS and ELKS	*160*
PARRS	*161*
Hedge Funds	*162*
Commercial Paper, Bankers Acceptances, and Repos	*164*
Collateralized Debt	*164*

9
Other Topics of Interest   *167*

Bankruptcy   *167*
Endgame Strategies   *173*
Tax Strategies   *174*
Dividend Strategies   *175*
Taxation and Mandatory Convertible Preferreds   *176*
Tax Reporting   *177*
Original Issue Discount   *180*

10
Summing Up   *183*

A Long-Term Strategy for Income Investing   *183*

Appendix
Internet Investment Information Sources   *189*

Glossary   *199*
Index   *227*

FOREWORD

Richard Lehmann has written the ideal book for baby boomers, the demographically bulging generation (77 million strong) born between 1943 and 1958 that is about to retire or semiretire. He lucidly and painstakingly demonstrates how you can get both capital appreciation and income via carefully constructed portfolios of bonds, preferreds (and convertible versions of both), exchange-traded funds, closed-end mutual funds, various kinds of fixed-income trusts, and, occasionally, high-yield stocks. These can vary in quality from investment-grade to junk securities.

Active management is a necessary fact of life: Times and circumstances continually change. But Richard Lehmann masterfully demonstrates how you can proceed with *wise* and active management.

Richard is a seasoned, successful advisor in the vast income-producing sector of the financial markets. That's why *Forbes* approached him more than six years ago to produce a monthly newsletter, the *Forbes/Lehmann Income Securities Investor*. (It can be obtained—for a price!—at Forbes .com.) He also writes periodic columns for *Forbes* magazine.

Bottom line: Richard's record is excellent. His returns in the past five years have been more than a match for equities. And that's in no small part because he systematically and meticulously weighs risks and rewards. He also knows when to cut his losses on a security that falters. Readers and clients also appreciate Richard's acute awareness of the income tax status of all the securities he studies—for instance, some preferreds qualify for the dividend exclusion; others do not.

Richard is always scouting for the as-yet-unappreciated opportunities. When oil and gas prices started moving up in 2004, he advised clients to invest in Canadian energy trusts (as well as in some U.S. versions). These peculiar securities have thrown off immensely positive returns and have periodically paid back principal—a sort of Wild West version of a GNMA (without the U.S. government backing, of course). A little over a year ago, Richard courageously recommended that investors add preferred issues of Ford and GM to their portfolios. Great calls, both. As the two struggling giants have taken painful steps to return to profitability, the value of their preferreds have gone up smartly—and investors are enjoying attractively juicy yields, too.

Not every security Richard recommends is a winner—which is not unlikely in volatile times like these and when your universe includes companies whose finances are a bit dicey. But his *portfolios* do well.

There will again be periods of bubbling bull markets for stocks, and Richard's approach may strike some as a tad dull. But investors who have discipline and are clear in their financial goals will not succumb to yet another round of "irrational exuberance." They will, instead, find Richard Lehmann's sage approach rewarding, as well as providing a safe harbor for all kinds of economic weather.

STEVE FORBES

PREFACE

The market choices for income investing have become so dynamic and evolutionary that any book on the subject that is five years old is out of date. This book tries to avoid using the term *fixed-income investing* because, like economics, income investing is anything but fixed. The investment vehicles I will be reviewing and recommending range well beyond traditional fixed-income securities or creditor instruments such as bonds.

In the current low interest rate environment, achieving a high level of income without also assuming inordinate levels of risk requires a blending of investments that are dependent on diverse economic events, not just interest rates. This is much like the reasoning behind buying indexed stock funds, reducing risk through diversification across a range of sectors, not just companies.

Before beginning this book I asked myself, does the world really need another book on fixed-income investing? After reviewing the current offerings on the subject at Amazon.com, I realize that some of them are 500-page textbooks, written for those who want a course in fixed-income investing and are willing to try to learn the subject without an instructor. Other books focus on strategies that are defensive in nature: Feel good by settling for conservative (low) returns, generally through investing in bond funds. What is presented here is an introductory work that covers the minimum you need to know about fixed-income fundamentals, a sample of real-life situations where selection skills are helpful, and a discourse on just one strategy, geared to individual investors and the types of securities best suited for implementing that strategy.

The traditional vehicle for income investing, *bonds*, has been hijacked by the institutional market and shuns individual investors. In the process, due to massive institutional demand, the yields on bonds no longer provide an adequate rate of return. On the other hand, a variety of new products are available that are ideally suited for individuals but that are not well understood and therefore are underutilized by those seeking high dividends and interest income.

It is widely reported that the baby boomers have not adequately saved for their rapidly approaching retirement years. Because of this, many boomers believe the only way to catch up is by investing in common stocks. This book provides a safer alternative—income securities that can provide a 7 to 8 percent annual cash income without the downside risks inherent in the stock market. For the past six years, and probably for quite a few years to come, this has proven to be a winning approach.

From over 20 years of fixed-income investing and writing about fixed income, I have learned a few lessons that will help individual investors cut through the complexities inherent in income securities. In giving investment advice, I have always strived to couple such advice with how I came to a conclusion. Teaching investors the habit of looking for this in all the free advice available on TV, the Internet, and publications will help them to differentiate advice they can act on from advice to ignore.

INTRODUCTION

Since their 1982 high, interest rates have been on a relentless decline. In such an environment, buy and hold investing proved to be a very successful investment concept. Alas, all good things must come to an end. Interest rates have come down to a level where there is little room for further declines, but a lot of room for rate rises. A buy and hold strategy now faces serious risk of capital erosion. A strategy based on income source diversification offers greater opportunities and safety.

For 20 years I have been writing and advising on fixed-income securities in a monthly newsletter. Nothing so sharpens the mind on a subject as the need to produce a newsletter, month after month, on a subject most investors think of as boring. Finding new material and recommendations in the fixed-income area is no longer boring, thanks to the universe of new and hybrid preferreds that are fast coming to dominate the retail fixed-income market. Likewise, Exchange Traded Funds (ETFs) and various common stocks have become vehicles for generating cash income and not just capital appreciation. The very nature of these securities, their high liquidity (NYSE-traded) and low unit value (generally $25), has opened up opportunities for entirely new income investment strategies. It's not your father's bond market anymore.

For those new to income investing, it is worth noting how it differs from investing in stocks. Stocks, as an investment vehicle, are easy to understand because they are almost uniform in their rights and features. A share of IBM is the same instrument as a share of Exxon. Bonds and preferreds, on the other hand, differ significantly from one another, even for different issues from the same company, and require study and understanding of their unique features. The virtue of income securities and what makes them worth studying is that, once you understand them, the selection process is substantially easier and safer than for stocks. This is mainly because credit ratings make risk evaluation highly reliable. You also aren't as vulnerable to price fluctuations due to quarterly earnings forecasts and missed forecasts, since the company's survival, not its prosperity, is your main exposure. You won't often see a bond or preferred drop by 20 percent when a company misses its sales or earnings forecasts, but when this happens it probably represents a buying opportunity.

The book broadly addresses three subjects: income investing concepts you need to understand, the various investment vehicles currently attractive, and investment strategies. Note that I will touch on only those vehicles I prefer for my newsletter subscribers and advisory clients. It leaves out much more than it includes. Unlike other books on income investments, I have chosen to advocate herein the approaches I use every day rather than providing a 500-page guide to all the investment vehicles, techniques, and jargon that populates these markets. Thus, readers will find here a guide of the minimum they need to know and, I hope, guidance in how to then use that knowledge.

My goal is to show readers that, far from all they may have read about stock versus fixed-income investing, it is not an either/or choice. Properly done, a portfolio with a diversification of income securities can, over time, equal or exceed the returns from common stock investing—and with much lower risk. For the past six years, at any rate, that has been the case.

The Why and How of Fixed Income

Why Consider Fixed Income?

Growth versus Income (Stocks versus Bonds)

Experts have been saying for years how much better stocks have been in providing long-term profits than bonds. Depending on which study you read, stocks have returned an estimated 7 to 11 percent a year for the past 100 to 200 years. Bonds, on the other hand, are credited with returns of just 2 to 4 percent, again depending on the study. The obvious conclusion the investor is supposed to draw from these studies is that a choice between stocks or bonds is a no-brainer. Why, then, are the fixed-income markets several times bigger than the stock market? Why do many more investment dollars go into bonds and preferreds rather than stock? There are many ways to answer this question, and in those answers, you may just find your reason for considering fixed-income securities.

The principal reason fixed-income securities have faired badly in these studies is inflation. Inflation has historically sapped anywhere from 20 percent to more than 100 percent of the return paid by bonds. While this remains a perennial weakness of fixed-income securities, it has become less so over time. The ravages of inflation are much better understood today by those in government whose responsibility is to control it. More important, the tools for controlling it are in place and not as vulnerable to the political forces of the day. Another reason for the poor showing for bonds is that such studies used U.S. Treasuries as the fixed-income benchmark. While this is the premier bond instrument in the world, it is hardly representative of the fixed-income universe. Because of its high quality, it is easily 1 to 4 percent below most other debt instruments in its rate of return. Today's bonds and preferreds offer an array of risks and yields for which no historic equivalent exists for comparison. This book focuses on many of these investment instruments, many yielding relatively low-risk returns of 8 percent or more.

A second consideration in evaluating stock-versus-bond studies is volatility. The returns cited for equities include years in which they were as much as plus or minus 20 percent. Additionally, within any given year, price fluctuations of plus or minus 50 percent are not uncommon. Hence, any given investor, depending on when and how much he or she invested, could average less than half or more than twice the 7 percent return rate, which has been cited by studies as a long-term average. Buying into a mutual fund can mitigate some of the intrayear volatility, but not the interyear volatility. Bonds, on the other hand, have only a fraction of this volatility. In fact, you control much of it by virtue of how long a maturity date or credit quality you select.

With stocks, the investor is putting his or her future into the hands of company managers whose skills, priorities, and loyalties are constantly shifting and open to question. While high salaries and generous options are given to them to ensure loyalty, this has proven only partially successful and may serve to encourage risk taking beyond their management skills in order to enhance stock prices. With bonds and preferreds, investors are insulated against most mismanagement unless it proves fatal, but even then, they stand ahead of shareholders in being repaid in any corporate reorganization or liquidation. Investing via a mutual fund further removes the investors' control over their funds, since now the judgments and priorities of the fund managers are a factor as well.

Looking forward, I doubt whether past history is the best way to predict future performance. The principal reason for this is that past stock performance was in large part due to high dividend payments. According to a recent study by Robert Arnott and Peter Bernstein in the *Financial Analysts Journal*, as much as 5 percent of the 7 percent historic return for stocks came through dividend yields. During the 1990s this percentage dwindled to 1.5 percent. This is one of the unintended consequences of management stock options. Since stock options become valuable through price appreciation, not dividends, profits are going to be used either to buy back shares or launch new ventures, no matter how marginal. The study went on to note that only 1.4 percent of the 7 percent historic return came from earnings growth. Since economic growth has been over 2 percent for most of this century, it means public companies are not keeping pace with the economy as a whole. Hence, the money retained by corporations got a poorer return for investors than the 5 percent that they distributed. What then can we expect now that dividend payouts have slipped to only 1.5 percent? Although recent tax law changes have made dividends more attractive, increases in dividend payouts have been slow to gain momentum, which has not been helped by the fact that the tax law change is set to expire in 2010 unless extended by Congress.

The main reason, though, why bonds will continue to outsell common stocks is that they reflect the wisdom expressed best by Ben Franklin: "A bird in the hand is worth two in the bush." Fixed-income securities offer a definite rate of return and a definite date in the future when they will return a definite amount owed. These are, or should be, of ever-increasing importance the closer one gets to retirement.

Selecting stock investments differs from selecting a fixed-income security in one critical respect. *In order to profit in stocks, the company must prosper. Not so for fixed income. To make money in fixed-income investments, the company need only survive.* Making a judgment about a company's ability to prosper is often extremely complex, because it is so dependent on such intangibles as the general economy, the legal environment, industry trends, management ability, and just plain good luck.

Judging a company's ability to survive is more dependent on data and much less dependent on intangibles. Learn how to understand the data and you've learned how to invest.

Understanding the data, however, does require learning how to interpret it. This is not to say that the intangibles affecting stocks don't also affect bonds, but rather that the effect is generally not as severe and takes place over a longer period of time.

What Kind of Investor Are You?

You may have picked up this book precisely because you don't know the answer to this question. Hopefully, you will be able to answer it before you are finished reading. The question usually comes up because many individuals fail or even resist putting themselves into a defined category. Yeah, I'm unique. But I haven't saved enough for my retirement, and I'm getting close enough to retirement to worry, and I don't have a clear plan for saving or a clear investment strategy, and I don't even know how much I'll need to retire, and my present investments are going nowhere. Sure, you're unique, but maybe you can find your spouse or an anonymous friend in the following investor types.

The first and most common investor species is the *buy and hold investor*. These investors buy good, safe things like Treasuries, munis, CDs, money market funds, and investment-grade bonds. They want to sleep well at night, so they take no risks. They also get a lousy rate of return. Ideally, we'd all like to be so blasé about investing, but most of us don't have enough resources to afford that, as evidenced by the fact you are reading this book. (Just kidding!)

The second investor type is the *total return investor*. These individuals want to grow their portfolio by both income and capital appreciation and have no current urgency for cash income. They have a broader array of investment choices and a bit higher risk tolerance level. They are generally still working full-time and growing their portfolio as much by new savings as by portfolio growth. *This group will get the most benefit from this book*.

The third type of investor is the *scared investor*. These individuals are scared of any risk, probably because of bad personal experience, or they are scared because they haven't a clue about investing. This group is the most sought after by financial industry people because they can be talked into buying the most expensive or risky investments. They buy mutual funds and whatever else a broker can talk them into because they won't take the time or effort to learn investment fundamentals such as are found in this book. *I can help scared investors if they are willing to learn, because mentally they have the most important attribute an income investor can have—fear.*

The fourth type of investor is the *desperate investor*. These people know they are way behind in planning for their retirement and are looking to hit a home run to catch up. They differ from the scared investor in that they think they know what they're doing because they've had some successes in the past. What they've really had in the past was a smattering of luck and selective memory. The fact that they're desperate means their luck comes only now and again. If you are one of these investors, you are beyond my help. Return this book to where you bought it and ask for your money back. And this time, I'm not kidding!

It's not my goal to fit everyone into my formula for income investing. You need to develop a strategy with which you can be comfortable for years or even decades—one that can succeed across different business cycles and financial downturns. If you learn the fundamentals detailed in this book, I'm sure a more confident you will emerge. And that new you will become a more successful income investor.

Investment Strategies

Asset Allocation

How many investors can tell you what their asset allocation is? For that matter, how many investors can tell you what asset allocation is? To appreciate the importance of this investment basic, let's first define it. *Asset allocation* is how you distribute the discretionary portion of your net worth among various categories of assets. By *discretionary* portion, I mean the assets that you own and that you could reallocate without having to change your lifestyle. The easiest system consists of the following six categories:

1. *Cash*. Includes CDs and money market funds.
2. *Fixed-income securities*. Includes bonds, preferreds, and convertibles.
3. *Common stocks*. Includes all equities in public companies or in mutual funds. The family business is not included.
4. *Collectibles*. Includes art, gold, diamonds, postage stamps, coins, and other tangible assets with an investment value.
5. *Real estate*. Includes only your nonresidential real estate.
6. *Other assets*. Includes partnership investments, tax shelters, and any asset you hold that is not part of your lifestyle or business.

It is a worthwhile exercise for everyone to take the time to list their asset holdings under each of the preceding six categories. Exact values are not important at this stage—just be sure you count everything.

Once you have completed this exercise, determine what percentage of the whole (100 percent) each category represents. Let's evaluate the results. Add up the dollar amount of categories 1, 2, and 3. These are the assets that can provide you with a steady retirement income. Multiply the dollar value by 7 percent (a theoretical rate of return and drawdown of your capital that can be maintained over a normal life expectancy) and ask yourself whether the resulting amount is sufficient, when added to your pension benefits, to supplement the income you expect to need when you retire. If not, then look at categories 4, 5, and 6 and ask yourself which of these you should consider selling in order to increase your income. Too often, we find ourselves holding assets in the 4, 5, and 6 categories that we inherited or purchased for reasons that no longer matter. This is not the time to be sentimental, unless you can afford it.

The Right Allocation for You

The right answer to the allocation question is clearly personal (i.e., the combination that will help you achieve your investment goal). If you are a 55-year-old baby boomer who has not saved enough to retire comfortably by age 67, you may be tempted to allocate 100 percent to stocks in hopes of catching up. As I point out later in the chapter, under "Retirement Planning," this is not the time in your life to test your luck, because you have little room to err. If you are well along in saving for your retirement, and all future appreciation will only fatten the estate you will leave behind, then you have room to take a heavier stock position. My advice to someone 55 or older who needs to catch up is, start with a 50/50 (stock/income) allocation and reduce the stock allocation by 1 percent each year, so that by age 67 your allocation will be 38/62. This approach may or may not work for you. An important consideration here is your comfort level with whatever strategy you pursue. Keep in mind, however, that finding comfort through buying one or more mutual funds is not a sound strategy for reducing stock market risk. More on this later.

Diversification

Diversification is easily the most important subject in income investing. When you bring up the subject of diversification to an audience of fixed-income investors, they tend to think of traditional mantras such as the following:

- Don't investment too much in any one security or issuer or industry.
- Spread your investment among different rating qualities and instruments
- Ladder your maturities.

These guidelines are meant to help investors minimize their exposure to loss from defaults, credit crunches, and inflation. *In principle, these traditional guidelines are inherently good ideas, but much too limiting for today's investing climate. The problem with them is that they are basically defensive in scope.* They assume fixed-income investors must constantly protect against declines in the value of their portfolio, since, with traditional fixed-income instruments, the par value and maturity of the instrument limits any upside appreciation while downside risks are limitless.

Looking at these diversification guidelines in greater detail, well, yes, it's never a good idea to have too large a stake in the fortunes of any one company. Generally, 5 percent is a good upper limit on any one security or issuer. Such a policy, however, makes no exception for special-situation investments, which I cover later in this section. Diversification by industry makes sense only because the market is irrational. Right now fixed-income investments in the auto industry are taking a beating, in part because it is receiving so much bad press. Fixed-income investors often run from an industry when this occurs, even though the doom and gloom the media is talking about falls almost exclusively on shareholders and not on debt holders. This is a downside risk for income investors mainly because any eventual good news gives little upside boost to a company's debt until the whole industry turns around.

Spreading risk among different rating qualities is an attempt to offset the dismal returns on A- to AAA-rated issues by blending in some BBB and BB issues. As I explain later in the chapter under "Credit Ratings," all that investors should be concerned with is getting their interest payments on time and recovering their principal at maturity. Only if there is reasonable doubt about a company's survival should investors be concerned with the credit instrument and its terms (i.e., how senior is the debt, what is the collateral, and which debt issues are first in line if the company does go bankrupt?).

Laddering maturities is a strategy that spreads your maturities over short-term and longer-term issues so that in the case of any interest rate spike you take a lot of little hits instead of one big one. It also provides a continual cycle of maturing issues that can then be reinvested at current interest yields. The flaw here is that when the interest rate yield curve is flat or negative, as it is at the time of this writing, you get no premium yield for buying longer maturities. Laddering makes sense mainly if your selection of maturities coincides with your expected drawdown of the funds involved (i.e., if you plan to spend everything as it matures).

My definition of *diversification* is "allocating capital over a selection of instruments that are responsive to widely different economic events." I call this *diversification over different income drivers*. This means that you should not rely on some guru's forecast of what interest rates are going to do or whether default risks are rising—assume they are just guessing, because they are. Today's investment market offers individual investors a vast array of often confusing products. However, this array of products also offers the opportunity to diversify your holdings among a variety of securities that have only a passing link to interest rates or credit quality. Hence, you can build a fixed-income portfolio much like you build a stock portfolio. But rather than diversifying over a variety of companies and industries, which may currently be hot or countercyclical (or may not), you diversify over a variety of prospective economic events. Let me demonstrate using the investment climate as it looked at the beginning of 2007 as an example.

Begin with a selection of interest rate–sensitive issues. If you consider yourself a medium-risk investor, start by allocating 40 percent of your portfolio to investment-grade bonds and preferreds down to a rating of BB. Don't get hung up on the concept of investment-grade versus junk-rated issues (ratings are discussed later in the chapter). Don't overload on very highly rated bond issues, either—most are currently overpriced. Shoot for a composite return of at least 2.00 percent over U.S. Treasuries. It is difficult to avoid exposure to interest rate swings, and occasionally (e.g., 1982 to the present) long-term rates actually declined, boosting the value of your holdings. True, many analysts promote investing in U.S. Treasury Indexed Performance Securities (TIPS) and adjustable-rate bonds as the perfect way to offset inflation and rising interest rates. But in the present low-inflation environment, what you give up in current yield in exchange for protection against the possibility of rising inflation is just not worth it (see Chapter 3, "Bonds," for a discussion of these securities).

At the beginning of 2007, the stock market looks promising, so a portion of your portfolio (I recommend 20 percent) should be allocated to convertible bonds and preferreds. Should the stock market continue rising, these securities will look to the stock price rather than interest rates for their valuation. In 2005, even with a relatively flat stock market, convertibles were among my clients' best-performing securities.

I recommend a 20 percent allocation to high-dividend-income securities tied to the price of natural resources. Energy and other natural resources price increases were among the most significant economic events of 2005–6. Canadian oil and gas trusts (PWE, PVX, PWI, and ERF) were up 11 percent, on average, while also paying out double-digit dividends. Exposure to metallurgical coal, through Fording Canadian Coal (FDG), and to copper, through Southern Copper (PCU), offers similar payouts and further diversification. Will the price increases in these raw materials continue? I don't know, but unless prices fall substantially, the dividend payouts alone make them worth holding through a downdraft.

I recommend a 20 percent allocation to special situations, situations that may or may not be high risk. These situation come about for a variety of reasons. Here are a few examples.

We are all aware of the emotional factors that enter into stock pricing. Journalists interview analysts, fund managers, or brokers to flesh out an article or video segment they may be doing about a company, an industry, or a market situation. What they get from such pundits is either an opinion (biased or sometimes even unbiased) or sound bytes (if you don't want to be edited out, make it brief and catchy). This process of creating news is flawed, mainly because the journalists may have no more than a passing knowledge of the subject they are trying to cover. Fewer still bother to get a second opinion or to verify that the first opinion was unbiased. The few who do make the effort often ask the person being interviewed for the names of other sources (like I'm going to share who they should *really* be talking to and lose my 15 minutes of fame!). The bottom line here is that this same emotional element exists with income securities because there are just as many nervous Nellies in fixed income as in stocks.

The beating up of GM since 2005 serves as a good example of the media driving values into the ground. For the media, there's nothing like predicting the inevitable bankruptcy of the largest car company in the world to sell advertising. It's a lot more exciting to predict this than to listen to a boring dissertation of all the steps that are being taken to turn GM around. The hype grew and grew as reporters tried to outdo one another, so that by year-end 2005, GM debt was trading at 60 cents on the dollar, well below the recovery one could reasonably expect from a GM bankruptcy. However, you can keep investors scared only so long before greed sets in. Once investors realized that GM is going to be around for a while, and once the nervous Nellies had dumped their positions, a more realistic valuation for GM debt issues prevailed.

Another recent example of special situations arose with closed-end income funds. The Federal Reserve in 2004 announced that it would increase the short-term borrowing rate by 25 basis points at every open markets committee meeting until further notice. Closed-end income funds, which leverage their balance sheets with short-term borrowings, found that these rate increases eventually forced them to cut their dividends. This resulted in their share price moving from a premium over the net asset value (NAV) per share to a sizable discount. Such an outcome was fairly predictable, namely, that once the Fed stops raising short-term rates, the dividends of these funds are no longer subject to downward pressure, and the price will migrate back to NAV. This presents the opportunity for high yield as well as capital gain. More on this when we cover closed-end funds.

Retirement Planning

There is an unspoken conspiracy afoot to scare baby boomers into saving for their retirement. Most visible are government officials and media pundits who tell us that baby boomers are unprepared and likely to suffer dramatic reductions in their lifestyle once they retire from their day jobs. More subtle are the brokerage firms, mutual funds, financial planners, and so on with their handy-dandy online retirement planning guides that let you plug in your age, when you plan to retire, and what income you expect to need in retirement for the next 30 years. You may, of course, elect to die sooner, especially after you've taken your first cut at any of these retirement asset calculators, which invariably tell you how many millions of dollars you will need to ensure that you do not run out of money. *Most of this free retirement advice is designed to scare you into saving more (i.e., putting more money into your brokerage or mutual fund account where these advisors make their fees).* However, true retirement planning requires a little more introspection and a sharp pencil.

In order to test out one of these planning calculators, I indicated I was married, age 55, with $60,000 in savings, $150,000 in homeowner's equity, and $1,800 in expected monthly Social Security payments. (Note that I had to offer up my e-mail address to access this system, which means I have condemned myself to a nonstop flow of reminders for the next 12 years about how far behind I'm falling.) I used what I considered to be a fair monthly expense level of $5,000 and indicated that I planned to leave no estate when my wife and I punched out. My only commitment to savings between now and age 67, when I could retire on full benefits, was $5,000 a year to my IRA account. After 30 seconds of what, per the site's description, was something close to rocket science, I was greeted with the results. Retire? Forget about it! I was going to need $1.2 million in savings by age 67 in order to have a 95 percent probability of reaching my goal. I also received the cheerful news that my proposed savings program gave me less than a 5 percent chance of reaching my goal. And that's based on my odds of winning the state lottery if I buy one ticket each month between now and retirement! No wonder people buy lottery tickets. You can save yourself the effort of using one of these asset calculators if you just multiply your first year's expected expense level by 25. You can also save yourself a lot of needless stressing since there is no real science to these calculations. Whatever you plan to spend per year above your various pension incomes times 25 is going to be the answer, more or less.

Real retirement planning is not just an asset counting exercise. There are five variables in retirement planning and they need to be considered jointly since all can be modified until you get the desired mix:

1. The age at which you want to retire
2. The lifestyle you plan to lead
3. How much in savings you can expect to have
4. What level of investment income you need
5. What level of risk you must assume to achieve that income

Most boomers probably are behind in accumulating a nest egg that will last them for up to 30 years of retirement and therefore may feel that only the stock market can help them catch up. If the past six years is any guide, and I think it is, that is a big risk. *The closer you get to retirement without sufficient savings, the less risk you can afford.*

Before trying to determine your retirement income needs, first take a realistic look at your and your spouse's life expectancy, health, and desired lifestyle. Take into consideration that after you pass age 70, your desire for traveling, living in a large house, maintaining a second house, and buying new cars or new gadgets decreases. Hence, your actual cost of living, other than for health care, should decline. If your retirement income looks today as though it will not meet the lifestyle you envision, it is better to scale back your expectations or even postpone your retirement date than to pursue a high-risk investment plan that leaves you even fewer choices if it fails. Yes, we hate to contemplate scaling back, but hey, that's life.

In determining how much income you can look forward to upon retirement, first add up all your pensions. Consider whether to take Social Security at age 62 or delay until later and receive the higher payout, especially if you are in good health and your spouse is not, or vice versa. In determining your cost of living, factor in the lower income tax rate you will be paying once you retire and therefore the lower tax benefit you will have from a home mortgage interest deduction or from holding tax-exempt securities such as municipal bonds. Although your house is a good savings vehicle, that equity can be invested to return a 6 to 8 percent cash income if extra income is needed. Aside from this, the carrying cost of owning that house is probably a significant portion of your lifestyle expense.

Too many retirees have as a goal leaving an estate for their children. While this is a noble thought, it should always be secondary to planning for your needs. After all, *children should be motivated to strive to achieve their dreams, not to believe that an inheritance means they won't have to.*

Most of us contemplate a retirement free from the need to work. However, many find that part-time work gives them a reason to get up each day and brings more diverse social contact as well. They don't work just for the extra money, although that extra money can help; they do it because they want to. Leave yourself open for this possibility, especially with your current employer. Future opportunities for such work will only increase as the nation's workforce ages.

Investment-grade-rated debt securities today provide a steady 5 to 7 percent payout without stock market-like risks. Look for ways to improve your returns today in a steady, predictable manner *Sure, there may be more-exotic, higher-yielding stuff out there, but this is the stage in life to count your blessings, not test your luck.*

Investment Strategies

What's Exciting about 6 Percent Returns?

Those Wall Street types who have suffered enough to learn from the experience will advise any investor, no matter their age or wealth, to include fixed-income securities in their portfolio. In fact, they have made a game of it by recommending ratios of fixed income to equities and then periodically announcing shifts in such ratios. A common mantra is 60/30/10, which means having 60 percent of your investment capital in equity securities, 30 percent in fixed-income securities, and 10 percent in cash. As markets move, they announce new ratios (e.g., 70/20/10). What is often behind such ratio shifts, I suspect, is that a stock market rise has already brought the typical investor to a 70/20 relationship, so what they are really saying is, "Don't start selling stocks in order to get back to the previously recommended 60/30/10 relationship."

Those advocating portfolio balancing never fully explain why such a balancing approach is not just prudent, but is more profitable than an all-stock approach. Let me demonstrate this by example:

- Portfolio A has $100,000 invested, 100 percent in stocks.
- Portfolio B has $100,000 invested, 65 percent in stocks and 35 percent in bonds and preferreds yielding a constant 6 percent.

Scenario 1. Stocks appreciate 10 percent a year for four years, then drop 20 percent in year 5 due to an economic slowdown. Then for years 6 and 7, stocks resume their growth, appreciating 10 percent in each year. Fixed-income investments are assumed to remain steady in the first four years, then interest rates drop to an average yield of 5 percent during the economic slowdown, rising again to the 6 percent level in years 6 and 7. A key assumption here is that the Portfolio B investor adheres to the 65/35 fixed-income-to-equity ratio throughout the seven-year time period. Hence, at the end of years 1 through 4, when stocks are appreciating, he reallocates earnings from stocks to fixed income. (Note that the new breed of hybrid bonds and preferreds I expand on in this book are ideal for just such a strategy because they are exchange traded and come in $25 denominations). In year 5, when the value of the stocks falls, our investor reverses the allocation back into stock. Note that when interest rates fall, the price of fixed-income securities increases; in this case a drop in rates from 6 percent to 5 percent means fixed-income securities would be sold at about 17 percent more than their cost. See Table 1.1.

There are two reasons for Portfolio B's superior performance. The ability to reallocate assets from fixed income back into stocks when the stock market is depressed allows

Table 1.1
Why a Balanced Approach Matters

	Year-End Value		Ratio
	Portfolio A	Portfolio B	A/B percent
Year 1	110,000	108,600	+1.3
Year 2	121,000	117,939	+2.6
Year 3	133,100	128,082	+3.9
Year 4	146,410	139,097	+5.3
Year 5	117,128	131,836	−11.1
Year 6	128,840	136,864	−5.9
Year 7	141,725	148,635	−4.6

for a much more rapid recovery. This is because the Portfolio B investor has buying power derived from his fixed-income portfolio. In addition, he has suffered less of a loss because fixed-income investments tend to appreciate as interest rates fall, as they do in an economic slowdown. This is because a lower demand for credit as well as Federal Reserve policy will drive rates down.

A reallocation out of fixed income into stocks when interest rates are low is prudent, given that an economic and stock market recovery generally means interest rates will rise and fixed-income securities will decline in price. It should also be pointed out that making a shift in your portfolio from fixed income into equities in a year when stocks have dropped is probably also a good move for tax purposes. It reduces the buildup of future tax liability and allows you to take capital gains on fixed-income investments, gains that you had not counted on and that will disappear when rates rise. The ability to reduce your taxable income through a balanced strategy is an additional plus to your overall return that has not been factored into this comparison.

Scenario 2. Were the investor in Portfolio B more aggressive, he would change his asset allocation to, say 80/20 in year 5 to take advantage of the buying opportunity in stocks. His portfolio value at the end of year 7 would thus be even higher ($152,198 instead of $148,634).

Scenario 3. Should it turn out that the stock market did not recover for three years (e.g., the growth in years 6 and 7 was 0 percent) the difference in results at the end of year 7 would be dramatic. Portfolio A would be worth $117,128, versus $129,930 for Portfolio B, or an 11.7 percent difference.

In short, portfolio diversification recognizes the fact that stock markets go up and down in an unpredictable way. Through diversification investors have a means of taking advantage of downturns to minimize the long-term effect on their portfolio.

What's exciting about 6 percent? It's low-cost (no-cost?) principal protection insurance.

Diehard stock-only investors may argue with the assumption that a market correction will occur every seven years (as in this model) or that the stock market will grow an average of only 10 percent a year. If they are correct and no stock market correction occurs, then, in my scenario 1 example, they would be ahead in year 7 by $194,871 versus $171,306 for Portfolio B. Now then, how lucky do you feel?

As for the growth rate assumption for equities, stocks have had a long-term growth record in the 9 to 11 percent range for the past several decades. Their ability to sustain that rate in the future is probable, although assumptions that they can grow any faster are dubious.

You have to ask yourself, given your present age, how many 20 percent stock market drops can you recover from and still feel comfortable in retiring when you planned. The bear market of 2000 to 2002 was a wake-up call for many. While some may choose to abandon stocks altogether in favor of fixed-income securities, this is not the right solution for everyone.

Equities will always be an important investment tool, but two significant changes in the equity markets over the past 20 years will make stock markets much more volatile in the future. The first factor is the huge concentration of buy/sell decision making in the hands of less than 10,000 fund and asset managers. Added to this is the advent of electronic information services and the Internet, which makes news and information about individual companies and industries simultaneously available to all these market participants, often on a real-time basis. Today's market makers are individuals with similar backgrounds and experience (or lack thereof) using similar information tools and with a shared bias toward short-term results. If ever there were a reason to predict greater future stock market volatility, that is it. If ever there were a reason to keep a good share of your investment portfolio in fixed-income securities available to take advantage of future volatility, that is it.

Regarding use of a 6 percent rate of return for fixed-income investments in the preceding demonstration, I believe this to be quite conservative. I used it to demonstrate the soundness of an asset allocation strategy even at such low return levels. There is no reason an actively managed portfolio of fixed-income securities cannot earn 8 percent or more without taking on high risk. This can be done with the new breed of hybrid bonds and preferreds, which I address later. The goal of this book, then, is not just to sell you on my investment newsletter, but to give you the skills to build a portfolio with built-in protection against stock market declines and the opportunity to take advantage of market volatility in the stock markets as, and when, they are sure to occur.

What You Need to Know about Risk and Uncertainty

Ask 10 investors how they define *risk* and chances are you will get at least five different answers. In a recent prospectus for a new mutual fund I counted no fewer than 28 defined risks, and this did not include risks based on dishonesty, such as after-hours trading in fund shares, over-pricing infrequently traded holdings, or front-running (buying for your own account before making market-moving trades for your fund) fund purchases. The point is, while 28 different risks may exist, the degree of each fluctuates according to economic, political, or market conditions. The most common concern among investors is credit (payment) risk. That's why many investors buy only government-backed debt or FDIC-insured CDs. Yet today, when I rank the various risks by their likelihood, credit risk is quite low.

Think about it this way: Investment risk is a moving target that can be parsed into as many as 28 components. Taken to the extreme, each of these 28 risks can cause major short-term or long-term damage to your portfolio. The challenge for investors is in identifying which risks are currently the highest and whether they should or should not react to them. For example, if credit risk were suddenly a great concern, every-one would likely react. However, if the risk is one of interest rates ris-ing, not all investors would react. Income investors with portfolios wouldn't be concerned because their income remains the same and so does their principal maturity value. On the other hand, investors seek-ing growth and income would despair, because the market value of their holdings would contract.

Looking to the future, I see the following risks as high: interest rate risk, industry-specific risks (e.g., mortgage REITS, financial institutions), political risk (e.g., due to elections and Fed policy), financial system risk (e.g., related to derivatives and currency issues), market disruption risk (e.g., terrorism-related), and inflation risk. This is even more compli-cated when you consider that the risk result can appear to be positive or negative, and the consequences can be predictable (e.g., interest rates rise and bond prices fall) or contrary (e.g., control of Congress changes hands, leaving uncertainty and stock prices rise!). It is precisely because risks come in such varieties that forecasting accuracy is so poor.

Subjective Risks

Risk is one of those words like *love*, *hate*, *fear*, and *dread*; in short, a word that often has a different meanings to speakers than to their listeners. In investments, it is a word with a very personal definition, shaped by a person's experience, much like an acquired taste. One of the principal tasks of an investment advisor is to gauge an investor's tolerance for risk, both perceived and actual. Needless to say, it would behoove investors to make this determination on their own, beforehand, since it will determine what kind of advice they should seek in the first place.

Risk is subjective in that it is defined by your personal tolerances, but it is also objective as it pertains to the actual selection of investments. Looked at from its subjective aspect, it is a phrase that encompasses two emotions that drive individuals: fear and greed. The emotional element of risk is strictly personal, and you need to give serious thought to your own tolerance for risk because it is unique to you. No one can tell you which investments will make you comfortable, nor is your level of comfort the same all the time. As you get older and as your economic wealth rises or shrinks, your comfort level will change. The two ways you define your comfort level in investments is through your portfolio balance and through your quality selection. Quality selection for fixed income is generally defined by bond ratings, a subject addressed later in the chapter under "Credit Ratings."

Greed has gotten a bad rap throughout history, but like it or not, it is the driving force behind capitalism. It is not as portrayed in the movie *Wall Street* by the line "Greed is good," but think of it instead as unavoidable. *The main emotion a smart investor should have is fear*. Fear is the emotion you must overcome to invest when opportunities appear risky but usually are at their best. Fear is also the emotion you need to consciously recall when things are going really well and seem to have no end. Greed is the emotion you must always work to keep in check. It clouds judgment and is sustained by rationalization. It therefore depends mainly on luck for its outcome. Both fear and greed can skew your investment discipline and must be kept in check.

It is the ability to quantify risk with reliable and comparative yard-sticks that gives fixed-income investments a degree of comfort not found with equity securities. Ratings provide the investor with a grading system of a company that has proven to be highly reliable over time. Credit ratings break down broadly into investment-grade and non-investment-grade categories, which are then further refined to show relative risk and, through rating changes, whether that risk is rising or falling over time. Interest rate risk is also a highly quantifiable risk, which can be managed in several ways, as I explain later. While few people can predict the direction interest rates will move, the good news is that the rates move slowly. Therefore, you can use both time and technique to minimize the damage.

Objective Risks

As with equities, there is an element of unquantifiable risks with fixed income, albeit these risks are significantly less. There is *market risk,* which is the inability to sell a security quickly or at a reasonable price. This varies according to the type of security. For example, municipal bonds that are not AAA insured can be difficult to sell quickly at a reasonable price if it is not a well-known issue or if you have less than a $25,000 lot to sell. This is because, with munis, brokers who want to buy lots of less than $100,000 are few, and they will demand a sizable discount to do the trade. Corporate bonds face a similar problem.

Fixed-income securities also face periodic flights to quality. This *flight to quality risk* is when uncertainty causes the fixed-income investors to suddenly sell lower-quality bonds and buy higher-investment-grade issues. Such a flight to quality took place when the first Gulf War started in 1991. Once the initial crisis passed, values drifted back to normal relationships. Hence, these flights matter only if you need to sell; they represent an opportunity if you are buying.

Another risk that has received prominent attention recently is what is graciously termed *accounting risk,* although it has always been around under the more familiar term, *fraud.* Modern innovations in finance and accounting have managed to create a huge gray area wherein "creative accounting" becomes difficult to distinguish from fraud. While recently implemented penalties have made it more onerous for company executives to engage in blatant misstatements, the problem will always be just under the surface. *Fraud and securities are so closely linked because it is one of the easiest and most lucrative crimes to commit.* Securities represent the exchange of money for a promise. The only skill required by the thief is an ability to talk convincingly and be brazen. With careful execution, the perpetrators can even come up with a convincing exit strategy that leaves investors thinking that the failure was not predestined. Don't get me wrong, the vast majority of business failures are honest failures, even if the accounting was manipulated along the way to stave off the inevitable.

Often, careful analysis will uncover accounting risk; however, markets tend to take a dim view of misstatement disclosures and rating agencies, and the SEC takes an even dimmer view. Thus the erosion in the price of a company's securities when misstatements are disclosed can be severe. The only good thing that can be said here is that price erosion in fixed-income securities is much lower, and their recovery much swifter, than for common stocks.

Uncertainty

Added to risk is uncertainty (i.e., the disruptions that can't be anticipated, such as floods, earthquakes, hurricanes, pandemics, assassinations, and wars). In fact, no less an American icon than General Electric picked as the cover theme of its 2003 annual report, "Growing in an Uncertain World." The distinguishing feature of uncertainty is that when such disruptions occur, the market consequences cannot readily be identified or quantified, not to mention the immediate knee-jerk reactions, which in themselves create short-term investment opportunities or losses.

The one idea to take away from this discourse is that in investing, very little is highly predictable and nothing is certain. Don't put too much reliance into any forecast or too much money into any one investment, or even into a single asset class. Sure, we all read stories about the investor who bet it all on a company or idea and made a fortune. No one writes about the 99 other investors who did the same and were wiped out. Why is that, I wonder? Uncertainty in investing will always exist, especially the negative kind, but through proper diversification, its long-term effects can be considerably reduced.

Understanding Interest Rates: General Features

Interest is a convenient way to characterize what to a borrower is the cost of money and to a lender is the time value of money. It is one of the simplest concepts to understand and one of the most complex to implement. It has been around since biblical times and has been maligned to the point of being criminalized. Those who lend money have historically been looked down on and even persecuted, except when their services were needed by the king or another ruler of the day. Today interest is recognized as the lifeblood of the capitalist system. It is the motivation for those who have money they don't currently need to lend it to those who do. Those who lend money (versus investing it in, say, equities) are showing a preference not to participate in the risks of the borrowing enterprise. Of course, all risk cannot be avoided, but as a lender, their risk is limited by virtue of the fact, written into law, that they have first claim to any assets still remaining should the enterprise fail.

Practically everyone understands interest as being the cost of borrowing money. How much this cost will be depends on (1) what is being financed, (2) how it will be repaid, (3) the length of the loan period, (4) the tax treatment of the income, (5) the prevailing cost of money at that point in time, (6) the conditions of repayment, and (7) the currency of payment. These seven variables allow for an infinite number of ways to structure an interest-paying security. They also make comparisons quite complex. Still, quantifiable comparisons are possible, which is more than can be said for most common stocks.

Before I go into these seven aspects of interest, an investor needs to become familiar with certain terms. The list of terms used is extensive, but I mention here only those that are absolutely essential:

Yield. This term refers to how much interest a security will earn for you. It is a number expressed as a percentage, so that it can be readily compared to all other securities and so that it is the same number no matter how much you are investing. You may also see it referred to by another term: *rate of return*. For example, an 8 percent bond pays $80 a year interest on its $1,000 face value, but its yield to you is only 8 percent if that is what you paid for it. If you paid $900 for the bond you still get the same $80 a year interest payment, but your yield would be 8.88 percent rather than 8.00 percent ($80/$900). Likewise, if the bond sold for $1,100, your yield would drop to 7.27 percent ($80/1100). *Current yield* or *current rate of return* are other terms you will see used to describe this same amount. You may ask, why does the price of a bond change if its quality remains unchanged? The answer is that securities' market prices reflect the prevailing rates of interest that day. The prevailing rate is what a bond issuer would have to pay today to sell new bonds. If that rate is 8.88 percent, a new bond would come out as an 8.88 percent bond paying annual interest of $88.80 per $1,000 bond. However, since the 8 percent bond will still be outstanding and has a fixed payment of only $80, the price adjusts downward to $900 to put it on an equal footing with the new bond. Unless this happens, no one would buy the 8 percent bond, so it would become illiquid.

Yield to Maturity. Now that you understand yield, its time to complicate things further. Yield to maturity refers to how much a security will earn for you if you hold it to its maturity date. Using the preceding example, if you bought the 8 percent bond for $1,000, the yield and the yield to maturity would both be 8 percent. However, if you bought it for $900, you will be entitled to an additional $100 payment over your cost at maturity. This additional payment is income that needs to be expressed in a percentage form (again, so the security can be compared to all other bonds), but it needs to have a different defining term, since this additional $100 yield is paid only at maturity. The yield to maturity is more complex to calculate, but you don't need to do it, because yield to maturity should be disclosed to you as part of the price quote before you buy. In our example, assume the 8 percent bond has 10 more years to maturity. In that case, if you paid $900 for it, your yield to maturity is 9.64 percent. If you paid $1,100, you will actually lose $100 of your purchase price at maturity, so the yield to maturity is less than the current yield, or 6.54 percent. Note that you don't have to wait until the last year to realize the additional $100 payment (or $100 loss). This is because, as the maturity date approaches, the current price of the bond rises or falls to keep the yield to maturity fairly constant. Two other yield calculations you should also ask for before you buy are the *yield to call*, which is what your yield would be if the issue is called at the next call date, and the *yield to worst*, which is the yield if the security is paid off at the worst possible time for you.

Yield to Call. This is the yield a security will give over its remaining life, assuming it is called at the next call date and price.

Yield to Worst. This is the yield a security will give assuming the worst maturity and call price combination for the buyer.

Maturity Date. This is the future date when the face amount of the bond or preferred will be redeemed or paid in cash.

Call Date. This is the date prior to maturity when the company may redeem a security early. A corporation will usually call a security early because interest rates have declined from what it is paying, allowing it to refinance the debt at lower rates. This right to call a security early, however, may come with a penalty to the company, called the *call premium*. Such a call premium may be 5 percent above face value, meaning the company in our example would pay a bondholder $1,050 if it calls the bond, say, five years early. Call dates generally run the life of the security, with a diminishing premium at each call date as you get closer to the maturity date. This list of call dates and prices is called the *call schedule*. Note, there are no hard-and-fast rules about call dates and call premiums, so you need to thoroughly understand them before you buy a security, because they can greatly influence the fairness of the asking price. For example, a security can have a tempting 9 percent current yield, but be callable in six months, in which case the yield becomes a negative 1 percent!

Preferreds. Preferred securities, often termed *preferred stocks*, make their payments as dividends. This is true despite the fact that they are fixed-payment securities. Many of today's preferreds are actually bonds. This is a market convenience that can cause confusion with the more familiar concept of the dividend payments on common stock, which are discretionary. The various types and features of preferreds are discussed in detail in Chapter 4.

Now that you know these basic terms, its time to address the variables that affect the structure of interest paying securities.

Variable 1: What Is Being Financed

Over time, different borrowing needs have developed mass markets of buyers and sellers, and this in turn affects overall interest rates. Three prominent markets are the U.S government debt market, the mortgage debt market, and the commercial paper market. These are all highly liquid markets selling debt instruments with negligible credit risk. The buyers are mostly institutions that value liquidity and low risk and therefore accept a lower rate of return than they could earn on debt instruments that would require subjective evaluation. This is not to say that these markets are no-brainers. You still have to compare and value the maturity and redemption or call features from among these securities. However, such choices are more like picking the color and upholstery on a car once you have decided on the model.

Aside from these three very large markets exists an informal, or over-the-counter (OTC), market for a variety of other fixed-income securities composed mostly of corporate bonds and various derivative instruments such as collateralized mortgage obligations (CMOs) or collateralized debt obligations (CDOs). These securities are not homogenous except for the features they are required to have by law. Most important, they vary hugely in their rate of return. As a convenience to those who make the markets in these securities, they break down into investment-grade and non-investment-grade, commonly referred to as *junk bonds*. Don't be put off by the denigrating term *junk bonds*, whose stigma is undeserved, especially considering that these can easily add 2 to 4 percentage points or more to your yield.

Variable 2: How It Will Be Paid

Interest payments can be monthly, quarterly, semiannually, annually, or not at all. As a rule of thumb, bonds pay interest semiannually and preferreds pay interest/dividends quarterly. The variety in payment features, however, is generally provided to appeal to the different purposes of buyers. *One major difference between bonds and preferreds is that when you buy a bond, you pay the agreed purchase price plus the amount of the next cash interest payment that has accrued up to the trade date.* If a bond's next interest payment will be $40, and three months of the six-month payment period have passed, you would have to pay an additional $20, above the price being quoted, to the bond seller. With preferreds, this is not the case. Preferred interest/dividends belong wholly to whoever owns the security on the last day before the *ex-dividend date*, which is a date set by the stock exchange to determine who gets the payment. On preferreds, the market value is expected to, and usually does, adjust to reflect the change in the value of the security the day after it's no longer eligible for the dividend.

When I say that sometimes interest is not paid at all, I am referring to what are termed *zero-coupon bonds*. These are bonds sold at a discount to their face value. In effect, you receive only one payment at maturity, generally the face amount of the security, that represents your purchase price and all the interest on that price and interest on the interest you would have received if interest had been paid semiannually and then reinvested.

Another unusual interest payment feature is an *original-issue discount bond*, or OID bond, which comes about in one of two ways: It can represent the discount at which a bond was sold at the time of original issue (e.g., a $1,000 bond that is sold for $950 when issued). It can also be a bond that pays no cash interest for the first year or more. The purpose in this arrangement is to give the borrower time to employ the bond issue proceeds for their intended purpose and begin to generate the income needed to make cash interest payments. Here again, the purchase price is something less than face value in order to compensate the buyer fairly. Such bonds often originate as part of a bankruptcy settlement.

Some securities, termed *convertible bonds*, or *convertible preferreds*, are issued with a stated rate of interest and maturity, but are never intended to be redeemed. Such securities have a redemption clause that provides for the holder to be paid in common stock or cash when the bonds mature or are called. Such redemption may be at the option of the seller or the buyer. More on this in Chapter 5.

Finally we have securities that pay interest by issuing the holder more of the same security, commonly called *pay-in-kind (PIK) securities*. Such securities are generally issued by companies with very low credit ratings, or they may have been issued as part of a previous distress situation such as a bankruptcy settlement. The pay provisions generally allow the issuer to pay in cash or in kind for a defined period of time, according to that issuer's financial fortunes.

Variable 3: The Length of the Loan Period

The length of time a security has between its issue and its date of maturity affects both its rate of return and its price volatility. This is because the greatest cause of interest rate fluctuation is inflation. Inflation has historically been difficult to predict and has been financially devastating several times in history. A security with a far-off maturity date traditionally yields a higher rate of return than one with only a short maturity. The relative relationship of security yields over time is expressed by a graphic called the *yield curve*.

During times of low inflation, this yield curve will be almost flat, while during times of great concern it will become quite steep. During periods of changing expectations regarding inflation, the curve can even become inverted (i.e., short-term rates are higher than long-term rates). This yield curve graphic is like a weather barometer, forecasting change the more it varies from its traditional slope. (This is because short-term rates will react much more quickly to economic change than long-term rates.)

Although inflation is hard to predict, its effect on the price of a given security is not. The tool that the fixed-income markets use to measure this effect is called *duration*. The concept of duration is explained in detail in Chapter 3. The reason you want to understand duration is that while interest rate movements are hard to forecast precisely, the direction of change is generally slow and lasts over an extended period of time. Hence, if interest rates are predicted to rise in the foreseeable future, you should look toward buying securities that will decline less in price. Likewise, when rates are high, look for longer-maturity securities, because they will likely appreciate when rates fall. Note, however, that if you buy a fixed-income security with the intention of holding it to its maturity, you need have little concern about which way interest rates are going or their effect on the price of your security. This is because at maturity, you will get the face or par value in cash no matter what happens in between.

Variable 4: Tax Treatment

Coupon rates, or rates of return, are directly affected by how the recipient of the payments is taxed. Generally speaking, all interest in the United States is subject to federal, state, and local income taxes. That being said, let's address the more notable exceptions. Debt issued by the federal government is exempt from state and local taxes. This includes Treasury bills, notes, and bonds and federal agency debt. Debt issued by municipalities is exempt from federal income taxes and from state and local taxes if held by residents of that state. This exemption from federal tax is limited in its total amount and is not true for all municipal debt. Likewise, municipal debt interest on a New Jersey bond does not help a New York city resident with his or her state and city income taxes. This is why the municipal bond market is very regional. Investors need to ask the seller of any municipal bond purchase about its specific tax limitations as a matter of routine, since it has a direct effect on its price and its value to them individually. For more on this subject see Chapter 3 in the sections on municipal bonds.

Interest does not have to be paid in order to give rise to a tax liability. For example, zero-coupon debt has an imputed interest rate even though no payment is received until the year of maturity. The annual imputed interest must be reported as taxable income for each year the bond is held, despite the lack of any actual payment.

Variable 5: The Cost of Money

Various studies that have been done on the cost of money through the centuries have concluded that before factoring in inflation and the other variables, real returns have averaged between 2 and 3 percent. I am personally puzzled by how anyone can make this determination, as some claim, over a period of 1,000 years. Nevertheless, it has become an accepted convention to assume the cost of money is 2 to 3 percent and then attribute all the rest to assorted variables. In fact, there may be a current precedent for this convention in the form of U.S. Treasury Indexed Performance Securities, or TIPS. These securities are as good as it gets, quality-wise, and fully adjust for U.S. inflation. Their yield fluctuates in a 2 to 3 percent range. Fluctuations in their yield can therefore be seen as a barometer of interest rates in the future.

While in theory the cost of money is determined by the free market, the Federal Reserve Bank, in the name of economic stability, is the visible hand that helps the market make its decisions. It does this by controlling the short-term cost of money through its power to set the rate at which banks can borrow from it and through control over the supply of money and credit. The Fed controls the supply of money through buying and selling U.S. Treasury debt and through setting the banks' reserve requirements, which determines the amounts available for lending by member banks. Note that this rate setting and credit supply management only indirectly affect the market of greatest interest to investors, the fixed-income securities markets that are driven by long-term rates. Here the free market still operates, although it shows a healthy respect for the message the Fed sends out with each short-term rate change. Likewise, the Fed pays close attention to what the long-term markets are saying by their rate movement. In short, you can never be sure when the Fed is going to lead the way and when it's following the markets.

While this management of short-term rates by the Fed may not sound like much, it has proven to be the principal tool available to the government in managing our economic growth. For this reason, the actions by the Fed and the pronouncements by its chairman are closely followed by market participants. It is also why every attempt has been made to insulate the Fed from politics by appointing its governors to nonconcurrent 14-year terms. The Fed reports to Congress, but Congress doesn't set its agenda. It's not a perfect system for economic management, and it's still highly dependent on the skills of those in charge, but few would advocate its demise.

Variable 6: The Conditions of Repayment

The most complicated aspects of fixed-income securities are often the repayment provisions. When you are lending money to the U.S. Treasury, there is little concern about repayment provisions, because you have the confidence that the United States as an entity will outlive you. Not so for any other borrower. The repayment provisions are quantified in the call schedule. As stated in my definition of the call date, most bonds make provision for the early redemption of the security. Such provisions are designed to provide the borrower with an opportunity to

retire the debt early should interest rates or other fortuitous circumstances make this advantageous. Aside from this, many fixed-income
securities are backed by a revenue stream that is not wholly predictable
(e.g., mortgage-backed securities). In these cases, there may be a provision for earlier repayment because the underlying mortgages were
repaid early. Bonds may also have sinking fund provisions, whereby
monies are deposited periodically with the bond trustee for the redemption of the bonds. Bonds are then redeemed piecemeal based on a pro
rata or random selection process. Generally, this is done by random
selection of serial numbers. On rare occasions, issuers may choose to
pay, say, $80, on each $1,000 bond, leaving the holder with a $920 par
value bond, which now may be a little hard to sell.

Securities generally provide for early repayment upon the occurrence
of some event that changes the ownership or nature of the business.
Such provisions may be for the protection of the lenders, but may also
work against them if the issuer is acquired by an investment grade company who calls the security because it can borrow at lower interest rates.

Variable 7: The Currency of Payment

Fixed-income markets have become truly international in scope, so a
caution about currency of payment as well as the nationality of the borrower is in order. Bonds denominated in other than U.S. dollars include
a variable that the investor must also consider. Bonds denominated in a
foreign currency are quoted with yields that assume no change in
exchange rates between now and the maturity date. This can be misleading, given that a currency play would be one reason the investor chooses
to buy a bond denominated in another currency. The yields on foreign
currency—denominated debt will reflect the anticipation that further currency appreciation or depreciation may occur. The advent of the euro
has created a huge market of securities in a currency that should prove
to rival the dollar over time. Recent strength in this currency means that
investors receiving, say, a 5 percent interest yield would also have a
security that has appreciated 7 percent in price due to the appreciation
of the euro against the U.S. dollar. Such currency aspects introduce a
wholly different risk, as well as a profit opportunity, that needs to be
evaluated.

Recent events in Argentina also point out that the risks associated with the nationality of the issuer are a consideration. Although a company based in Argentina borrows U.S. dollars, it is doing business in Argentina, in pesos, and is subject to the remittance rules of that country. A financial crisis in that country can lead to a suspension of foreign exchange remittances, including interest payments on the borrowings of the country itself. Ironically, companies that were financially capable of making interest and principal payments were prevented from doing so because of these currency restrictions, and their debt was also declared in default.

Summing Up

Figure 1.1 demonstrates that since 1981, when long-term rates in the United States hit a peak of 14 percent with inflation of 12 percent, interest rates have been on an unprecedented 25-year decline. During this time, investors were able to earn huge real interest returns as well as capital appreciation on securities as safe as long-term U.S. Treasuries. This decline to a present level in the 4 to 5 percent range is pretty much at an end now, and rates should stay relatively benign for the foreseeable future. This means that the days of 7 and 8 percent rates of return on riskless Treasuries is at an end for the expected lifetime of investors

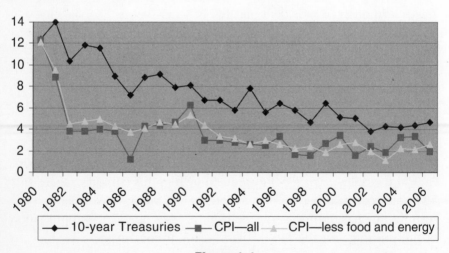

Figure 1.1
Inflation versus 10-Year Treasuries, Annual Percentages

over 50 years old. *Building a nest egg for the next 25 years at more than a 4 percent compounded rate of return will therefore require an investor to look at alternative instruments, strategies, and risks.*

Compound Interest

If you are saving for your retirement through income securities, you need to become familiar with the concept of compound interest. Einstein is famously quoted as saying that compound interest is the most powerful force on earth, relatively speaking. The past five years have certainly demonstrated this, in spades. To understand what compounding can do for you, start with Table 1.2.

Great, now how do you double your money? By compounding! The secret of compounding is time and interest rates. As shown in Table 1.2, $100,000 must double three times in order to make about $1 million nest egg, but how long will that take?

Even in the present environment of low interest rates, a 7 percent yield is available in corporate bonds and preferred stocks. At this rate it will double in 10 years, double again in the twenty-first year and reach $1 million in 34 years. Another approach would be starting with nothing and saving $10,000 a year from your current income. To reach $1 million in this instance would take 31.5 years. Okay, let's say you can't save more than the $4,000 that the IRS allows you to put in an IRA ($5,000 if you're age 50 or older). Even this amount of savings per year, compounded at 7 percent, can grow to $23,000 in 5 years, $55,000 in 10 years, $164,000 in 20 years, and $253,000 in 25 years. Not bad growth considering the IRS is giving you a free ride to save at least that much.

Table 1.2
How to Become a Millionaire

Starting Amount	Number of Doublings Required to Reach $1 million
$1,000	10
$10,000	7
$100,000	3 plus a little

For me, building a nest egg by relying on interest rate compounding is more satisfying than investing in common stocks, where your main satisfaction is selling what you hold, when you so choose, for more than you paid. This is infinitely more risky because your timing has to be right when you buy the stock as well as when you sell it. This means you must be right about the company's prospects and right about the market in general. These same risks exist in fixed-income investing, but to a much lesser degree.

Fixed-income investors are no different than equity investors in their ultimate goal: to build wealth and make the most profit they can. The principal difference is in how ready they are to risk their capital to achieve that end. I know from dealing with numerous investment advisory clients that there is also an underlying "animal" spirit in many of them. Few are content to settle for the returns promised by our model portfolios. They want to have some fun. Well, *investing is about making money, and Las Vegas is about having fun.* But, if Las Vegas is not your bag, or you are between trips, at least discipline your urge to make the stock market your casino. Mentally set aside, say, 5 percent of your capital for taking flyers. If they pay off, you've satisfied your urge; if not, you can shrug it off. In any case, you haven't killed your total return for the year as have those who have invested 100 percent in stocks the past five years.

When Interest Rates Rise

When interest rates begin to rise, the market reaction can be sudden and sharp. Worse yet, the decline in prices is likely to continue for a while. The question you may ask yourself is, "What should I do?" The answer to this question depends greatly on why you bought your fixed-income securities. If you bought them for their cash income, the answer is to do nothing. While the monthly brokerage account valuations may rise or fall, your monthly income will not change. Likewise, if you are a buy and hold investor, your eventual return of capital from a maturing security or one with an early call will not change. But if you need to protect against any erosion in the value of your portfolio, then you have a number of options. If the rising rate threat is during a time when the yield curve is fairly flat (i.e., short-term rates are about the same as long-term rates), then you can simply opt to sell your longer-maturity investments and park the funds in a CD, Treasury bills, or a money market fund. The advantage here is that if a rate increase comes quickly, you avoid the initial hit to your account and can then reinvest the money parked on the sidelines at the new, higher interest rates and actually get higher cash income than before. To help you determine which securities to sell, go to Chapter 3, the section on "Duration."

A second question you may ask when rates are rising is, "Where do I put new money?" There are several choices here: adjustable-rate securities, convertibles, and securities likely to be called.

Adjustable-rate securities pay a rate of return that is adjusted periodically based on some cost-of-living index or a short-term interest rate such as the London Interbank Offered Rate (LIBOR). Such securities pay a rate that may be adjusted anywhere from monthly to as long as five years. They generally feature a minimum and a maximum rate within which they can vary. They also may come with an initial coupon rate that looks irresistible as a sweetener to get you to buy them without reading the fine print. But *do* read the fine print. Such sweetener issues can be very misleading and may actually lock you into a below-market interest rate after the initial two or three years, much like some of the adjustable rate home mortgages currently being peddled. Make sure the reset provisions of any security being considered will keep the price near its par value and that the reset schedule is at least quarterly. If it's only once a year, the price should be lower than for one that resets four times a year. Also look at the floor and ceiling reset limits. If the issue has been outstanding for a few years, there's a good chance the current reset price is well below the floor price for the issue. What's wrong with that, you say? It means that the interest rate will have to rise by several rate resets before it rises above the floor and you see your first payout increase. That may be one or two percentage points away, or as much as you are likely to see rates rise in the current low-interest-rate environment.

I also recommend buying convertibles as a way to protect against rate rises, since the conversion feature provides downside protection and provides possible upside gain should the underlying stock rise. That's not uncommon, given that interest rates can also rise because stock prices are strong, thereby drawing capital away from income securities forcing yields up.

Another alternative to buying short maturities when yields are low is to look for bonds and preferreds that are likely to be called in the next year or two. Such issues may provide more yield than comparable issues that definitely mature in the next few years. Note that in evaluating such issues you need to know the yield to call rather than the current yield, which is generally higher. Buy only those priced at or below the call price. Often, such issues are not called at the earliest call date. In such a case, the rate of return going forward is generally better than what you could have gotten at the time from having to reinvest your call proceeds. This is because the securities were priced on the assumption they would be called away, hence any additional time beyond the call date is a bonus yield.

Investment Strategies

Comparative Yields Explained

For years I have published a monthly "Comparative Current Market Yields" table in the *Forbes/Lehmann Income Securities Investor Newsletter* to demonstrate the diversity of yields and instruments that investors need to be aware of in selecting various income securities. Too many investors embrace the concept of buying investment-grade securities as if it were a model of prudence, ignoring the fact that default risk is only one (and a minor one at that) of the factors they need to consider in making an investment choice.

Our newsletter table uses the yield on 10-year Treasuries as the benchmark interest rate and compares it to the rates for other popular instruments via the spread columns. Spread is stated in basis points, where 100 basis points equals 1 percent in yield. The 10-year Treasury is used as the benchmark because it is the most liquid security in the world and is free of default or call risk. This does not mean, however, that the difference between it and all other rates represents default risk. This is because many of the buyers of Treasuries are foreign central banks that don't buy corporate bonds. Their yardstick for comparison is something closer to the 10-year euro bonds, also quoted in the table, and currently yielding below Treasuries. These investors want a higher return on Treasuries because of a perceived currency risk in dollar-denominated debt. If the dollar begins to show sustained appreciation, vis-à-vis the euro spot rate, you will see this relationship reverse. The table also quotes the return on inflation-protected Treasuries (TIPS) since the yield difference (spread) between them and straight Treasuries is a proxy for how high a rate of inflation the market is expecting. As you can see in Table 1.3, as of December 31, 2006, the spread between the 10-year and the inflation-adjusted Treasuries stood at 230 basis points, which implies that investors think inflation will be 2.30 percent, from 2.34 percent at the beginning of the year.

Moving down the table, you will note the various quality levels of corporate bonds. Note here how the investment-grade issues closely track (see the Net Change column) the change in the 10-year Treasuries, but the below-investment-grade issues do not. This is because below-investment-grade issues are driven more by perceptions of credit and liquidity risks than by inflation concerns. In Table 1.3, the spreads for investment grade issues are fairly constant year to year. Not so for the below-investment-grade issues, where spreads have narrowed as default concerns wane. The danger here is that investors in below-investment-grade bonds are not of the buy and hold school of investment. They will cut and run if they see a downturn or better opportunities elsewhere.

Preferred yields are significantly higher than comparable bonds despite the fact that most of them are actually bonds held in trust. This is due to a variety of factors, the principal one being that large institutions ignore this market because they cannot make purchases in large quantities. These securities are ideal for individual investors making small purchases, especially given the better yield and pricing visibility, since most issues are exchange traded. The table breaks out yield returns for preferreds eligible for the 15 percent tax treatment. I consider these securities an attractive alternative to municipal bonds because of their liquidity and higher pretax and after-tax yields. When interest rates are low, muni yields are so low that they provide little return after allowing for inflation. Also, having some tax liability provides opportunity to offset tax-deductible losses elsewhere.

The municipal rates listed feature the yield spreads from Treasuries expressed as a percentage. This percentage subtracted from 100 is roughly the marginal tax rate you are paying to make munis attractive. As this percentage rises, the benefit of tax-free income rises. Keep in mind, however, that the assumption in all these comparisons is that you would invest in Treasuries if you did not buy munis. If, however, you would consider investment-grade 15 percent taxable qualified dividend income (QDI) preferreds as an alternative to BBB munis, the yield percentage would increase to 110 percent, versus 97 percent for munis, a clear after-tax advantage for preferreds. See Table 1.3.

For readers who are more comfortable with graphics, Figure 1.2 shows, in a graphic explanation of comparative yield, how corporate bond rates have fluctuated since 2000. Note how the gaps between rating qualities widen and shrink for below-investment-grade categories. I do not show a yield for AAA bonds because there are so few issues. It seems that in order to get a AAA rating, you have to be strong enough not to need any borrowings.

The preferred yields (Figure 1.3) demonstrate how yields have come down since 2000. Note the comparative differences between the yields by rating category in Figures 1.2 and 1.3. Since most of the preferreds in Table 1.3 are also debt issues, this illustrates the absolute yield advantage for preferreds over bonds, in addition to the yield differential by rating category.

Table 1.3
Comparative Current Market Yields
(Net Changes and Spreads in Basis Points)

Rating	Yields	Net Change	Net Change	Spread	Spread
Category	12/31/06	Month	YTD	12/31/05	12/31/06
U.S. TREASURIES AND EURO BENCHMARKS					
10-year	4.70	24	31		
Inflation indexed	2.40	25	35	−234	−230
10-year euro[1]	3.94	25	64	−109	−76
Euro spot rate	1.320	−29	1152		
Corporate Bonds[2]					
AAA	5.36	21	31	66	66
A	5.63	21	33	91	93
BBB	5.99	22	13	147	129
BB	6.83	−5	−49	293	213
B	7.91	−13	−32	384	321
CCC	10.24	−27	−188	773	554
Preferreds[3]					
AA and A	6.36	−2	−25	192	166
BBB	7.22	29	−27	310	252
BB	8.08	−19	−83	452	338
B	8.84	−19	−140	585	414
QDI Preferreds[4]			Yields	Yields	
Investment.grade	5.69	−11	−23	115 percent	103 percent
Below inv. grade	6.42	20	41	116 percent	116 percent
MUNICIPAL BONDS[5]			Yields	Yields	
AAA (insured)	3.79	11	−10	89 percent	81 percent
A	4.16	3	5	94 percent	89 percent
BBB	4.28	3	−16	101 percent	91 percent

1. Rate for 10-year German government bonds.
2. Per Merrill Lynch bond index by rating.
3. Per Income Securities Investor Index by rating.
4. Eligible for 15 percent tax rate. Yields shown at after-tax percent of U.S. Treasuries rate.
5. Per Bloomberg. Yields shown at after-tax percent of U.S. Treasuries rate.

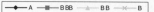

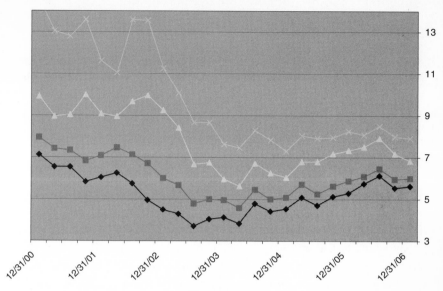

Figure 1.2
Corporate Bond Yields

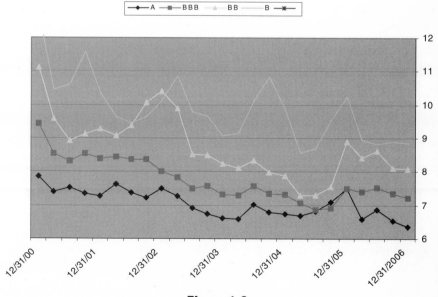

Figure 1.3
Preferred Yields

What to Pay: Fair Value Pricing

One area in which income securities have equities beat cold is pricing, or I should say *fair value pricing*. A stock that has never paid a dividend and makes no promises it will ever pay a dividend is a pretty subjective thing to price. Its price is based on such factors as how many analysts follow it, how well they are wined and dined, how good a job the company does on PR, how well known its products are, how hot its industry is currently perceived, and how much money it makes, even if it doesn't share any of it with its shareholders.

Income investors have it much easier. They couldn't care less what the company makes (unless they are environmentally, politically, or ethnically sensitive). For them, the right price is how much a comparably rated security with the same yield, maturity, and call features is priced. And since prices generally move quite slowly, last week's or yesterday's price is as good a benchmark as they need. This is why you will see numerous yield indexes published on a daily basis. Most such indexes key off the 10-year U.S. Treasury rate, although this is becoming more problematic given the vast audience of overseas buyers for this particular security. We assist our newsletter readers in this regard by publishing monthly a "Comparative Current Yields" table (used in the preceding example), which shows the yield spreads between the benchmark Treasury securities and the various alternative instruments. This provides an investor with a rough starting point for evaluating the offering price of a security he or she is considering. Factor in the rating, call features, maturity differences, and accrued interest, and you have a pretty good approximation of what you should be paying. If the price is significantly different, you need to look for what might cause this difference. If nothing stands out and the price is below expectation, it's a real buy. If the price varies on the upside, you may want to wait for a price drop or, alternatively, put in a good-till-canceled order for the security at its estimated fair value.

One area where this fair valuation exercise is particularly valuable is when a company has a number of similar securities outstanding. Here you have an opportunity to exploit pricing differences caused in large part by temporary supply/demand imbalances. Table 1.4 shows an example of

Table 1.4
Ford Preferreds—Comparative Pricing 12/31/2006

Ticker	Coupon	Maturity	Actual Price	Fair Value Price	Variance	% Variance	Dividend Accrual	Last Ex-date	Current Yield
PJE	8.25	2031	19.94	19.86	0.08	0.42%	0.97	7/12/06	10.87%
DKL	8.125	2031	19.9	19.57	0.33	1.68%	0.97	7/10/06	10.73%
KVU	8	2031	19.59	19.25	0.34	1.71%	0.94	7/12/06	10.73%
XVF	8	2031	19.8	19.25	0.55	2.76%	0.94	7/12/06	10.61%
TZK	7.7	2097	17.17	17.90	−0.73	−4.28%	0.28	11/8/06	11.40%
XKN	7.55	2097	17.04	17.56	−0.52	−3.03%	0.27	11/8/06	11.26%
KSK*	7.4	2046	17	17.27	−0.27	−1.58%	0.33	10/27/06	11.10%
FpA	7.5	2043	18.05	17.38	0.67	3.69%	0.22	11/19/06	10.51%
PIJ*	7.4	2046	17	17.27	−0.27	−1.58%	0.33	10/27/06	11.10%
Average for the Above									**10.92%**

various Ford Motor Company preferred and trust preferred issues and how they were priced on December 31, 2006. Since Ford is in the rating agency doghouse, all of its preferreds are way below comparable fair valuations of other companies with similar ratings. The game, then, is among the Ford issues, which one is the cheapest of the lot on any given day. The variance on December 31, 2006, between the cheapest (TZK) at—4.28 percent and the dearest (FpA) at 3.69 percent is a price disparity of 7.97 percent (4.28 percent plus 3.69 percent). If you buy only 20 shares of TZK instead of FpA, you'd have saved the price of this book!

In this exercise, the 11.90 percent average current yield for all these securities is used as the substitute fair value benchmark. However, because of various market anomalies, the current yields vary from 11.09 percent to 12.39 percent. Why is this? You will note that most of these preferreds are third-party trust preferreds sold under such names as Preferred Plus Trust FMX-1 (ticker PJE), Saturns—F 2003–5 (ticker DKL), Corts Trust for Ford Motor (ticker KVU), and Trust CERTS 02–1 (ticker TZK). An investor has quite a challenge even knowing that all these varieties exist and then understanding from these descriptions that this is a Ford bond repackaged as a $25 preferred. Also, the KSK and PIJ preferreds are a repackaging of the same Ford bond, but they will fluctuate as much as 25 cents from one another. That's a 1.5 percent price difference, not a lot—but trade 500 shares once a month and at the end of the year you may make enough for the down payment on a new Ford car. Even the one issue actually put out by Ford (FA) has a variety of ticker symbols, depending on the designator used by the brokerage firm (FpA, F_A, FprA, F+A, F/A, to name them all). Given these identity obstacles, you can assume that few buyers have a handy chart in front of them to tell them which is the bargain of the day. Hence, the FpA issue, because it's the easiest to identify, is frequently the most overpriced. The other issues fluctuate in value from day to day, so investors should trade them based on dividend payment dates and price fluctuations by using good-till-canceled buy and sell orders.

When to Sell

Much has been written about, how, when, and at what price to buy stocks. Less frequently addressed is when to sell a stock; and never addressed is when you should sell an income security. Hence, what you read next is in itself worth the price of the book.

Most advice on selling focuses on the investor's tax situation and need for cash income. Rarely do we see articles that give the investors credit for being able to anticipate a declining situation on their own and choosing to get out before the roof falls in. Certainly, we know from the dearth of written sell recommendations by Wall Street analysts that such recommendations are generally slow in coming. Frequently, this is because the brokerage houses are more concerned with their relationships with the companies involved than with their relationship with client investors, or at least small investors.

Here are five reasons to change a fixed-income security position:

1. *Potential declines in the ratings of a company.* Such ratings are often based on a deteriorating balance sheet, cash flow, return on capital, price earnings ratios, or operating results. You may not want to wait until the big three rating agencies get up to speed. Look for early alerts from agencies such as Rapid Ratings International, Inc., to provide an early alert.
2. *Radical changes in management or a company's business.* Nothing

changes the fortunes of a company faster than good or bad management. Witness the stock run-ups when a prominent business executive accepts a leadership position with a new company. Witness also the decline in value when he or she leaves a company.

3. *Changes in the prospects that a security will be called.* As one approaches the call date for a security, review the coupon or dividend rate to determine whether it is above current market rates. If so, chances are the security will be called. If the yield to call is substantially below the current yield, it may be time to sell.

4. *Frequent trading of preferreds or bonds to take advantage of price fluctuations.* This tactic generally enriches only the broker. However, you should be open to replacement of an issue that will better serve the objectives of a portfolio. Some examples are comparable issues offering better income or extended call protection, issues with better growth potential (especially true with capped adjustable-rate securities that are trading near their maximum interest rate), and growth and income issues with better ratings but equal returns. Any given holding can become temporarily overpriced, especially with convertible securities, relative to other issues of comparable or better quality. Trading up in such a circumstance is advisable. Use the fair value approach detailed in the previous section to determine when a security may be overpriced. Since price spikes are fleeting, you may place good-till-canceled sell orders at your desired price and catch any opportunities.

5. *A corporate event that has an effect on a company's stock and is of concern to the company's fixed-income investors as well.* Monitor media reports about corporate events. Frequently, an event that is a negative for shareholders can be a real positive for bondholders. For example, a new stock offering or share dilution may cause the stock price to decline, but this is a positive for bondholders since it puts more collateral behind their claim.

On the one hand, a corporate takeover announcement can cause either an increase or decline in the value of a company's fixed-income obligations. The key to the direction of the change is whether the acquiring party is more highly rated and the degree to which it intends to pay for the acquisition with new debt rather than stock and cash. There is often an immediate price reaction when such takeovers are announced. If the reaction is positive, consider selling into euphoria. Many such deals fall apart or deteriorate, from the creditors' perspective, as the bidding goes up. On the other hand, if the immediate reaction is a strong negative, it is already too late to avoid loss. Generally you should hold on to see whether the pressure from large creditors could improve or kill the proposed acquisition.

Don't be lulled into thinking that, as an income investor, you will not be affected by a corporate takeover or merger just because the price of your security does not immediately react. This may be due to a lack of initial disclosure details or the fact that there are no large institutional holders of the debt issue. Mergers don't happen unless someone sees a profit in the combination. The announcements of such mergers will carry the usual mantra of creating value through synergism and economies to be achieved. However, more often than not, they also are founded on the principal of making a profit at the expense of someone else. That someone else is often the bondholder or preferred stockholder. Hence, be skeptical about the announced reasoning behind corporate takeovers. When evaluating a corporate event and its consequences to you, keep in mind the order of priority for a typical business enterprise. That order is, first, the interest of management, next the interest of shareholders, then the interest of bank creditors, and last of all the bondholders and other creditors. Company employees also fit in there somewhere, but their positioning varies.

There are, of course, an array of personal reasons why an investor may decide it is time to sell. These tend to be the focus of most articles on this subject. Our discussion here on some of the investment-related reasons to sell is intended mainly to make you realize you must be alert for such events if you intend to be successful in managing your own account. A company announcement of plans to open a huge number of new stores next year may be designed to give the common stock a lift, but it means more debt and more risk for debt holders. When such changes are announced, it is generally time to look for the door.

Using Leverage and Margin

Investing using margin borrowing, like short selling, carries a negative connotation for most income investors. Margin is the amount a brokerage firm will lend you against your investments in order to invest even more. This use of borrowings against your investments is also referred to as *using leverage*. Typically, a brokerage firm will allow you to buy $2 worth of securities for every $1 of capital in the account. Against holdings of bonds and Treasuries, you can borrow even more. The interest rate the broker will charge you for this borrowing is negotiable and goes down as the amount increases. Use of leverage by fixed-income investors is a common strategy and has been broadly categorized as the *carry trade*. This is when investors borrow at generally lower short-term rates in order to reinvest at generally higher long-term rates. Hedge funds carry this to an extreme by borrowing 10 to 30 times their capital and may even borrow in a different currency than they invest in. Borrowing yen and investing in junk bonds are an example of the extremes here.

By definition, using leverage is high-risk investing. When the yield curve is flat, as it is at the time of this writing, it is also only marginally profitable. Leverage is useful, however, to exploit short-term opportunities and for year-end tax strategies. As you become more comfortable in your investment strategies, occasional use of leverage, such as to take advantage of year-end opportunities created by tax-loss selling by others can be an effective way to boost your total return. A word of caution here: Using leverage can be addictive, especially if you have success the first few times out, so be careful.

Credit Ratings

One of the marvels of fixed-income investing is credit ratings. They have traditionally been the single most important tool that investors have for defining their risk tolerance, making individual selections that fit that tolerance, and monitoring their portfolios for sell candidates due to changes in risk. Credit ratings are made by independent agencies that are recognized for that purpose by the SEC. They specialize in analyzing and comparing the financial data of companies and rendering their objective opinions. The most prominent of these agencies are Moody's, Standard & Poor's, and Fitch. The ratings are standardized with letters that denote increasing levels of risk. The categories run from Aaa (Moody's)/AAA (S&P or Fitch) to C/CCC. Also, plus (+) and minus (–) symbols are used to further refine the ratings and, more important, to allow for more frequent rating changes, changes that signal the direction in which the credit standing of a company is moving. Note that credit ratings are of limited value in predicting the future prospects of a company. They are assigned today to debt issues that may be outstanding for 30 years or more, a time period during which most corporations will suffer a trauma or two. Also, the ratings are based on the numbers supplied to the agencies by the companies themselves. The agencies do not audit or verify such numbers, although they may employ skepticism derived from experience in valuing any unaudited reports they receive.

To put these ratings into perspective, Ratings of Aaa/AAA to Baa/BBB are called investment-grade ratings. Ratings of Ba/BB to C/CCC are considered below-investment-grade ratings, or, in the vernacular of the popular media, "junk." As I stated earlier, this misleading pejorative can be the source of significant profit to savvy investors. See Table 1.5.

The reason I describe ratings as a marvel in my opening comments is

Table 1.5
Credit Ratings and What They Mean

Agency/ Risk	Standard Moodys	Rapid & Poor's	Fitch	Ratings
Investment Grade				
Highest quality	Aaa	AAA	AAA	A1
High quality	Aa	AA	AA	A2
Upper medium grade	A	A	A	A4
Medium grade	Baa	BBB	BBB	B2
Below Investment Grade				
Lower medium grade	Ba	BB	BB	C1
Low grade	B	B	B	C4
Poor quality	Caa	CCC	CCC	D3
Most speculative	Ca	CC	CC	E1
In default	C	D	D	

that they are a remarkably accurate indicator of default risk. Historic studies of default rates for the past 20 years show that securities rated investment grade have a default rate of less than 1 percent. And when such securities do default, the average eventual recovery of principal is 50 percent or more. *One shortcoming of ratings is that it is hard for a one-dimensional rating to predict a two-dimensional risk.* By this I mean that the risk of default is one concern, and the other is the likely level of recovery in a bankruptcy. Clearly, these differ when one company has a ton of goodwill on its books and another has mostly hard assets. A second element to this problem is that a company may have different levels of seniority of debt. In a bankruptcy, that seniority determines who gets paid first. Rating agencies try to address this problem by rating the junior debt lower than the more senior. But this can be misleading because, if there are not enough assets to settle all debt claims (never mind shareholders), junior debt holders can often end up getting nothing, while those more senior make almost a full recovery. There is no clear answer for this problem, so when trouble begins to appear, a closer examination of the company balance sheet is in order.

When comparing the higher yield of corporate securities to U.S. Treasuries, yes, Treasuries have zero default or call risk, and therefore inflationary considerations are the principal cause of price movements. However, is this worth giving up 100 to 200 basis points of additional yield? Clearly, on this merit alone, the answer is no. The additional yield is justified mainly by the fact that corporate securities can suffer price declines due to rating changes that fall short of an actual default. In this respect, ratings can be a curse in that changes in the rating become an additional factor influencing the price of a security.

Ratings are essential for large institutional investors mainly to help determine the price to pay for a given security. *Individual investors have a much simpler concern when it comes to ratings: Their major concern is whether they can be confident of getting their principal back at maturity.* If the answer is yes, all the periodic ratings adjustments are just so much noise. It is, however, noise that has consequences on the price movement of the security. But such price movements, if properly interpreted as just noise, can represent buying opportunities for capital gain and additional income.

Note that while a company's debt may be rated, say A3/A–, it is the practice of rating agencies to rate the preferred stock of the same company one notch lower, or Baa1/BBB+ in this example. This practice has created a special opportunity for investors, since the yield difference between the preferreds and the bonds of an investment-grade issuer can be 100 basis points or more. The reason for this rating disparity and yield difference is that, should a company default or go into bankruptcy, the recovery a preferred stockholder can expect may be significantly lower, although more than that of common shareholders.

Below-Investment-Grade Ratings

Below-investment-grade, or "junk," ratings denote securities with a significantly higher risk of default, in addition to other risks. To compensate investors for this added risk, the yield on these securities is from 100 to 800 basis points (1 to 8 percent) higher than for U.S. Treasuries. Such a huge yield difference is clearly worthy of a second look. But just how much more risky are these securities?

One of the activities I have been involved in since the early 1980s has been tracking and reporting on bond defaults. Over the years we have accumulated a mass of statistical data on corporate defaults. This data indicates that default rates over the life of Ba/BB-, B/B-, and C/CCC-rated issues run about 1.5 percent, 4.5 percent, and 12 percent, respectively. Since I previously indicated that the yields on these securities are from 100 to 800 basis points higher, there must be other factors to account for these relatively higher yields.

Second to default risk is the marketability risk of high-yield bonds. This is the risk that, when you want to sell them, there would be no takers to buy them, except at drastically reduced prices. This happens because the high-yield bond market is almost wholly an institutional investor market. By this I mean that the bonds are mainly bought by a few thousand mutual or pension funds that buy in million-dollar-plus lots. When a piece of bad news comes out about an issuer, thanks to our modern information technologies, all these institutional holders see it at about the same time, and the reaction is pretty much uniform: They all want to sell. Would-be buyers, who also see the news, will offer prices below comparably rated securities because they know there are many more sellers than buyers. Clearly, the risk of such an eventuality demands a yield premium by the original buyers.

Another cause of illiquidity in this market is a phenomenon called *flight to quality*, which occurs when uncertainty causes an across-the-board exodus from junk securities. For example, both of the Persian Gulf wars triggered such a flight. The flight-to-quality characterization is used because these investors tend to move into investment-grade bonds rather than out of bonds altogether.

As with investment-grade securities, junk-rated preferred stocks are rated one notch below the bond issues of the company. (Note also, when a company has senior and junior or convertible bond debt, the company will sport three rating grades to reflect the relative rank of these three types of securities.) It is in applying this across-the-board approach to ratings by the agencies that an opportunity opens up for investors.

I should point out that the yield difference between the lowest category of investment-grade bonds (Baa3/BBB–) and the highest-rated category of so-called junk bonds (Ba1/BB+) is generally 150 or more basis points. This jump in yield is more a reflection of the higher demand for investment-grade securities than it is a higher tendency to default. It also reflects the fact that many pension and mutual funds are not allowed to hold below-investment-grade securities, so the number of buyers shrinks and sellers increases when this relatively meaningless threshold is crossed. My bond default research indicates that the default rate difference between BBB and BB ratings would justify a difference of only about a 50 basis points, so investors interested in BBB-rated issues can buy BB- and BB-plus-rated issues and view the other 100-plus basis points as found money.

An additional lesson that can be drawn from how ratings are derived is the fact that when a preferred is rated Ba/BB, it means that the issuer is rated investment grade. Few issuers default only on their preferreds and not (eventually) on their bonds as well. Since the yield difference between a Baa/BBB bond and a Ba/BB preferred is 150 or more basis points, an investor who is comfortable with BBB bonds should be downright ecstatic with the comparable risk and higher yield for BB preferreds.

A few brief comments about rating changes. As I noted at the start, ratings often carry a plus (+) or a minus (–) (S&P) or a 1, 2, or 3 (Moody's) suffix to denote small variances. More important, their existence allows the rating agencies to make smaller changes to signal to investors which direction a company's fortunes are headed. Most rating changes in securities rated A—or higher are of small concern. To further alert investors to credit changes are the issuance of *credit outlooks* (negative or positive) and *credit watch* alerts (meaning a review is under way with positive or negative implications). Much of this has little market effect, but things do start to heat up when ratings go from A– to BBB+ or lower. The most jolting rating change is to Baa3/BBB—from any previous higher rating. This is the lowest investment-grade rating and often means that a downgrade to junk status is imminent. In fact, *I would argue that Baa3/BBB—is often a proxy for junk* to those in the know. It's a delay by rating agencies who want to postpone the blowback they get from the issuer when they finally drop the junk rating hammer. A downgrade to BB+, or junk, generally means a substantial price drop in both stock and debt prices and may be cause for the investor to reevaluate his or her holding. The market is aware that, at least in the recent past, rating agencies took pains not to downgrade an issuer to below investment grade until such a designation was long overdue, because issuers tend to become quite offended when this happens. After all, it is the issuers who pay the agencies to rate them, and shopping around for agencies is not unheard of. Since the Enron debacle, agency attitudes have changed, but the consequences are still playing out. See "Credit Ratings Drift: An Ongoing Problem" later in this chapter.

Since the yield difference between investment grade and below investment grade is 150 to 300 basis points, it is important to avoid securities that are making this rating transition downward (called *fallen angels* in Wall Street jargon). More to the point, however, it is a windfall to hold a security that makes the transition upward (called a *rising star*). Such upward transitions are only about half as frequent as the downward ones, but they do happen. Most come about due to an acquisition of another company by the issuer or a similar fortuitous event. Once in a while, they even result from hard work. In any case, securities of companies that are showing a series of rating improvements carry a premium for potential future price increases. In the below-investment-grade category, that bonus can be sizable, since the chances of an issuer on the upswing in ratings going bust are significantly lower than its peers.

Investment Strategies

How to Read the Ratings

The huge default rates for corporate debt from 2000 to 2002 seem to have accelerated the credit downgrading process by the three major credit rating agencies (Moodys, S&P, and Fitch). This is particularly true for downgrades from investment grade to below investment grade. Published statistics indicate that once downgraded to below investment grade, most such fallen angel issuers never recover their investment-grade status. A recent study by Standard & Poor's, titled "Rating Performance 2002," gave the data needed to construct Table 1.6, which shows the percentage of all debt issuers upgraded or downgraded in three-year periods for 1981–1983, 1990–1992, and 2000–2002. It demonstrates that such downgrades have had a cumulative erosional effect on debt quality and thereby have increased the cost of debt refinancing for corporate America as a whole. And that effect is accelerating.

Adding to the problem is that credit agency reports and rating actions are sounding more and more like brokerage house analysts focusing on the prospects for a company's equity rather than on its ability to service its debt. Witness a recent credit agency's wholesale downgrading of utilities and its announced threat to do likewise to 14 aerospace companies. Such actions have the distorting effect of raising the borrowing cost for a company because its prospects have dimmed rather than because its financial condition has deteriorated. In a number of cases, the downgrading greases the skids for the very problems that has been projected.

Table 1.7 was constructed from the same previously cited S&P study and reflects the total market percentages of debt by the issuers' rating for the same three time periods.

Table 1.6
Rating Changes for Corporate America Over Time

% of Issuers	1981–1983	1990–1992	2000–2002
Upgraded	7.6 percent	7.0 percent	5.4 percent
Downgraded	12.2 percent	13.7 percent	13.6 percent
Net erosion	–6.4 percent	–5.6 percent	–8.2 percent

Table 1.7
Ratings of Corporate America Over Time

% of Issuers	1981–1983	1990–1992	2000–2002
Rated			
AAA	19.4 percent	10.2 percent	1.5 percent
AA	15.6 percent	25.2 percent	5.8 percent
A	19.9 percent	24.9 percent	15.7 percent
BBB	13.3 percent	14.2 percent	25.4 percent
Total inv. grade issues	68.2 percent	74.5 percent	48.4 percent
BB	13.4 percent	12.2 percent	25.5 percent
B	16.4 percent	10.5 percent	23.3 percent
CCC	2.0 percent	2.8 percent	2.8 percent
Total non inv.-grade issues	31.8 percent	25.5 percent	51.6 percent

It demonstrates that the percentage of U.S. industry rated as investment grade has slipped from 68.2 percent to 48.4 percent over 20 years. Corporate debt is essential to fuel America's growth, since corporations use it to leverage the earnings of shareholders. The value companies can create for shareholders by borrowing will be substantially less, assuming it does not become an outright negative. This is killing equity prices of mature companies, which find more and more of their earnings are needed just to maintain the current level of debt. It also encourages growth through acquisitions rather than internal expansion, activities that don't help to grow our economy. Put another way, more companies are finding they cannot justify the capital expenditures that fuel economic growth. A side effect of this diminishing universe of investment-grade issuers is that there is, today, a shortage of such debt resulting in low yields. On the other hand, the downgrading to below investment grade creates a supply of junk bonds that crowds out new issues meant to finance new endeavors. Some will argue that the companies themselves are to blame for this credit deterioration. While there is truth to this, I believe the credit agencies role needs to be reevaluated.

The lessons for investors in all this are several. First, investment-grade bonds face far more price risk from rating cuts by trigger-happy rating agencies than from default. Second, don't let the term *junk bonds* frighten you. Most of corporate America today is junk if you believe this warped description. Finally, after three years of watching most of the stock market suffer massive value meltdowns, bond default loss and risk pales by comparison. As I've said here before, the biggest investment risk today, which credit rating can't reflect, is uncertainty. So increase your so-called risk and consider buying securities rated Ba/BB or those one or two notches below investment grade. The higher return that comes with them will provide a cushion against that uncertainty. See Table 1.6.

Investment Strategies

Credit Ratings Drift: An Ongoing Problem

On March 13, 2006, Fitch Ratings cut the credit rating of Ford Motor Company further, from BB+ to BB, based on recent parts suppliers' bankruptcies. It cited rationale such as, "The potential for labor actions, potential financial support, and costs related to re-sourcing and double-sourcing all point toward potentially higher direct costs from Ford's supplier base," and "Clearly the deep stresses [among auto-parts suppliers] will make the cost cutting more difficult." The luminary at Fitch responsible for these nuggets of wisdom goes on to opine that Ford's cash reserves would be depleted quickly should suppliers begin requiring Ford to pay cash for parts and services, because suppliers could soon grow wary about Ford's ability to stay current on pay-ments. And, not to leave anyone out, GM was thrown into the mix for having the same problems.

What is wrong with this picture? Why does my 23 years of tracking and reporting on corporate bankruptcies make me skeptical of these broad indictments by a credit rating agency, an organization that is supposed to give objective opinions based on known, or at least knowable, facts? Some of those knowable facts are these: Ford has $25 billion dollars of cash in the bank versus debts of only $18 billion; it earned $2 billion world-wide last year despite huge losses in the U.S. market; its balance sheet still sports $13.9 billion of shareholder equity; and it owns one of the largest, most profitable finance companies in the world. At this rate, Ford could continue losing money for a decade and survive. Although long before then, the credit rating agencies will have run out of rating letters and symbols.

Its not as though Ford and GM aren't aware of their problems and aren't busy trying to fix them. It's just that what the companies are doing doesn't seem to matter to the credit police. Ever since the Enron debacle, credit agencies have been on a campaign to restore their credibility. They have an agenda of their own, and it's all about ratings' competition. They are now in a race to outshine their competitors, even though there are only three players in this race.

A closer reading of the aforementioned statements by Fitch allows for some entirely different interpretations. Fitch is saying that because of its perceptions of Ford's out-look, parts suppliers will be more demanding on the company, thereby weakening Ford's financial position. Hence, Fitch feels it needs to anticipate the fallout from its dis-mal forecast by downgrading the company now and projecting more bad news for the future. This is the classic example of a self-fulfilling prophecy. Fitch executives might as well say, "We are cutting Ford's ratings because of possible future rating declines." Sim-ilar rating actions such as these lead to weaker players, such as Calpine and Mirant, hav-ing their credit cut off, precipitating eventual bankruptcy.

What is missing from the Fitch interpretation of events is recognition of business realities. A parts supplier to Ford or GM is a weak-to-strong relationship that does not change just because the weak member goes into bankruptcy. The strong member still determine how much it will buy only—now that the weaker is in bankruptcy and in a position to dramatically lower its costs, the strong partner will be looking to share those cost savings through lower component costs in the future. Yes, the weak partner can terminate the supply contracts and ask for higher prices, but the strong one can feel free to multisource in the future and use supplier competition to its advantage. Airline bankruptcies drove fares *down*, they didn't increase them. As for that nugget about how suppliers are going to demand cash payments and stricter terms in the future, this is sheer nonsense. It's a well-known truism that he who has the gold make the rules.

If credit agencies were of a mind to fairly weigh all the factors currently in play in the auto industry, the bankruptcy of the suppliers could just as easily be interpreted as a fortuitous event. In effect, the quote from Fitch could read, "Bankruptcy of parts suppliers will speed up Ford's plans to downsize and reduce component costs and will serve as the model for concessions in its own labor negotiations. Once the UAW sees how painful contract concessions in bankruptcy are, they will be reluctant to push GM or Ford into a similar negotiating position." In effect, the ratings outlook for Ford could just as easily have changed from negative to positive, and no rating change need have occurred. But then, such a scenario does not fit into the strategic plans of the credit agencies, in which Fitch is lagging Moody's and S&P in the derby to downgrade Ford and GM to the bottom.

The latest downgrade of Ford illustrates how credit rating agencies have drifted from their traditional function of evaluating a company's ability to survive to now evaluating a company's ability to prosper. The two things are very different, as long-term dogs Kodak and Xerox can attest. The shift has led to debt instruments acquiring stocklike volatility in their pricing. Investors who see and understand that this is what is happening can profit from the uncertainty.

The Federal Reserve Bank

The official role of the Federal Reserve Bank is to stimulate full employment and maintain price stability (i.e., dampen inflation). The principal tools it uses to achieve these goals is to manage short-term interest rates and the money supply. It manages short-term interest rates by setting the discount rate at which banks can borrow funds to meet their daily reserve requirements. It manages the money supply through buying and selling U.S. Treasuries. While this is a simplified explanation of what the Fed does, the consequences of its actions go well beyond its official goals. Its policies and public statements influence Congress, the economy, and the securities markets. It has this influence not so much because of its regulatory tools, but more because society and the markets want Fed leadership as a beacon into the future. Industry decision makers hate making decisions in a vacuum, so being able to tie their decisions to a Fed statement or policy move provides cover from critics of that decision, thereby enhancing job security when they are wrong. However, Fed pronouncements are often opaque. They don't want to be definitive on matters outside their control. It's a game of the blind leading the dumb, but you didn't hear that from me.

Because of America's dominant role in world trade, the Fed is influential in maintaining worldwide confidence in the U.S. dollar and securities markets. It is the organization the world looks to when national and international financial crises arise. It's no wonder that the role of the Fed chairman, as chief spokesman for the organization, has been described as the second most powerful job in the world.

Why am I addressing this subject in a book on income investing? Because the Fed is an organization that must do some of the long-range thinking on economic matters in this country. Congresses and presidents come and go, and their policy and budget decisions, more often than not, are short-term political expedients and compromises. The United States, along with most of the rest of the industrialized world, faces a mounting problem of an aging population that will soon translate into a declining workforce and a booming retiree population. The funds to pay the cost of maintaining these retirees, Social Security and Medicare, don't exist. Sure, there are assets in the Social Security fund, but they're not assets like stocks in profit-making companies or bonds backed by company assets, they're U.S. Treasuries. Treasuries are a debt the government issues backed by the full faith and credit of the United States of America. In short, they're debt issued by the government to itself, so that the actual cash collected as Social Security taxes can be spent currently. Its repayment (i.e., turning it back into cash that can be used to pay retirees) is totally dependent on a stream of future taxes withheld from people still working and economic growth. Since the ratio of working people is declining relative to retirees, we will reach a point, some time around 2040, when the country will need to either cut back on what are considered essentials (e.g., national defense) in order to pay for the retirees, or the politicians will alternatively take the easy way out and just print more money. While this is self-destructive, it is not uncommon in world history. It is how politicians renege on promises they have inherited from their predecessors and can't afford to keep. The only alternative to this bleak scenario is economic growth, which will fuel ever-greater tax revenues.

The Fed is aware of this demographic problem and the Social Security shortfall. More important, it has a role in making the problem less severe. Case in point, we all recall Chairman Alan Greenspan's comment in 1996 about the stock market showing "irrational exuberance." This expression of concern was not a protest against people getting rich playing the stock market. It was an expression of concern for the long-term effects of inflated stock prices. Those who lived through that era will recall the media infatuation with day traders and overnight millionaires. This was leading to a growing segment of the public thinking seriously about retiring at age 55.

The hard facts are that the Social Security and Medicare shortfalls are not going to be solved by Congress, by economic growth, or by any governmental agency—they are going to be solved by the public itself. The solution is both simple and elegant: *The baby boomer generation is going to reach minimum retirement age and continue to work. Why? Because they fear they don't have enough to last them for their remaining years. And for the most part they are right.* This may seem like a broken promise leading to a dismal future, but think again.

Through the advances of medicine and diet, we have an average life expectancy of over 80 years. In 1935 when Social Security was started, the average life expectancy for a male was 64, so targeting retirement at 65 was no gift. Today, you may have to be 67 to 70 before the same benefits are allowed, but that is still well before today's workers can be expected to die or lose their ability to function well. While Congress could push out the minimum retirement age even more, it doesn't have to. People will continue to work—and pay into Social Security while doing so—in order to save more in their private accounts. This is an elegant solution because it is a voluntary decision; it continues employment for the most experienced segment of our workforce; it continues an inflow of money into Social Security from these workers; and it diminishes the unfunded burden Social Security has to bear, given that these people will collect from the system for fewer years. Even the Medicare system will benefit, assuming these people continue under their employee-sponsored health insurance plans. Aside from this, people who work have less time to talk themselves into ailments or visit doctors. By now you may wonder what all this has to do with the Federal Reserve Bank.

Well, the Fed can meet its official mandate while also taking certain subtle actions that can lead to major economic changes, including retirement plans. For example, the stock market collapse in 2000, while traumatic for millions of people, was an important event for the long-term health of the country. When a 55- or 62-year-old worker retires, the workforce loses an experienced, highly paid worker who was paying into Social Security, not drawing on it. The stock market collapse forced millions of workers to rethink their retirement plans. Bad for those workers, but good for the country.

While the Fed has not been directly accused of causing the 2000 stock market collapse, its policies certainly helped. Be sure that the Fed is no fan of early retirement, nor should it be. As a government organization concerned with the long-term health of the country, such a policy concern is correct. If you've done a good job planning your retirement and can retire early, God has blessed you. But if you are counting on catching the next stock market or housing boom to make it happen, don't look to the policymakers at the Fed for help. Low interest rates, moderate stock growth, and slower house price appreciation are important ways to avoid premature retirements. Expect the Fed to clamp down on any "irrational exuberance," be it in stocks or housing, and plan on getting rich slowly. And all this will be done in the name of stimulating personal savings, albeit such personal savings will come about mainly from boomers staying on the job a lot longer than they planned.

If the preceding analysis leaves you depressed, think about those poor Europeans. In their socialist systems of government, the public has come to depend on the state to provide for their welfare, come what may. Europeans have come to feel they are entitled to retire as soon as allowed (which is too soon for the same reasons as exist in the United

States), and they expect the state to somehow come up with the resources to support them. In short, they have no fear of running out of savings, because the state will provide. Well, the state will not be able to provide in those countries any more than Uncle Sam can provide here. Nor do any of the governments show the courage to push back the retirement age. In Europe, people will retire from their jobs too soon, leaving them with no fallback. Governments will not be able to provide the promised levels of pensions and support from their current revenue, so they will resort to the only alternative: they will print money. Yes, this will lead to rampant inflation and erosion of the euro currency, but by then it will be the only politically workable solution. It leaves pensioners with a declining real income level with no likelihood that payments will keep up with the cost of living. The investment lesson here for U.S. investors is, don't look to Europe or euro-denominated investments for long-term income opportunities. As for those European pensioners who rely so much on their governments, it's not too late to give God a second chance.

Security Dealers and Brokers

Smart income investing is all about getting a high cash return on your money while assuming the lowest possible level of risk. There is, however, a third element to this investment objective, and that is *fees*. Unless your idea of income investing is lending the money to a relative, you are going to have to pay some fees. Fees come in many names, shapes, and sizes, may be hidden or boldly advertised ($8.95 a trade), and can be paid up front, at the end of a transaction, or both, with monthly stops in between. Why do we put up with all these fees? Because we are scared of losing. Because we are constantly being told that the best never comes cheap. *We take comfort in paying the high fees because it allows us to believe we must be buying the best. If such were the case, the fees would be money well spent. Alas, there is little correlation between fee levels and performance levels.* In fact, those authors who enjoy playing on the fears of their readers would state here that often the relationship is inverted, but I would never do such a thing. Let's just say that income investors who don't closely monitor where and how much they are paying in fees may well be earning less on their capital than the various people providing so-called help.

An investor should understand that brokers make their living from fees. In the old days this meant they were constantly offering you new opportunities to pay them fees. Today, with low commission rates, they look to making fees by selling you on the concept of a wrap account whereby, in return for a flat 1 or 1.5 percent, you can have their expert advice for free and pay no trading commissions (i.e., they're paid even if you do nothing all year!). The problem with wrap accounts is that the brokers want to wrap you in mutual funds from which they collect a fee as well. You are also a prime candidate for the new security underwritings the firm does. Actually, I should say all the new underwritings, not just the one or two hot ones each year, of which you might get 100 shares if you make enough noise. In fact, your allocation of a hot new issue is the true test of just how high you rate with these guys.

As a fixed-income investor, look for a discount broker and forget about all the supposed benefits of a wrap account. If you need advice on what to buy, then buy a newsletter like mine, which will cost you more than $8.95 but less than a wrap fee. Best of all, I'll even tell you when to sell. But enough self promotion—I just caution you that you will rarely find all your needs being met efficiently by using a full-service broker. Its very neat and comforting, but rarely is it cost effective. In fact, the big-name firms have a big name to protect so they put severe constraints on what their brokers are even allowed to talk about with you. This is because their number one concern is being sued for giving bad advice. Not that they lose very many cases, given the way the arbitration system for settling disputes works. Rather, they know investors will settle for mediocre returns as long as they don't have significant losses. Hence, you will rarely see them recommend a junk bond to you unless they need to unload it out of inventory. If you should insist on buying them, the order will be clearly marked "unsolicited," even when the broker brings it to your attention.

In deciding who to use as a broker, look at what you intend to do. If you plan to buy mostly mutual funds, go with someone like Fidelity and use it for brokerage services as well. If you intend to buy municipal bonds, use someone like Joe Brady at William Blair & Company. If you like to buy and hold bonds, go to a strong bond house like Merrill Lynch or Bear Sterns. But, if you plan to actively manage your own account, go with a Charles Schwab, Scott Trade, or an E*Trade.

Finally, if you're in poor health and need someone you can rely on to look after your account for a spouse or children, look to retaining an investment advisor you can trust, or use a bank trust department or company such as Northern Trust. In this situation there is no low-cost solution, but, then, it's not a time you should be seeking one.

2

INFORMATION SOURCES AND HOW TO USE THEM

Investment Advice via the Media

In today's multimedia world, investment advice as a topic of writing or discussion is exceeded only by news about politics and crime. Entire publications, Web sites, and TV shows are dedicated to giving free advice. The advertisers for such media are often firms trying to trumpet their advisory services as part of opening an account with them. I am particularly struck with the overnight success of Jim Cramer's *Mad Money* TV show. Here's someone who has an opinion on every security out there—even *way* out there. His colorful and entertaining style (at least some people think it is colorful and entertaining!) begs the question of how good advice can be from someone who tries to cover the universe. Much of his success is due to his success (i.e., his picks become self-fulfilling prophecies). Hence, if you are a day trader, you can probably make money at the expense of those who don't know how the game is played. The game is baseball, and during a game, some 90 pitches are thrown at you. Even if you swing at every pitch Cramer throws at you, you will still miss, foul, or pop out more often than you will get a base hit. And if you get a base hit, when do you run for home (cash out)?

I pick Mr. Booyah (Cramer) as an example because, while he may have the best of intentions, he personifies all that is wrong with media-generated investment advice. What's lacking in such advice is an understanding by the listener of who it is really suitable for. Fortunately for income investors, you are of little interest to media pundits (bonds are boring, as we all know!). This is fortunate, because most fixed-income media advice assumes you are risk averse and therefore focuses on instruments (CDs, Treasuries, bonds, CMOs, etc.), timing (buy now because rates are going up), or strategies (laddering, diversification, tax free versus taxable, etc).

The major concern for income investors is when the individuals giving the advice are genuine income gurus. Then you have to contend with the fact that their advice may be perfectly suitable for a large institutional buyer, but may be impractical for an individual managing his or her own account. For example, recently a prominent income fund manager was touting the virtue of buying Treasury Indexed Performance Securities (TIPS). For him the strategy made perfect sense. He picked up 25 basis points on $1 billion in a month. For an individual investor who doesn't want to buy and sell from one month to the next, it would be a lot of effort for a small reward. On a $10,000 investment, 25 basis points will buy lunch, provided you skip dessert.

Prospectuses

Every new issue of public securities, be they stocks or bonds, has an offering prospectus. This document is supposed to be a source of all the reasons you should want to buy the security, but is often anything but. The prospectus is an SEC requirement that must provide all the information an investor needs to know in order to make an informed decision.

It must be placed in the hands of the purchaser before a sale can be finalized. Don't think, however, that you will necessarily receive or read this document before you place your order. Yes, you will receive the prospectus more or less before you buy, but you will not read it. And if you read it, you will not understand it. And if you read it and understand it, you will probably not want to buy the security.

If you subscribe to any financial newspaper, you will also see full-page "tombstones" announcing a new company's stock or bond offering. At the bottom of that ad you will see wording to the effect that this ad is not an offer to sell the security, which can be made only via a prospectus. Yeah, right. That's why they pay the *Wall Street Journal* upward of $50,000 for that nonadvertisement. It's like those drug ads you see on television promoting a medicine you can buy only with a doctor's prescription. In fact, I wondered for months what that purple pill was for. With tombstone ads you get all the information you need to place your order, or at least all the underwriter thinks is needed to pique your interest and to get you to call one of its selling underwriters, who will in turn tell you the rest of the story, or at least as much as he knows. If you really press him with detailed questions about the issue beyond the facts on his two-page sales spiel, you'll find that he has never read the prospectus. But then, why should he? Very few people do—and fewer still understand what they've read.

Brokerage houses are notorious for taking orders on the phone and making a meticulous record of when they sent you the prospectus. This covers them, since your trade is legally not settled for three days, by which time they can assume you have received the prospectus in the morning mail, all 300 pages. These requirements are meticulously observed by underwriters for one reason: If the security offering goes bad, it is the main protection the underwriter has that it did everything required to alert the investor of the risks.

While a stock prospectus is trying to interest you in the company and provide an incentive to invest, a prospectus for a debt issue is all about risk. This focus on disclosure of adversities makes most prospectuses for debt issues read like warning labels that come with medicines. However, unlike those warning labels, which are fairly brief, prospectus warnings go on forever. This is because they are written in large part by attorneys whose total perspective is negative. In fact, if one reads the prospectus of most fixed-income securities today, one would probably not buy the offering. Knowing this, the prospectuses are often written in legalese, using very long sentence structures and with a page count that defies reading. That is, of course, their purpose. I recall one prospectus that defined no less than 28 separate risks that could affect the subject security. That could be a record, of which some attorney out there is justly proud. In securities law, the road to partnership seems to be defined by how many new pages of nonsense you can add to the hundreds of pages of boilerplate already considered accepted fare, but nevertheless paid for by the page.

What the underwriter wants you to read is the one- or two-page summary sheet that addresses all the things you should want to know about the issue. All the good things, that is. The bad things, called *debt covenants*, must generally be dug out of the prospectus. Debt covenants are the dos and don'ts under which a debt issuer must operate. Things like the call provisions, exceptions to the call provisions, dividend restrictions, restrictions on the issuance of more senior debt than this issue (or the lack thereof), sinking fund provisions, collateral provisions, exceptions thereto, and on and on. These debt covenants determine the relative seniority of a debt issue, which is all-critical should bankruptcy occur. For it is in bankruptcy that relative seniority of the various parties' claims is defined. This is discussed further in Chapter 9.

Debt covenants tend to be fairly standard, in part because credit rating agencies pay close attention to them and are influenced in their rating of the issue by differences in covenants, such as between various issues of a company as well as variance from the norm. You should compare where a company's specific debt issue ranks relative to others from the same company. If lower, even slightly, it means you would probably stand in line behind more senior claims in case of bankruptcy. The recent issuance by Ford of new debt secured by the company's assets is a classic example of where existing unsecured debt is downgraded because the claim value of all existing debt has been significantly undercut.

While a prospectus must be given to you before the sale is consummated, no such requirement exists once you buy the security in the secondary market. Prior to the SEC making such documents available online through the Edgar system, getting a prospectus on an older issue was difficult. Reviewing the prospectus of an older issue is particularly important when an issuer gets in trouble. It is then that you truly need to know where you stand if things get worse. This is particularly true of below-investment-grade bonds, especially those that do not start life that way. Issues that start out as junk issues often have restrictive covenants that anticipate trouble. Issues that start life as investment grade and fall from grace (i.e., *fallen angels*, in investment terminology) generally don't need to provide the same level of protection and therefore are often higher risk issue. Of course, you may say, why bother? Why not just sell the issue when it looks like trouble rather than doing all this research. *The answer is that when trouble begins to show, the price of the security will overreact and you face a serious loss of capital if you sell.* Clearly it would be better to evaluate where you stand based on the finances and relative strength of the security you hold rather than selling into a knee-jerk market judgment. I can't tell you how many securities I've seen fall into the teens when default or bankruptcy threatened, only to recover almost all, if not all, of their face value. In fact, bankruptcy can often promise a quicker recovery in value than if the company continues to struggle.

One of the things a prospectus should tell you about is the use of proceeds. While for most large corporations this is not particularly significant, this is not so when buying a below-investment-grade or junk issue. Statistics on past defaults show that there was a higher predictability for a bond to default from its purpose than from the issue's credit rating. High-default-risk purposes include funding for an acquisition, both past or contemplated. Making acquisitions work is notoriously difficult, even for the best of companies. When that company has no cushion of financial strength, failure is unforgiving. Many times, companies don't want to tell you why they are issuing debt and offer up as explanation "general corporate purposes." While this may be acceptable from an investment-grade issuer, it is a red flag when done by a junk issuer. The most egregious example of this is when a company uses such proceeds to pay out a large cash dividend to a controlling shareholder group. This not only demonstrates a lack of faith in the company's future, it also severely weakens the company's finances. In contrast, bonds issued to pay down bank debt is one of the safest use of funds. This is because paying down bank debt increases the company's borrowing capacity, which may be needed in the future. Again, do your homework. Study the company's financial history. The company may be forced to pay down its loans because banks that have lost faith in the company's ability to survive want an early out.

Another thing to look for in the indenture is the relative seniority of the bond you are buying. This is especially important when you are buying preferred issues that are designated as debt. Debt issues come with various titles, but you can't rely on them to define your relative seniority. One thing you can be sure of is that any bank debt will be the senior debt, although sometimes the debt you are buying is on par (*pari passu*, in Street talk) with the banks. The only way to get ahead of banks is via a bond that has a lien on specific company assets. This happens when such debt is issued before the banks come along, except in certain industries where they have become common practice (e.g., railroad cars, airplanes, and airport gates).

Behind the most senior debt can be bond issues misleadingly titled *senior debt*, *senior-subordinated debt*, and *junior debt*. These titles are also applied to the debt issues of a subsidiary of a company, where they have even less claim value. If bankruptcy comes, the court makes short shrift of these various titles. You are generally thrown into one of three categories: Class 1, the senior secured creditors; Class 2, the senior unsecured creditors; or Class 3, the unsecured creditors. The offering prospectus should allow you to identify where you might be classified before the hammer falls.

Misuse of the English Language

I always look forward to the end of the biannual national election campaign cycle. Think of all the outlandish headlines we're forced to suffer. Take, for example, a recent AP news headline, "Economy Grows at Weakest Rate in a Year." It was a catchy headline, but the real news in the article was that the second-quarter growth was revised upward to 3.3 percent rather than the 2.8 percent previously reported by the Commerce Department. Another recent example in the *Wall Street Journal*, "Efforts to Reduce U.S. Addiction to Oil Are Few," would better read, "Efforts to Reduce Dependence on Foreign Oil Are Few." These are subtle ways the media tries to inject personal agendas or biases into our thinking. This is a constant problem, but always reaches its zenith in an election year. The effect of this on investors is to put investment decisions on hold and encourage caution. Now caution is something I constantly stress and it is something any fixed-income investor should value. It is not, however, a sentiment that grows economies or drives up stock markets.

Unfortunately, one thing that doesn't end after November is all the disclaimer language we will be reading with every press release, financial report, or financial analysis. Thanks to the Sarbanes-Oxley legislation, we can all sleep better knowing that what we are reading is now so much more reliable. This, not withstanding such new disclaimer language as, *"When used in these presentations, the words 'expects,' 'anticipates,' 'intends,' 'plans,' ' believes,' 'seeks,' 'estimates' or words of similar meaning, or future or conditional verbs, such as 'will,' 'would,' 'should,' 'could,' or 'may' are generally intended to identify forward-looking statements. These forward-looking statements are inherently subject to significant business, economic and competitive uncertainties and contingencies, many of which are beyond our control."* I take that back, we will not be sleeping at all, because most of us do know the meaning of the word *is*, and you won't find it in any document issued by these people.

The preceding extract is from a 300-word disclaimer that not only takes on the task of defining the English language, but also then reminds you of some 14 risk factors that could affect anything the company says. This disclaimer language is probably attached to every communication issued by that company. It was written by well-paid attorneys who can be fairly confident that it will never be read. This leaves the door wide open for burying some really significant caveat without fear of repercussions. This does little to inspire confidence . I dare say, the effect is quite the opposite.

I suspect that corporate officers will soon be taking public speaking classes in how to sound convincing while remaining noncommittal and spewing the preceding safe-haven words. The Sarbanes-Oxley Act's attempt to legislate integrity leads to the most minor accounting infractions being disclosed and played up in the press. This is a problem, because neither the media nor most investors are smart enough to know what qualifies as minor and what does not. This leads to media overplay of a story whenever it's a slow news day or they have an ax to grind. In any case, the volume of such disclosures will cause price swings, which will trigger class-action lawsuits and generally reduce confidence. You cannot legislate honesty and you cannot legislate investor confidence. You can only legislate obfuscation. How long before we read, "In the interest of full disclosure, I certify that no animals were harmed in the drafting of this disclaimer"?

Case Study

Getting Railroaded by China

Here's what a close reading of an actual prospectus can reveal.

A recent full-page tombstone for a $543 million new stock issue caught our eye because of its impressive size and sponsorship. It seems every major house on Wall Street had a piece of this issue, called the Guangshen Railway Company Limited. Yes, in this high-tech era, these folks are telling us there is opportunity and profit in low-tech railroads.

The appeal here is that this railroad is in China, a country on every international fund's short list. And why not? Page 5 of the prospectus (under such headings as "High Profitability," "Leader in Railway Reform," "Modern Technology," and the high-sounding "Strategic Investments in Infrastructure") tells about this very profitable railroad in a high-growth-region market. Page 6 tells us that this railroad enjoyed operating margins of 63 percent in 1995 compared to 17 percent for a comparable U.S. railroad. Also, we are told that the area served by this railroad is the fastest-growing province in China, with an average annual GDP growth rate of 20 percent for the past five years. In case the potential investor is worried about government control of this company's prices, we are assured on page 8, under the section headed "New Autonomy," that the government has given the company new autonomy in the pricing of its transport services. We are left to speculate what the old autonomy might have been if this company currently enjoys a 63 percent operating margin.

Like all well-written prospectuses, this one has all the good news and color pictures up front. If you can restrain your enthusiasm long enough to get past page 6, a true reality check awaits you. In fact, your suspicions may begin early, about page 10, where you see for the first time that the $543 million being ponied up by foreign investors will buy only 30 percent of the railroad. The other 70 percent will continue to be owned by the "parent company" (i.e., the Chinese government). By definition, then, this railroad, with a book equity of $317 million is being valued at $1.81 billion. We also find out under "Use of Proceeds" that, after about $30 million in underwriting fees and expenses is deducted, the balance of the stock offering is to be used to fund equipment purchases, track and facility renovations, and repayment of loans from the so-called parent company. Curious, however, things don't get really disturbing until you get to pages 12 and 13, where hard numbers in the form of summary financials begin to appear. At first we see operating results that show passenger revenues increasing 36 percent over the past two years, freight revenues increasing 41 percent, and net income increasing 25 percent. We also now learn that the additional capital being contributed by foreign investors is equivalent to 79 percent of the total assets of the company. In short, they will almost double in size overnight. Pretty ambitious for a low-tech business like railroading. However, isn't the prospect that such assets will be effectively employed implicit, given that the new shares are being sold at four times book value? No matter, this is a high-earning, high-growth investment where book value doesn't matter. Or does it?

The reality check continues on page 13. Here we see that the company's passenger traffic over the past four years has decreased 20 percent in number of passengers and 24 percent in passenger miles. Freight tonnage per mile in this time period has also declined, by 2 percent. How is this possible in light of the reported passenger and freight revenue increases? Well, it seems all the fabulous growth statistics cited so far in this prospectus are calculated in renminbi, the currency of China. If you skip ahead to page 17, you find that this currency was subject to some inflation and devaluation pressures during the previous two years. In fact, the fabulous growth in local currency is offset by the fact that it lost 45 percent of its exchange value in U.S. dollar equivalents. If a Brazilian railroad tried to pull such a numbers game, we would call it flimflam.

Still and all, when you calculate the earnings per share based on the dollar numbers reported for the year 1995, you get a price-earnings ratio of 11.7 times. As you get deeper into the accounting policies in China, however, this, too, begins to look inflated. For one thing, the company began to depreciate its assets for accounting purposes only in 1993. Would anyone like to guess the average age and depreciated value of its assets given the stated need to modernize? We also see that in the past three years, the government has paid out in dividends 100 percent of the earnings—earnings that equal the total amount supposedly needed to finance the modernization that foreign investors are now being asked to fund. The prospectus notes that future earnings could be subject to income taxes payable at 15 percent, thus potentially further decreasing the price-earnings ratio, albeit an improvement over the de facto 100 percent tax rate it has been paying as "dividends" for the last three years. As for the prospect of dividends in the future, beyond a promised payout of about 1.5 percent in 1996, there is no statement of dividend policy. We are told dividends will be declared in local currency and paid in Hong Kong dollars. How this will translate into U.S. dollars is a big question given the outlook for Hong Kong beyond 1997 (when Britain handed it back to China). We can visualize a lot of games that can be played regarding such a payment arrangement once China controls both currencies.

The deeper you get into this prospectus, the more you suspect you are being had. Pulling a variety of disclosures together offers a picture of a Chinese government looking for ways to earn foreign exchange. It spins off a piece of its railway system into a separate entity and calls it "autonomous." Never mind that the company has so overpriced its services that buses and water transportation are taking market share from it—Wall Street will buy anyway. Sign on Bear, Stearns & Company as your global coordinator for a $1.6 million fee, pay up to 6 percent in underwriting costs, and the best names in the business will sign on. In fact, with international funds pulling in billions of dollars monthly, where can they invest except in megadeals such as this one? Furthermore, the success of this issue is likely to lead to similar offerings (e.g., the announced plans to build a chain of hotels across China), since, in addition to providing capital for low-tech projects, very little of the foreign exchange raised by these offerings is required to be used for the project itself.

However, don't fault the underwriters. After all, they fully disclosed all we gleaned from this prospectus—and much that we missed as well. Blame instead the investors and fund managers who never read past page 10 of a prospectus. Better to show these ignorant souls the list of some earlier China deals that are available for just pennies on the dollar. Deals like the 1914 Nanking-Hunan 7 percent railway bonds, the Chuchow-Chingchow 8 percent railway bonds of 1916, the Hukuang Railway 5 percent sinking fund bonds of 1911, or the various securities of the Shanghai-Nanking, the Honan, the Canton-Kowloon, the Tientsin-Pukow, and the Lung Tsing-u-Hai Railways. By issuing bonds instead of stock, these early Chinese issues at least pretended they were going to pay investors back.

International fund investors may want to peruse their fund's portfolio holdings in the next report they get. It would seem that Chinese railroads have been giving foreign investors a merry ride for a long, long time.

P. S. The preceding analysis was done by me and published in July 1996 in my *Defaulted Bonds Newsletter* at the time of the launch of this company on the NYSE at a price of $20 a share. Following a 14-month honeymoon with investors, the stock sank to a price of $5 a share, where it traded for the next two and a half years before rising to about $10 a share, where it traded for another five years. Today, after almost 10 years, it is threatening to break its initial $20 launch price. A careful reading of the prospectus, in this case, could have saved a lot of investors a long train ride to nowhere.

When to Worry about the Accounting

The recent wave of accounting concern is welcome because it instills caution in an investment market that too recently succeeded largely by shooting from the hip. Aside from this, it is a necessary comeuppance for those thirtysomething MBAs running their investment portfolios as though numbers told the whole truth. *Accounting is not an exact science, nor are corporate managers meticulous in tattling on themselves.* Manipulation of the accounts prior to Sarbanes-Oxley (SOX) was normal in most corporations, usually for the good of shareholders, due in no small part to the knee-jerk reaction of markets to short-term disappointments. No shareholder is benefited from the class-action suit automatically filed by predatory law firms the day after any unexpected earnings shortfall. Since auditors don't certify quarterly results, management had leeway to lag in reporting bad news while preparing shareholders for such news. Since SOX, industry practices have tightened considerably. This does not mean, however, that investors can lower their guard.

Aside from the financial numbers, there are any number of corporate events that provide a natural reason for skepticism and caution. Here are some examples:

- The year CEOs are scheduled to retire will generally be a bumper quarter or year for a company. They want to go out with a bang, as well as a big bonus and a high exercise price on their remaining options. Needless to say, the year after that should be a downer (e.g., General Electric CEO Jack Welch's retirement in 2001 led to a price decline from which the company took some time to recover).

- If a new CEO is an outside hire or replaces one who left under a cloud, look out! The first priority for such an executive, if he or she is at all smart, is to write off anything not nailed down. In that case, the follow-on year should look quite good.

- If a company begins talking about reorganizing or restructuring its businesses, expect bad news. Such talk is a euphuism for big-time screwups that need to be buried in a larger event. The news here is negative, but oddly enough, the market often reacts positively, perhaps because it's pretty good at knowing when management can't shoot straight, so the bad news is already factored in. Also, the write-offs have often unburdened future years' earnings.

- When a company's auditors resign voluntarily, run for the phone. This is almost always bad, and we are likely to see it happening a lot more often post-Enron.

- When a company changes auditors suddenly, look out. This can mean its auditors wouldn't go along with some questionable transactions or practices. In today's market there will be little tolerance for this.

- Watch out for the sudden departure of CFOs. These are the people with the front-row seat, and in today's SOX world, they're riding without a seat belts or an air bags. If they were fired, that's even worse.
- Be wary when company press releases become less frequent and start using words like "unforeseen," "may result in," "could portend," and the like.
- Special announcements are particularly worrisome. Assume the worst when you see wording such as, "We have retained the services of _____ to [investigate, explore, pursue, study] the [possibilities, alternatives, remedies] for . . ."
- Here's another red flag: "We have received an informal inquiry from the SEC . . ."

Many investors, having been burned by one of the preceding events or believing the world of Wall Street is beyond their comprehension, have retreated into mutual funds. The belief that a fund manager is better able to read these signs and take timely action may be correct. It does not, however, unburden the investor from having to make judgments. It merely shifts the investor to a different set of evaluations and judgments, the answers to which are not always found in the fund's share price or in a Morningstar publication.

Financial Statements

Reading and understanding the financial statements of a company is the principal way in which analysts and the public learn how well a company is doing. Over time, they provide a picture of hope or despair for the future, but only by guesswork, since the public financials are all historic and not prospective. Although companies will project their expectations one or two years forward in internal statements, the public rarely gets to see these. Still, it is worth looking at these historic results, since that is where management starts in making their projections for the future, projections you can sometimes make more objectively than they can. For an untrained reader, financial statements might as well be written in a foreign language. The assumption is that the reader is knowledgeable, and therefore these documents make few compromises for clarity. In fact, the more troubled a company is, the less it wants those problems understood and second-guessed. Hence, a lack of clarity should be taken as a warning sign.

Comprehending financial statements is a multiyear task and well beyond the scope of this book. My goal here is to provide an introduction to what these financial statements mean and to invite you to begin the journey toward comprehension by at least understanding what each of these reports is designed to do. Reading these financials is what is meant when you are advised to do your homework. Like homework, it's no fun, but it's possible that you may actually rise to the challenge, read a book and take a course on security analysis, and open up an entirely new life interest that can make and/or save you money. Unless you can comprehend these financial statements, you will always be dependent on the advice of advisors, newsletters, pundits, and analysts whose opinions may be compromised or unsuitable for your situation.

The four financial statements a company must produce and have certified each year by independent accountants are found in a company's annual report or its more comprehensive version, the 10-K report. The four statements are the *balance sheet*, the *income (operating) statement*, the *source and application of funds (cash flow) statement*, and the *shareholders' equity statement*. In addition, the financial statements have numerous pages of footnotes in which other statements, which include some of the most meaningful information, reside. Along with the financial statements is the opinion of the independent accountants. This is normally a boilerplate letter stating that the financial statements fairly present the operations and condition of the company. Only when that opinion has any sort of qualifying language in it do you need to give it a second thought. Normally, a company will move heaven and earth to avoid such language, since it is a well-known red flag. Failure to provide such a standardized opinion is therefore that much more significant.

Before you get to these statements in the annual report, there is an explanation of the year's results as seen by the company management. It is generally titled "Management's Discussion." Here the management takes you through the year, pointing out what went right and/or what went wrong and why. It is certainly a help in that it anticipates many of the questions an astute reader will have and therefore provides answers as well the questions a novice doesn't know to ask. But it may not answer all your questions, especially those relating to what you can expect the company to do about any negatives. Still, it is a good gauge of how forthcoming the company management is and whether they are being honest with themselves when they have serious problems.

Balance Sheet

For income investors, the most important financial statement is the balance sheet. It is the best measure of a company's ability to survive. The left side of the balance sheet lists all of the assets of the company in the order of their liquidity. The variety of assets a company may have and in what detail it may choose to display them varies, so this overview discusses the most common.

The top item is always cash and marketable securities (i.e., cash that is being temporarily invested). This is followed by accounts receivable and inventories. The most liquid assets, as a group, are considered *current assets* and form the basis for many calculated measures of a company's health. If a company is manipulating its accounts, it will be in this part, since early warnings of trouble ahead will often show up here through deteriorations in accounts receivable and inventory ratios and relationships vis-à-vis sales, cost of sales, and each other.

After the current assets come the *fixed assets* (e.g., factories, buildings, and equipment used in producing the company's products). Next you have any investments the company has made in businesses or assets that are not consolidated into the company's own balance sheet. These are long-term investments related to the business and not investments of excess cash funds, which would be listed in current assets. The nature of these investments is generally explained in more detail in the footnotes to the financial statements.

Finally, you have the company's intangible assets, which include such items as research and development expenses not yet written off, patents, trademarks, and other rights, as well as goodwill. The most difficult asset to understand in this category is goodwill. It comes about when a company acquires another company or another company's assets for more than their book value. In this case, the extra purchase price amount is assigned as *goodwill* and valued each year thereafter by accounting rules you truly don't want me to explain. The makeup of the intangibles is also often explained in detail in the footnotes.

The right side of the balance sheet details all the claims by various stakeholders against the company's assets. It begins with the most current claims and ends with the least current, namely, the shareholders' equity or ownership stake in the company. The most current is short-term debt payable within the next 12 months, followed by accounts payable or trade payables. The sum of these obligations, called *current liabilities*, is the basis for a number of important financial measures. It is the company's ability to meet these obligations over the subsequent year that is key to its survival. Next come the company's obligations to its bondholders and workers via funding obligations for pensions and health care. And finally, we come to the shareholders' equity section, where the net results of all the years' past, as well as the current year, are summarized. If a company has been doing poorly for some time, shareholders' equity may actually be a negative amount. When this amount is negative, it means the company is insolvent and shareholders no longer have a financial stake in the company, although they still legally elect the company's management. When you buy the debt instruments of a company with negative shareholders' equity, you should recognize that there is a good chance you will soon become a shareholder in that company.

It's important to understand that the balance sheet representations of values are derived over many years. Accounting rules are focused on avoiding the overvaluation of a company's assets, but they fall well short in recognizing undervaluations. This is why, in mergers and acquisitions, the price paid for a company being acquired may be a multiple of the company's share price, which in turn may already be well above the balance sheet book value of those shares (*book value* is the shareholders' equity divided by the number of shares outstanding). The 2005 acquisition of AT&T by SBC Communications for $16 billion is a perfect example. AT&T had a dying business, long-distance telephone communications. It did, however, have a huge customer base that was ripe for conversion to newer technology, and it owned one of the most recognized brand names in the world. *Hence, a company whose balance sheet showed only $7 billion of shareholders' equity, which was valued at $12 billion by the stock market, was sold for $17 billion. Had that $17 billion been shown on the balance sheet of AT&T, I doubt its debt would have been lowered to BB+.* As a debt holder of AT&T, this is valuable information because it means AT&T debt, like its stock, was underpriced.

Income Statement

The second financial statement and the one of most concern to analysts and shareholders is the income statement. Technically, the income statement is a summary of the activities during a year that account for the changes in the balance sheets from the previous year end to the current year end. It is also, however, the truest measure of a company's ability to prosper. A company's balance sheet may be in shambles, with negative net worth and worse, but if it shows growth and profitability it is given wide discretion by the various stakeholders who provide the capital. To add meaning to these numbers, a three-year history is shown.

The income statement begins with the revenues received during the year from sale of the company's products. Deducted from this is the cost of the goods and services produced. The difference is called the *gross profit*. Deducted from this amount are the sales, general, and administrative (SG&A) expenses of the company. These are the costs to run the company and include research and development expenditures, which are forward-looking expenses. The net result of the gross profit minus the SG&A expenses is called the *operating income*. From here on, the income statement becomes a little more customized before we get to the all-important bottom line, or *net profit* (also called *profit after tax*, PAT, or *net loss*). Included here is an array of items such as interest expense, interest income, income taxes, gains or losses from securities transactions, gains or losses from asset sales or discontinued operations, minority interests, and the always dubious provisions for reorganization costs. Although these items are considered nonoperating, they can add up to more than the operating results. More, that is, in a negative sense, since this is the section of the income statement in which most of the big mistakes of the past and present show themselves. When you see big negatives in this section of the income statement, it is worth your while to read the management discussion and footnotes to see how they address the bad news and whether their explanations are reasonable. Look out for dubious explanations or no explanation at all. It tells you something about management's attitude.

Statement of Cash Flows

Cash is the lifeblood of any corporation, and management of a company's cash flow is particularly critical if the company is below investment grade. When a company does not generate sufficient cash from operations or borrowings to pay its bills, it is considered illiquid. Nothing leads to a bankruptcy filing quicker than a company being illiquid, so it needs to plan its sources of cash and push out its debt maturities well in advance of public awareness of its operating problems. At the time of this writing, GM and Ford were widely perceived as possible bankruptcies, but this perception fails to recognize that, with more than $20 billion in cash available for each company, they have avoided the need to raise cash, and they do not face large short-term debt maturities. This is what I mean by good fund flow management.

The cash flow statement begins with the bottom-line number from the income statement and starts adding back all the operating expenses that did not involve cash: items such as depreciation, inventory, and receivable loss provisions, deferred income taxes, and accounting change items. Added or deducted from this is the amount of that cash went to increasing or decreasing accounts receivable, inventories, and various payable amounts. The net of all these items is considered the cash generated from operations. Companies that are growing rapidly or those that are losing money will often show a negative number here. This means they need to look elsewhere for the additional money required to keep going.

Once we tally up what the cash requirements from operations are, the cash flow statement details the investment activities of the company. Here are shown the details of what the company spent for property, plant, and equipment, or acquisitions less the proceeds from any sales of the same. Then the company details its financing activities. These include new borrowings or debt retirements, purchases or sales of common stock, and dividend payments to shareholders.

The sum of all the preceding items explains the year-to-year change in the cash and cash equivalents number on the balance sheet. As a debt holder in a company, you would be concerned to see a company buying back large amounts of its shares or paying sizable dividends to shareholders, especially if this was funded through additional borrowings.

Shareholders' Equity Statement

The final statement, the shareholders' equity statement, is also the easiest to understand. Its purpose is to let the shareholders know what transpired during the year in regard to the number of shares outstanding and to reconcile the shareholders' equity with the balance from the previous year. This may not sound particularly significant until you realize that many corporations may show earnings growing by, say, 20 percent, while the per-share earnings are growing by only 10 percent. This is the report that will tell you why.

Shown here is the addition of the year's income to that equity (i.e., the bottom line really does go to the shareholders). However, during the year, a lot of other things can occur that don't go through the income statement. These include, for instance, the dividends paid to shareholders, new share issuance, share repurchases, stock option activities, translation gains and losses from consolidating foreign operations, and various other extraordinary items.

This report is useful in telling shareholders why their share price may not be increasing. Issuance of shares for executive stock options or acquisitions may cause enough dilution of ownership to offset earnings growth. Recent accounting changes require stock options to be shown as an expense on the income statement, which gives more transparency and market effect to exaggerated executive compensation via stock options.

Even if the number of shares goes down due to stock repurchases, these are normally done at share prices well above the share book value and thereby negatively impact the financial ratios used to evaluate the company's financial strength and credit rating. This report is presented in a three-year history format so it is easier to see how share issuance and purchase activity has affected the accounts of the company.

Defining Earnings

I note with interest a recent articles pointing out the creative definitions of earnings that corporations are coming up with to explain away their shortcomings. The standards for all public corporations are defined by *generally accepted accounting principles* (GAAP). These accounting principles are developed by a committee of the American Institute of Certified Public Accountants (AICPA) in consultation with industry and an occasional nudge from the SEC. In fact, the SEC has final say here should they disagree, so we can assume its influence is greater than that of industry.

Where once earnings was defined as profit after tax (PAT), now corporations measure "earnings before . . ." and then add a growing list of qualifiers. The most popular is *earnings before interest, taxes, depreciation, and amortizations* (EBITDA), but variants of this yardstick exist. Recently we saw EBITDAR when a company added back "rents" to its performance yardstick. The REIT industry has taken this shell game one step further by using a yardstick called *funds from operations* (FFO), the premise being that property doesn't depreciate and therefore this and similar charges can be ignored. While there may be some truth in this notion, it leaves REIT management with discretion regarding which expenditures add to the value of the property and which are essential just to avoid its deterioration. If you modernize a hotel lobby, does this enhance the value of the property, or is it merely a necessary expense to remain competitive? In short, it leaves us with an act of faith to trust that management knows what it is doing rather than relying on third-party-validated numbers. This flexibility in defining FFO is not good in times of economic stress.

Creative accounting is as old as accounting itself, so it's not fair to criticize management for engaging in self-serving practices. *Accounting is an art, not a science.* The question is whether the art being practiced by any given company is black, abstract, or just a nature scene. As I suggested some time back, anything other than profits measured by GAAP should be thought of as EBOLA—*earnings before occasional losses and adversities.*

More Important than the Numbers

While few investors have the skill to properly interpret or dissect the financial reports of corporations, a variety of events can alert them to a change of fortune, or at least to sudden changes in the price of not only its stock, but also its debt securities:

- Major changes in the short position of the stock
- Heavy volume in the put or call options on the stock
- Heavy buying or selling of the corporations stock by insiders
- The upcoming retirement of the chief executive officer
- The unexpected resignation/termination of the chief financial officer
- The expiration dates and price levels of existing management stock options
- The sudden replacement/resignation of the outside auditors
- Collapse or crisis at a major competitor (the Enron effect)
- Announcement of a business restructuring/reorganization
- Downgrades in its debt ratings

There are no hard-and-fast rules about what to do when any of the these events occur. As a fixed-income investor in a company going through one of these events, however, it is important to recognize that a conscious decision is called for, not just a wait-and-see approach. This means you need to reach out for additional information and not simply wait for it to come to you. Unlike with stocks, you may have more time to make a decision before a possible price decline occurs, but there's no guarantee of that. Keep in mind also that the initial price reactions are often wrong, so there may actually be opportunity here as well.

Summary

Thanks to Securities and Exchange Commission (SEC) requirements, we receive a stream of financial data on a quarterly as well as annual basis on all publicly traded companies. The SEC is also an enforcement agency for a set of laws and rules regulating the securities industry. In short, it requires standardized reporting and can scrutinize what is reported. This is no guarantee of anything, but, like having a cop on the streets, it does provide a level of comfort. The U.S. securities industry is the most trusted in the world because of the burdensome regulations. It's a high price to pay, but given the alternative, a necessary one. Securities fraud is still quite common outside the United States, and this will continue until foreign markets become more regulated. As I've said before, securities fraud is an easy crime to perpetrate. It involves the exchange of money for a promise represented by a piece of paper. This is why it attracts so many charming, persuasive people. This is also why you need to understand financial statements—to know when you're being had.

3

BONDS

Basic Features

Mention fixed-income investing and 9 out of 10 people think of bonds. Mention it to members of the media and 9 out of 10 think bonds. This knee-jerk reaction is based on the fact that, historically, bonds were pretty much it when you wanted fixed income. Today things are much different.

There are numerous different bond markets, but there are three you should be familiar with: the U.S Treasuries market, the corporate bond market, and the municipal bond market. Each of these markets provides very different products and serves a variety of investors. Yes, there are also government agency bonds, collateralized mortgage obligations (CMO), foreign bonds, sovereign bonds, and so on, but I promised to keep this book brief to focus on what is of interest to most individual investors. If you want to learn about these other markets, buy one of those 500-page bond market tomes.

Before talking about these different products, however, let's cover some of the basics. The first basic is that a *bond* is a credit instrument or contract between a lender (i.e., creditor) and a borrower (i.e., debtor). The contract provides that in return for the creditor lending money to the debtor, the debtor promises to repay the lender at some future date the amount of the loan plus a rate of interest. This is a simple concept to grasp—an investment for a specific amount with a specific rate of return for a specific period of time. However, today, only U.S. Treasuries maintain this simplicity (almost).

All other debt markets introduce an array of variations regarding when you get your interest or principal, how it is to be paid, what rate of interest it pays, and under what circumstances (even when, how, and whether) you get your principal back.

Bonds may also be called *notes* if the maturity is less than 10 years. Most bonds are denominated in $1,000 amounts for Treasuries and corporate bonds and $5,000 for municipal bonds. The prices you see quoted for these bonds, however, are always stated as though the bond is denominated in $100 amounts. Hence a $1,000 corporate that sells for $1,050 is quoted as 105. A municipal bond that is quoted at $105 would cost you $5,250. Well, actually, they will cost you a bit more. You see, since bonds generally pay interest only every six months, the price you pay would be the quoted price plus the amount of interest that has accrued since the last interest payment. This is done because, although you will be the holder of the bond on its next interest payment date, a portion of that interest was earned by the previous holder. By way of example, a bond with a 7 percent ($70) coupon, quoted at 105 and paying interest every January 31 and July 31, that you are buying on July 1 would cost you $1,050.00 plus $28.76 ($70 ÷ 365 days × 150 days since the last interest payment, which is the interest that accrues to the previous owner), or $1,078.76. To further complicate matters, the brokerage house will report as your income the entire $35 interest payment you received on July 1 as your income. You are, however, allowed to reduce the income it reported to the IRS by $28.76, with the explanation that this was purchased interest. Note that certain low-rated bonds or issues that may not make their next interest payment or that have had payment delays in the past or that are in default trade with no accrued interest. These bonds are quoted with the notation "FLAT" after the price to indicate that accrued interest will not be assessed on the trade. An issue may continue trading flat, even after it makes up any delayed payment, until the market makers feel comfortable that the uncertainties have cleared up. Note that zero-coupon bonds also trade with no accrued interest. More on this later.

Commissions on bond trades vary with transaction size. If you are buying a new bond issue, there is no commission charge. The same is also true if the brokerage firm is selling you a bond out of its inventory, since it is acting as a principal in that case rather than as your broker. If you ask your broker to find a bond for you, then you can expect to pay a minimum commission of $40 for the trade or $5 per bond, whichever is higher (rates will vary from one firm to the next). Because of this fee structure, it is not very economical to buy only one to five bonds. Not only do these commissions eat up the first three or four months of interest income, but you don't get as good a price as the buyer of a larger block, except when it's a new issue offering. This means you should buy in such small quantities only if you are sure you're going to hold the bonds to maturity, since you take an even bigger price hit when you try to sell such a small quantity.

There's an important understanding investors need to have about fixed-income securities. With common stocks, every stock is almost identical in the rights and privileges a share represents. *With fixed-income instruments, every instrument is different. Understanding those differences is the principal challenge the investor faces when making a selection. However, once the investor understands these differences the selection process is relatively simple.* Simple, that is, compared to the difficulties in evaluating and selecting a stock. This is because uncertainty and luck play a much smaller role in fixed-income investment risk. Also, credit ratings and stock price movements provide a much better early warning system. These are some of the reasons why the fixed-income investor prefers a bird in the hand (interest payment) to two birds in the bush (capital gains). You see, Ben Franklin was a bond investor.

U.S. Treasuries

The biggest bond market in the world is the $8 trillion market for U.S Treasuries. Much hand-wringing goes on in the media about the amount of this debt, and pundits compete for new ways to impress you with how much this represents for every man, woman, and child in America, or how much of our GNP this equates to, or how many millions of dollars an hour it is growing (or was that billions?). The bottom line to such comments is always the naive question: How can we ever pay this back?

Well, the answer is quite simple: We can't, nor should we want to, pay it back. The current system of world trade requires a place for all countries who export more than they import to invest their excess funds until they need them. We're talking here about hundreds of billions of dollars (China alone is now investing $1 trillion). There is no other market that has the liquidity, credit strength, or currency strength of the U.S. Treasury market, which is why foreign debt holders now hold half of this debt.

Treasuries are relatively simple and have changed little over time. The securities are bought at face value, and when they mature the investor is repaid the principal. During its life, it makes semiannual interest payments equal to half the stated interest rate. Interest earned on Treasuries is exempt from local and state taxes but not from federal income tax. Generally, Treasuries cannot be redeemed before maturity unless purchased on the secondary market rather than directly from the Treasury.

Treasuries come in bills, notes, bonds, and a variation on common bonds called *Treasury inflation-protected securities* (TIPS). Treasury bills, or T-bills, come with three-month and six-month maturity dates and are sold at weekly auctions held on Mondays. One-year T-bills are also available but are auctioned off only every four weeks, on a Thursday. T-bills are especially popular with banks and institutional investors and are essentially the same as zero-coupon bonds. They are sold at a discount to their face (par) value and do not pay interest prior to maturity. Savings bonds are a similar type of vehicle in that they have no coupon and are bought at a discount to par. Earnings are realized through compounded interest payments, which are paid out only upon the bond's redemption. Unlike other Treasuries, savings bonds cannot be traded on the secondary market. However, after holding them for a required minimum of 12 months, savings bonds can be redeemed at any time, which makes them a very liquid asset. Upon premature redemption, interest is paid on a prorated basis relative to the life of the bonds. They are also tax-deferred investments, as earnings are taxable only upon redemption of the bonds.

Treasury notes are commonly issued with maturity dates of 2, 3, 5, or 10 years, in denominations of between $1,000 and $1 million, with a coupon payment every six months. Note that, Treasuries are never called, adding to their value and predictability. The 2-year and 3-year notes are auctioned each month, while the 5-year notes are issued quarterly, and the 10-year notes are issued bimonthly. Ten-year notes have become extremely important securities in the government bond market, as they tend to reflect the market's expectations for the long-term macroeconomic environment. The yield on these bonds is also used as the benchmark for setting mortgage interest rates. Treasury bonds are longer-term securities issued with maturities of 10 years or more and are generally issued with 10- and 30-year maturities. Long-term bonds have declined in popularity over the past 10-years, and the 30-year bonds were reintroduced only in February 2006, after a 5-year hiatus caused by high demand from pension funds. Their lower coupon rates (due to a flat yield curve) make them an attractive fund raising vehicle for the Treasury.

A major drawback of Treasuries, especially the 30-year variety, is inflation. That's where TIPS come into play. Treasury-indexed performance securities (TIPS) are a variation of the traditional Treasury bonds. TIPS are designed to protect investors from inflation. The coupon rate remains constant, but the principal value of the bonds increases correspondingly as consumer prices rise, thus guaranteeing that the value of the bond will never decline in real-dollar terms. For example, if the consumer price index rises five percentage points, then the principal of a $1,000 bond would automatically be adjusted to $1,050 and the interest payment would then increase as a result of being calculated using this larger, inflation-adjusted figure. Interest is paid every six-months. Inversely, should the consumer index decline, the investor is still protected, as the value of the bond would remain the same. The price for this added protection, however, is lower interest rates relative to ordinary Treasury bonds of similar maturities.

One of the drawbacks of TIPS is the tax treatment. In addition to the annual taxation of the interest actually received, the rises in principal value attributed to inflationary gains are also subject to current taxation, even though they aren't received until maturity. This can prove costly should inflation soar. This taxation of unrealized appreciation cuts into after-tax earnings and diminishes the very element that makes these bonds attractive in the first place. One way to avoid this excess taxation is to place these investments in tax-protected retirement accounts. For taxable accounts, the way to avoid taxation on the inflationary gain is to buy a recent iShare product called iShares Lehman TIPS Bond Fund (symbol TIP). The fund holds an array of TIPS bonds and the accreted value comes to you via appreciation in the value of your shares. Hence, there is no tax on your holdings until you sell those shares, and then the gain may be long term if held over one year. The tax savings is certainly worth the 0.20 percent management fee. *You should note that in today's low interest rate environment, Treasury bonds are primarily an avenue to protect wealth, not to create it, and TIPS provide an effective way to do this, especially in times of high inflation.*

Figure 3.1 demonstrates how TIPS performed over the past six years for investors who purchased them at year-end 2000. They significantly outperformed 10-year Treasuries, delivering a cumulative 10.35 percent higher return. Note, however, this return was achieved because TIPS were yielding 3.72 percent before Consumer Price Index (CPI) adjustments at the end of 2000. Since then, their nominal yield has declined to 2.40 percent. Thus, to achieve a similar result for the next six years, inflation will have to be at least 1 percent higher than the 1.93 percent average for the past six years.

Surprisingly, this largest of markets with the biggest of investors is actually quite receptive to participation by small individual investors.

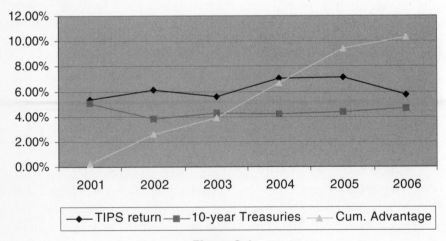

Figure 3.1
TIPS versus 10-Year Treasuries

Through the TreasuryDirect program, investors can have a personal account with the U.S. Treasury, from which they can buy and sell a wide range of maturities and participate in monthly Treasury auctions on a preferential basis, all without sale charges or commissions. You also need have no concern about the pricing of the issues you buy. The Treasuries market is the most transparent of the debt markets, and when you deal with the Treasury, there is no dealer markup. (It should be noted that for accounts over $100,000 there is a nominal annual maintenance fee of $25 per account.)

In today's high-tech world, setting up a TreasuryDirect account couldn't be easier. This can be performed over the phone or, for the computer literate, online. To set up an account over the phone, dial 1–800–722–2678 (1–304–480–7955 if outside the United States). To set up an account online, visit www.treasury.gov. You will be asked to provide certain personal details and bank information and may have to open a single or joint account. Having a personal TreasuryDirect account offers direct control over your assets and extreme convenience. Interest payments and principal payments at maturity are automatically deposited into your designated bank account(s). Additionally, your account can be accessed at any time via the Internet, and securities can be reinvested upon maturity with the click of a mouse. The minimum investment for TreasuryDirect accounts is $10,000 for T-bills, $5,000 for notes with maturities of less than five years, and $1,000 for securities with maturities of more than five years. It's an extremely efficient process that saves time and money and provides instant access and direct control over your accounts.

Treasury securities can also be bought on the secondary market. The advantage of bonds bought on the secondary market is that they can be bought or sold prior to maturity, an option not available with securities bought directly from the government. The secondary market also offers derivative products created by brokerage houses out of Treasury securities. One such product is zero-coupon bonds created out of the semiannual interest payments from an interest-paying bond. The interest-paying bond is placed in a trust and the rights to each interest payment are sold as separate securities. They are sold under such catchy names as TIGRs, CATS, LYONS, and STRIPS. They all do essentially the same thing, so the cute names are just a marketing gimmick. If you insist on knowing what nonsensical contrivances yielded these acronyms, I invite you to visit the appendix at the back of this book.

A TreasuryDirect account is a handy replacement for a traditional bank savings account, only the returns are higher. If you want to keep part of your capital in Treasuries, such an account is a real convenience. Individuals who get lump-sum amounts of money periodically and then have lump-sum payment obligations (e.g., on April 15) can buy Treasury bills that mature when those funds are needed, thus providing income on money often just left on account awaiting the payment date.

Corporate Bonds

The U.S. corporate bond market is a $5 trillion market of bond obligations issued by some 5,000 different public and private companies. Most of these bonds are traded over-the-counter, which means they are traded between dealers and not on an organized exchange (Note: The bond listings you see in the newspapers for the NYSE and American exchanges are quite sparse, and the prices shown are not always representative of the true bond market.)

The corporate bond market has evolved almost exclusively into an institutional market. This means small investors are not welcome. This is because large institutions do not want to trade in any debt securities in which they cannot take multi-million-dollar positions or trade in blocks of bonds this size without affecting the market. Bond traders and underwriters likewise don't want to do $10,000 or $20,000 trades, since their transaction costs are the same as when they sell a $1 million block. In fact, when bond traders suddenly entertain offers this size, chances are it's because institutions all want out. This is called a *market of adverse selection*.

Don't feel you are being discriminated against because you're a small investor. You will find in the section on preferred stocks that many bond issues are packaged into trust-preferred issues by brokerage firms for sale to small investors. Also, don't feel you are missing out. Today, corporate bond yields are terrible compared to most other alternatives. This is because there is a shortage of supply in corporate bonds as American corporations have been de-leveraging their balance sheets since the stock market collapse of 2000.

Still and all, if you call your broker today looking for a bond, she'll find you one—just not necessarily the one you want. When you ask your broker what's available in bonds, her search begins with the in-house inventory list. She zeros in first on today's specials (i.e., those issues on which she can earn extra commissions). These are either issues that haven't moved or are just dogs. When your broker quotes you a price on a bond, you want to know if she is acting as your broker or as a principal. You may have called her as your broker and agent, but in bonds, she can quietly mutate into the party selling you a bond her firm already owns. A favorite ploy for brokers is to quote clients a price and tell them (what a great deal!) they can buy the bond without having to pay any commission. This means your broker is acting as a principal in the transaction. When a broker sells you a bond as a principal, she is charging you a spread between what she paid for that bond and what she is selling it for. You can bet this is way more than a trade commission, but brokers need not divulge that to you. However, they do have to divulge, via the trade confirmation, often in fine print, whether they are acting as a broker or as a principal.

Acting as a principal is not necessarily bad, since it could simply be due to the fact that you are buying a bond from the house inventory. It does mean, however, that you need to get an independent valuation of the bond before you buy or sell. This can be via some quote service like a Bloomberg terminal or by comparing the current yield and yield to call of a comparable security or index for that quality of security. If you are a serious bond buyer you may want to establish accounts with two or more brokerage firms. For bonds this should be a bond specialist or wire house. A discount broker is of small help here. *For small investors, finding good bonds at fair prices is a challenge. You won't often be able to read about a good bond, then pick up a phone and order it, as you can do with stocks.* It's more like sifting through the merchandise at the discount counter at a department store. Lots of merchandise, but not the size, price, or quantity you are looking for.

One thing to remember when buying bonds is lot size. Never buy bonds in lots of less than $25,000 unless you plan to hold them to maturity. Don't make the mistake I see so often of trying to diversify your risk by buying small lots of many different bonds. Commissions on bond trades tend to be a flat amount plus a per-bond fee. When you go to sell them, this becomes a significant cost, provided you can find a buyer. If a broker is offering you a small lot of a bond issue, chances are he's unloading inventory, and you should ask for a better price than normal. Expect such treatment when you attempt to sell such a lot back to him.

Equipment Trust Certificates

Companies with low credit ratings but good assets may resort to using equipment trust certificates (ETCs) to lower their cost of financing. ETCs are first liens against specific assets, the most common being airplanes, shipping containers, and railroad cars. Not just any airplane, but a specific plane identified by serial number. While such certificate loans may appear to be safer, appearances can be deceptive. With aircraft, obsolescence often sets in well before the trust certificate is paid for. While you may have a claim for a specific aircraft, it does you little good if there is no resale demand for that generation of equipment. And if the equipment is new, chances are the bankruptcy judge will allow the airline to continue flying it until the bankruptcy is settled or a Chapter 7 liquidation is ordered. As for ETCs backed by railroad cars, in bankruptcy you entertain the risk that the railroad does not even know where your railroad car is. It may actually be operated by another railroad.

Direct Access Notes

Many investors want to build a laddered portfolio of bonds that is also diversified by issuers and maturity so they can hedge both interest rate and credit risk. Frankly, this is hard to do with bonds if your total portfolio is less than a $1 million. The institutionally dominated bond market is not interested in buyers who want to buy less than 50 or 100 thousand-dollar bonds. When they do offer them, it is at a price several points higher than the big players are asked to pay. It gets even worse when you want to sell. To remedy this situation and open up the market to small investors, a handful of blue-chip companies, starting in 1996, created a market for such small buyers. The products go by the name of InterNotes or Direct Access Notes (DANs), and they are offered by such well-known names as IBM, Caterpillar, UPS, Bank of America, Freddie Mac, John Hancock, GE, Dow Chemical, Prudential, and Daimler-Chrysler. This market has grown to over $70 billion and has a broad variety of offerings. Maturities range from 1 to 30 years, and quality ratings range from AAA to BBB. Yields might range from a low of 4.8 percent for an A2-rated Prudential three-year note to a high of 6.0 percent for a 10-year CIT Group note rated A. I recommend you shop around at the Web sites mentioned in this chapter for the best rates, since there can be significant spread differences for similarly rated notes of the same maturity available in the open market.

The yields offered at such online site are higher than for Treasuries. The AAA-rated Freddie Mac 10-year notes yield 134 basis points more than Treasuries, and the CIT Group notes yield a full 127 basis points more. However, these yields can be 40 to 50 basis points lower than for comparable bonds by the same company, although this varies greatly by issuer. The John Hancock product offerings I checked were in line with the bond market yields for the same securities. Such yield differences are unimportant if you are buying in small quantities, since the price spreads and transaction fees could easily be greater.

Investors who want to build a laddered portfolio with limited capital will find these notes a godsend. They allow you to buy as little as one bond for par value, and they offer a range of maturities and interest payment options (monthly, quarterly or annually). They also offer a range of maturities.

For those with estate planning in mind, these notes have an added attraction. If you have created a laddered portfolio with a dozen or more different bonds in quantities of as low as one or two bonds, you have a portfolio that will be hard to sell without incurring huge transaction costs. *These notes come to the rescue by providing for early redemption at full face value if one of the owners of the security dies.* This has the added advantage that, assuming you plan to hold the security until death, you can buy the longest maturities and get the highest yield without concern that interest rates may depress the value of the bond when your estate needs to sell them. Bonds with such a feature are referred to as *flower bonds*.

While these notes can be resold in the bond market before maturity, they are not a good choice for you if this is contemplated as a likely possibility. In that case, I recommend you buy PET bonds or trust preferreds, which are exchange traded and sell for $10 to $25 a share.

The Web sites where you can find out more about these notes are www.internotes.com and www.direct-notes.com. Companies such as Ford Motor offers its notes through its own Web site at www.ford.com. It sells notes directly to you without going through a broker, but you keep them on account with Ford, much like a TreasuryDirect account with the Federal Reserve Bank. Note that offerings change weekly, so if you don't see exactly what you like, wait a week and it may come up.

Junk Bonds

Prior to the Michael Milken–Drexel Burnham era of the 1980s, junk bonds were investment-grade bonds that had fallen on hard times. Original-issue junk bonds were mostly bonds that resulted as part of a bankruptcy reorganization, and there were few buyers. The genius of Michael Milken was in developing a market for such paper. This was done through his creation of bonds with a double-digit rate of return and with the implied assurance that if the issuer failed, Milken and his firm, Drexel Burnham, would refinance the debt and thereby bail out the holders. This created what was characterized as a daisy chain of buyers because they had an implicit assurance from the bond underwriter against default. This allowed Milken to launch bond issues that no thoughtful buyer would otherwise touch. In fact, a portion of this daisy chain was built from the very issuers of junk bonds themselves. If an issuer needed $100 million, it could be compelled to issue, say, $150 million in bonds with the understanding that the additional $50 million would be invested in the bonds of subsequent junk issuers. This was a type of pyramid scheme that might have worked, but like all such bright ideas, it was overdone. Too much junk debt for too many flaky takeover schemes finally caught the attention of regulators, and they shut Milken down. Unfortunately, shutting down Michael Milken led to a removal of the safety net and a collapse of confidence and bond pricing as issuers began to fail. Compounding the problem, many insurance companies and S&Ls were the holders of much of this junk debt, and as the debt issuers failed, so did some of these holders.

Despite this unfortunate beginning, the junk bond market (or as I prefer to call it, the *below-investment-grade market*) is here to stay. Today it is a trillion-dollar market of sophisticated institutional buyers. Because of the rigors of credit ratings, more than half of U.S. industry today falls into this category. Companies such as General Motors, Ford, J. C. Penney, and Sears Holding Corporation all sport below-investment-grade ratings and have large quantities of debt instruments outstanding that fit nicely into an individual's portfolio. The bond instruments of today contain more protective debt covenants than the instruments of the 1980s. These debt covenants are the dos and don'ts of what the bond issuers can do with the money and what additional debt they can take on.

As covered in Chapter 9, default and bankruptcy are more likely with junk securities, but the degree of risk and the magnitude of the losses are generally less than with most common stocks. You can buy an investment-grade security, accept the lower yield, and still face losses from credit downgrades. Credit upgrades of investment-grade issues are uncommon and don't pay well. Alternatively, you can buy a below-investment-grade issue, get a much higher yield, face loss from credit downgrades, but also have a chance at gains through a credit upgrade, especially back to investment grade if the issue is a fallen angel (i.e., was previously investment grade). But don't pursue investing in junk bonds unless you are willing to learn how to evaluate them and do your homework before you buy. *I return to junk-rated issues throughout this book because they are a maligned and misunderstood income instrument. For now, it is enough to understand that the risks and reward of junk bonds are generally superior to those of common stocks. You won't hear this from any broker, but the reason for that is another story covered elsewhere herein.*

Step-up and Pay-in-Kind Bonds

Step-up bonds are issued by investment-grade-rated corporate issuers at below-market interest rates, but with the promise that the rate will increase yearly according to a defined schedule. In this way, the buyer has some comfort that the yield will increase and thereby protect against a price decline should interest rates rise. There is, of course, the usual caveat that the issue can be called after a number of years, which happens if the step-up rate gets too far ahead of market interest rates. Step-up bonds differ from adjustable-rate bonds in the fact that the interest rate changes are not tied to current yields the way adjustable-rate bonds are. This is great if interest rates are falling, but means rate adjustments upward can lag if interest rates are rising. So you face a certain degree of uncertainty when you buy step-up bonds as inflation hedges.

Pay-in-kind bonds are generally issued by companies rated below investment grade and are often securities that came out of a bankruptcy reorganization. They are affirmations that the issuer does not expect to generate enough cash to service these securities for some time and is, therefore, building in an interest payment time-out at the front end. At some future date, they convert to cash pay bonds or they default. The problem is that the built-in discount, called the *original issue discount* (OID), is considered current income to the holder and declared as such by the brokerage house to the IRS. You get to adjust your cost basis to compensate for the nonincome. Its kind of like depletion allowance in reverse.

Pay-in-kind bonds are a common bankruptcy exit product because they allow for a company to get back on its feet without a heavy cash interest drain and they allow the bankruptcy claimants to believe they got a higher settlement value. Pay-in-kind is generally a cash-pay bond, where the issuers have the option to make the interest payment in more bonds if their financial condition so warrants. These bonds generally trade at significant discounts to cash-paying securities, as evidenced by the fact that they jump in value when cash interest payments actually kick in.

Zero-Coupon Bonds

Zero-coupon bonds pay no interest until they mature. They achieve this by selling at a significant discount from their face value. You may already have come into contact with these bonds if you've ever bought a U.S. Treasury Series EE bond at your local bank for a grandchild or nephew. It feels nice to give $100 bond and only pay $43, doesn't it? Zero-coupon bonds are convenient for IRA accounts because they require no administration, such as having to reinvest a $69 interest payment every six months into something you can't buy without a $19 commission charge. By laddering the maturities in one-year increments, you can also structure an IRA account such that the amount you must withdraw each year beginning at age 70½ will be available in cash without having to sell anything.

There are several drawbacks to zeros, however. First of all, it is difficult to calculate the interest rate you are receiving and how that compares to the yield you would get on a cash-paying bond. On the one hand, with zeros, you lock in not only your interest rate, but also the rate at which that theoretical interest is being reinvested. Hence, their implied yield tends to be lower than for a comparable cash-pay issue. This ability to lock in the reinvestment yield means they are a great buy when interest rates are high. On the other hand, when interest rates drop, no security is as sensitive to the interest rate decline as are zero-coupon bonds, so they are mainly attractive as investments you intend to hold to maturity. They are not attractive if you need to resell them, because the brokerage commission is based on the face value of the security. Hence, at a $500 asking price for a $1,000 bond, the commissions are twice as much to buy as interest-paying bonds. However, the worst drawback to zeros is that you have to declare as interest income each year the accreted interest attributable to the bond, even if the price has dropped because interest rates have risen. For this reason, they are not a good selection for a taxable investment account except in a high interest rate environment where rates can be expected to drop.

Put Bonds

So-called put bonds are generally issued by below-investment-grade issuers who want to reassure holders that their bonds will not decline in value because of deterioration of the company's credit quality or other foreseeable events. Issuers of such bonds are either desperate or dumb. Its hard to know whether a company may have issued such bonds because it was talked into it by its underwriters or because it was blindly confident of its future and saw the put provision as a way to precipitate an early call at an opportune time for the company. In any case, more than one company has been forced into bankruptcy because of such bonds.

A put provision may be constructed in different ways. It may require the company to maintain certain credit ratios or ratings or face the bonds being put back to the company. This can be traumatic, because few companies provide for such an eventuality in their cash flow planning. The provision may require the company to reset the interest rate on the issue in order to bring its price back to par value, or the bonds can be put back. However, if bonds are put back to the company, payment may not always be made in cash. A recent example of this was the Mirant Corporation, which had a put bond issue that allowed holders to put the bonds back to the company if its finances deteriorated below a certain point. Payment could be effected with stock or cash. As the put date neared, the company's finances were in shambles. It became obvious that the bonds would be put back to the company and that the company would have to redeem them with stock at the then-current market price. The problem was, the number of shares of stock the company would have to issue would so dilute the shareholding that the price would plummet to a level whereby the bondholders would own a majority stake in the company. An effort to avoid this led to a series of missteps that ended in bankruptcy for Mirant. While such bonds are appealing because they offer an apparent escape valve, when trouble comes they will as often as not precipitate a crisis in which everyone can lose.

Insured Municipal Bonds

Today's variety of tax-sheltered investment products makes municipal bonds mainly a choice for institutions or the very rich. While there are no other similar tax-free securities, since the dividend tax rate was reduced to 15 percent, there are many alternatives that provide a substantially higher after-tax return. And if that's not enough reason, you may find the alternative minimum tax (AMT) is making the tax-free promise of munis ring somewhat hollow. Nevertheless, if you live in states that have high local taxes, like California or New York, you may find municipal bonds a simpler solution.

My advice to those determined to buy municipal bonds is to buy AAA-insured munis from the state in which you reside. If you have very low local taxes, buy the AAA-insured issues offering the highest yield. Why AAA-insured? The simplest answer is that if you seek protection from default through buying into a bond fund or retaining an investment manager, you still suffer the loss if someone guesses wrong. *With insured municipal bonds, if a bond defaults, the insurer, not you, loses.* Best of all, the difference in yield between an insured and uninsured muni is less than the fees you pay to be in a fund or pay to an advisor.

Insured bonds have become a generic product much like U.S. Treasuries. The yield on uninsured AAA munis is often less than on those that are rated AAA because they are somehow perceived as better. But consider this, over the past 25 years the number of AAA muni issuers has gone from more than 40 to about 12. Hence, the real risk that high-quality-muni buyers have had to face is a deterioration of the credit rating and therefore of the price. Notice, I said *deterioration*, not fluctuation. AAA and AA credits can only decline in quality, and rarely are such ratings recovered. Insured bonds have defaulted, but the holders have always been made whole. Best of all, in their 25-year history, no bond insurer has lost its AAA rating. Uninsured AAA issues (also termed *natural* AAAs, as if this were a good thing) yield less because they are sought out by muni buyers as superior. This is because a government entity is considered by these investors as having infinite life, whereas an insurance company can be overwhelmed by events. What they fail to realize is that the events that would overwhelm these insurers would probably make pretty much everything else worthless as well.

Insured bonds come in three varieties. The best are issues insured by a monoline bond insurer such as Municipal Bond Insurance Association (MBIA), American Municipal Bond Assurance Corporation (AMBAC), Financial Guaranty Insurance Company (FGIC), or Financial Security Assurance Holdings (FSAH). These companies provide only credit insurance and no other products, so you don't need to worry about their hurricane or other exposures. They are all rated AAA and, therefore, so are any bond they insure. They are unlikely to suffer a rating decline (thereby affecting the price of the bonds they insure) because, if they don't do everything in their power to protect their AAA rating, they would be out of the new business market.

Many housing bonds are also guaranteed by a second type of insurer: the Federal Housing Administration (FHA) and Housing and Urban Development Agency (HUD). The protection here is not quite as good, since housing projects frequently fail, leading to bondholders being cashed out early when the project is refinanced.

The third type of insurance is by letter of credit issued by a bank. This type of guarantee is dependent on the bank's credit rating and can often lead to less than full recovery because of some technicality in the wording of the letter of credit. It is also not unusual for a bond issuer to use the failure to renew a letter of credit as a way to trigger an early call on bonds that are not otherwise callable. This is done when the opportunity to refinance at a lower cost presents itself.

The biggest risk with insured bonds is what I term *staged defaults*. This is a problem when interest rates fall. When the issuer of an insured bond finds it could refinance the bond issue at a lower rate or needs more money, it may decide to default intentionally in order to force the trustee to accelerate the bonds (i.e., declare them due and payable immediately). This is most often done when the bond issue has no early call provision. You know the default was staged because the issuer immediately reissues a new, insured issue at a lower interest rate to pay off the defaulted issue. So what's the harm? The issuer has a lower debt service cost and maybe even more money for its project. The bond insurer has a new piece of business for which the premium for the entire life of the bond is paid up front. It also has the remainder of the premium from the defaulted issue that was being amortized over the projected life of the defaulted issue but that can now be take into income immediately, since the issue was retired early, so the premium is fully earned (no refunds allowed). All in all, a nice piece of business. Nice, if you ignore the bondholders who just lost a bond that they may even have paid a premium for and for which they got back par. Nice, if you ignore the fact that the lower interest rate environment that often precipitates the default also means the bondholders will not be able to reinvest their principal at the same yield they were getting on their old bonds. This is what's known as moral hazard, and no AAA rating can protect you against it. A natural AAA bond issuer would not be able to get away with such a stratagem without losing its rating. Perhaps this is why investors hunt out such issues and accept the lower yields.

Lower-Rated Muni Bonds

Let's assume you refuse my sage advice about buying only insured AAAs, and assume further that you are determined to look for lower-quality issues to narrow the yield disadvantage between tax-free and taxable bonds. What else, then, do you need to know? You need to know plenty.

Most people in and out of the municipal bond business think muni bonds are all pretty much safe. This is true for certain types of bonds, especially those for general obligation bonds (i.e., bonds with the full faith and credit of a state, county, or city behind them). It's also true for essential service bonds such as schools, utilities, or public buildings. Also for bonds with dedicated, solid income streams such as sales taxes or property taxes. However, things become murky in the area of bonds where the only collateral for the issue is a very narrow revenue stream (e.g., bridge or highway tolls, stadium ticket sales, airport taxes, to name a few). Such issues often run into payment delays and rescheduling of maturities as the projected use runs into the real world. Keep in mind that such projects are often politically inspired or motivated and are being executed by government. There is no private company guarantee or oversight, nor does anyone have any money at risk or shareholders to hold them accountable. There are voters, yes, but I have yet to hear of a politician turned out of office because he or she built a road or baseball stadium that defaulted.

A note here about unrated muni bonds. They come in two types: bonds that would have been rated below investment grade, hence more difficult to sell to innocents, and bonds issued by municipalities that don't need a rating to sell (e.g., the town of Palm Beach, Florida). Also, certain issues of bonds are investment grade, but they could never achieve that rating because they are too small. Unrated munis are truly a mixed bag, but one with good and bad surprises. More on these in a moment.

Conduit Bonds

One interesting aspect of munis is that there does exist a large universe of bonds with various quality ratings that can provide up to double-digit yields. This is the world of conduit bonds or revenue bonds (although this term is used for true municipal revenue bonds as well). These are bonds whereby a municipality lends its name to what is fundamentally a private project by a nonprofit or for-profit organization. The municipality has no liability for the project and lends its name only because the project is deemed to be in the public interest. The range of projects involved is astounding, as is the quality of the issues. While many of these bonds are guaranteed by investment-grade public companies, most are backed by companies and individuals who could never borrow 10 cents under their own name or with the collateral value that the bonds offer. The failure rate for such projects approaches that for junk-rated corporate bonds, or as high as one project in three.

The best of these revenue issues are those from investment-grade companies who are issuing municipal bonds simply to obtain cheaper financing. Big users here are public utilities, retail stores, and hospitals. Revenue bonds come in various investment-grade rating categories, including AAA-insured, or they come unrated. Ratings provide little comfort here unless the bond issue is to refinance an existing project. New projects are dependent on financial projections by people who make projections for a living or who stand to be the ones executing the project. In short, they have an economic interest in seeing the project approved but have no economic risk if it fails. This is clearly not a formula for success.

Taxable Munis

All municipal bonds are not tax exempt. This comes about in two ways. The issuers of conduit bonds often have expenses incurred in launching the bond issue that exceed certain maximums allowed by the U.S. Treasury. In order not to disqualify the entire issue from tax exemption, the bond issue will have two bond series, an A bond, which is tax exempt, and a B bond, which is taxable, representing the excess underwriting and other fees not allowed by the Treasury. Such bonds may be exempt from state and local taxes but not from federal income tax. The second type of taxable munis are issued by a municipal authority as a financing mechanism rather than for a recognized public purpose. Recent examples are bonds issued by San Diego, California, and the State of New Jersey, who each sold taxable munis to generate funds for their government workers' pension funds. Again, the bonds are exempt from in-state income taxes, but not from federal income taxes.

While we're on the subject of taxation, all states exempt the interest income from in-state municipal bonds from state and local income taxes. This exemption extends as well to muncipal bonds issued by U.S. territories (e.g., Puerto Rico, Guam, and the Virgin Islands) under special exemptions designed to promote economic development there.

Unrated Munis

The current low interest environment combined with the steep decline in corporate bond defaults has tempted many investors to consider the unrated municipal market as an investment alternative. With their 7 and 8 percent coupon debt issues, a tax-free return of such amounts is an easy sell for an unscrupulous broker. But don't confuse the risks in high-yield munis with their corporate cousins. The risks are totally different, and defaults are not as seasonal or as predictable as with corporate junk bonds.

To begin with, unrated muni issues are generally below $20 million in size and usually represent the entire capitalization of an enterprise. That is to say, there is no share capital behind bondholders to cushion the risk or to motivate the enterprise operators to do a good job. The individuals sponsoring the enterprise often take their profits up front in various fees and sales to the venture. They often have little profit motive once the project is operational. We are talking about such projects as nursing homes, housing developments, water and sewer projects, and special facilities such as golf courses, skating rinks, zoos, manufacturing facilities, and so forth. Such bond issues are often the brainchild of investment bankers or a brokerage firm, who line up a project and do all the legal work required to then pitch it to a local municipal authority for support. Not that such authorities represent any sort of an obstacle. They often consist of prominent local citizens who seem to be selected based on their good resumes and lack of knowledge. In fact, underwriters sometimes create an authority where none exists precisely to facilitate and control the process of issuing bonds.

As a potential buyer of bonds with a poor foundation or overblown business plan, you may pick up clues from reading the *official statement* (also referred to as the OS.) This document is similar to the prospectus for a corporate bond issue, but suffers from the fact that it does not need to be submitted to the SEC for scrutiny because municipal bonds are exempt from SEC oversight. This is all the more reason to be diligent when you buy an unrated muni: You don't even have the comfort of knowing that the SEC or a credit agency has reviewed the issue.

As with corporate bonds, each muni issue has a bond indenture. The irony is that this document, which defines the role of the bond trustee and the rights of the bondholders, is written by the bond issuer and the underwriter. Abusive practices I have seen here are limitations on a trustee's power to declare a default or foreclose on the project assets. The bond indenture can even limit what the trustee can tell bondholders and nonholders. A red flag is when consent of 100 percent of the bondholders is required for any action. This is a sure sign that trouble has been anticipated from inception. Don't think that bank trustees of bond issues are your friend. They are well aware of who is paying their annual fees. When trouble comes, they generally become very legalistic to minimize their fiduciary liability. In many cases, they hand the default over to an outside attorney rather than working out a consensual arrangement with the project managers. Such an attorney will generally pursue the longest, most litigious route to a settlement.

Defaults of unrated municipals are far from rare. I have been tracking municipal defaults for over 20 years, and there have been few years with less than 100 defaults, mostly of unrated issues. The default rate is not unlike that for corporate junk bonds, but they come at a much steadier rate. This is because there is little cushion in most municipal projects for missing projected growth. As previously indicated, there is no equity capital here and no borrowing from to a bank for short-term financing. All cash flow shortfalls are for the account of the bondholders. It is ludicrous to call such securities muni bonds. They are, in fact if not in title, equity since there is no capital claim behind such bond investors. *Most conduit bond issuers couldn't borrow money from a bank on the kind of collateral or business plan they get approved by a municipal authority, but then, those authorities are only lending their name and have no liability whatsoever.*

If I have not yet thoroughly discouraged you from investing in such bonds, consider this. News about the status of a municipal project is, for the most part, nonpublic. Bank trustees often will not share such information with anyone other than a registered bondholder. Hence, the payment status of any given project is insider information. Not that this discourages buying on bad information—quite the opposite. It creates an opportunity for unscrupulous brokers to buy a failing issue on the cheap and then remarket it to unsuspecting new buyers at, or above, par value. When the project's failure is finally made public, they can pretend ignorance. The point is that the secondary market for unrated munis is, to a great extent, a market of adverse selection where bad news is heard first by the local brokers or the issue underwriter. Yes, you could do your due diligence, but keep in mind the trustee will often not tell you about invasions of the reserve accounts or other shortfalls until after you have bought the bonds.

There are many ways to lose money in investing. However, you can usually take solace with most such losses in the fact that hundreds of others, including smart money managers, shared in the loss. When you lose on in unrated muni, however, expect to cry alone.

Buying Municipal Bonds

Most municipal bond investors are high-net-worth individuals with big tax bills. They are interested in preserving what they have and minimizing their tax bite. Such investors should establish an account with a brokerage house specializing in munis, since they will likely receive better service, pricing, and commission rates there. For the rest of us, buying munis through a discount broker is normally a trying exercise. The Internet provides a valuable service here, and any buyer of munis in the secondary market (i.e., previously owned issues) should become familiar with the following Web sites. Three sites that show what is currently available are www.BondDesk.com, www.MuniBond.com, and www.ValuBond.com. You should shop all three sites for availability and pricing. You may find the same bonds being offered at strikingly different prices. To confirm the pricing, you can go to www.Investinginbonds.com, which is a Web site sponsored by a government-backed entity, the Municipal Bonds Rulemaking Board (MSRB). Here you will find past trades in specific bonds in real time. The site is also good for checking corporate bond pricing. If you are interested in buying municipal bonds through a mutual fund, read the section on municipal bond funds in Chapter 7.

Municipal Bond Defaults

One of the biggest drawbacks to municipal bonds is the treatment bondholders receive when an issuer defaults. The first drawback is that you may not know about the default until many months after it commenced. This is because the bank, which is acting as the bond trustee, may decide to fund interest payments out of reserve funds rather than declaring a default. This may be because the trustee is barred from telling the bondholders by the bond indenture. Trustees are comfortable with this arrangement because the more closely their role is defined, the less responsibility (read *liability*) they have. Nevertheless, at some point reserve funds run out and the trustee must then disclose the bad news to the bondholders. What happens next depends greatly on how seriously the bank trustees takes their role. I have noticed over the years that banks with weakly staffed trust departments will either try to pass the trustee role off to another bank or to outside counsel. In the first instance, this is a positive move; in the latter case, it spells a long drawn-out legal process. A business approach is almost always preferable.

A common approach trustees take is to notify bondholders of the situation and then advise them that they await instruction from any group that can get together bondholders representing 25 percent or more of the issue. Trustees show little professionalism by accepting a bond indenture that will clearly ties their hands. In fact, many don't really get riled up until the issuer stops paying them their fees.

Those trustees who recognize their responsibility will seek some sort of accommodation with the bond issuer or, failing that, foreclose on the property. This frequently triggers a bankruptcy filing by the issuer despite a mortgage lien on the property by the bondholders. This is a tactic issuers frequently resort to in order to induce the trustee to forego pursuing personal claims against the issues' sponsors who gave personal guarantees at the time the bonds were brought out. Other bankruptcies are filed just to buy time and continue to collect paychecks. The usual scenario, once the trustee gains control of the property, is an attempt to sell the property. Since the properties are often dilapidated, such sales generally produce bids at only a fraction of the value of the bonds outstanding. This should be of no surprise, since bidders at a bankruptcy sale are there for bargains. Once in a while, a project still retains enough promise to allow for a refinancing of the bonds. In these cases, bondholders often manage to walk away whole. In any case, few of these defaults settle quickly, and while there is an active market in defaulted bonds, most valuations are below 30 cents on the dollar until near the end, when the recovery valuation is in sight.

If you should happen to get caught in the default of a true municipal bond issue, the bankruptcy process is a little different. Municipalities file bankruptcy under Chapter 9 of the Bankruptcy Code rather than Chapter 11. Since a municipality cannot go out of business, the resolution of the default is left completely in the hands of a judge, who has an evaluation of the finances of the project or municipality done and determines its ability to pay. The judge then redefines the bond issue that investors hold, either regarding its interest rate, its maturity, or even a reduction of principal for the bondholders. It's quicker than Chapter 11 settlements and, fair to say, more judicious.

Miscellaneous Topics

The Bond Indenture and Trustee

The bond indenture is the actual contract between the bondholder and the issuer. It is described in detail in the offering prospectus, but no copy is included there. The key features of an indenture are defining what an issuer must do in the way of financial reporting and maintenance of certain financial ratios. Restrictions may also exist on how much debt the company may take on in the future and how senior such debt may be relative to the subject issue. Call and put provisions are also defined here with, the call prices established based on the number of years outstanding. Provisions for extraordinary calls in case of mergers or change of control are also defined.

The role of the trustees is defined, along with their responsibilities to bondholders. These responsibilities are also defined to some extent by state law, especially once an issuer is in violation of the bond indenture or is in default. It is the trustee's job to demand required financial reports and to signal when a given financial ratio is not being met. It is also the trustee's responsibility to decide when to declare an issue in default and accelerate the debt. Accelerating the debt issue means declaring it immediately due and payable. It is an action that usually triggers a bankruptcy filing unless the bond issuer was inviting such a debt acceleration in order to get rid of a high coupon issue that had an expensive call or no call provision. While the trustee is the bondholders' fiduciary agent, in practice, it is the large institutional bondholders who do the negotiation with the company and who decide when to declare a default. Once these holders negotiate an agreement with the company, they try to get all other holders to go along. Once a majority in each class of creditors agree, the company will frequently file what is termed a *prepackaged* Chapter 11 bankruptcy: All the parties march into court with a plan in hand and have the court confirm the plan and the voter approval, thereby forcing all creditors to go along. No holdouts here—an attractive way for small investors to make money in a default situation in the good old days.

Call Provisions

Unlike almost every other type of investment, fixed-income securities generally have a provision whereby the issuer can take its security back and refund you a specified amount of money. This feature is a *call* provision, and it may be triggered by the passage of time or the occurrence of any of a series of defined events. It is a feature in bonds, trust preferreds, and equity preferreds. Even if the security has 30 years until its maturity, the right to call an issue early may begin only a few years after the issue date, and the issuer may or may not pay the holder a premium over the face value for this privilege. There are various reasons a corporation may exercise such an early call provision, but the most common is that it can reissue a similar security at a lower coupon rate. *For the investor, calls usually mean you are being handed back your capital at a time when it cannot be reinvested at a similar rate of return.* For some investors that can be disruptive, because it upsets a laddered portfolio, which can be hard to rebalance.

Call and put provisions are defined in the bond indenture with a schedule of call prices based on years outstanding. Provisions for extraordinary calls in case of mergers or change of control may also be defined. *You need to know these call provisions, because they have a direct bearing on how the security should be priced.* While we tend to focus on a bond's current yield, the market is more interested in the yield to call. Hence, a high-coupon security sells at a premium to its face value, but may still look like a good buy because of a high current yield. However, that premium to face value will drop to the call price or disappear altogether between then and the date of the first call. This means the yield to call may be significantly less attractive, yet that is all you stand to earn. When calls are possible within the subsequent year or so, the yield to call can be zero or even negative.

The current interest rate environment is the best refinancing environment corporations have seen in the past decade. We face a period when investors must reexamine their portfolios with calls in mind. It's a safe bet that the bonds and preferreds offering you the best yield are also those most likely to be called away. At every year-end, investors should review each of their holdings for the likelihood of a call. While there's nothing you can do to prevent a call, you can do some tax planning to possibly offset the tax bite. If you hold securities trading well above their par value, you may want to take a capital gain now at a 15 percent tax rate versus allowing them to continue to pay an above-market rate of interest income (taxed at personal income tax rates) as they depreciate toward par (call) value.

To spot which of your securities may be called early, check the yields of similarly rated securities. If the coupon rate is 1 percent or more above this yield, you can assume a call is likely. Check the next call date and price of the security, something you can find on our web site (www.incomesecurities.com) or even on some brokerage statements. Note that once the first call date is reached, a security is usually callable anytime thereafter at an ever-declining premium. One clue to an early call is the current yield. If this is above the yield for comparable securities, it may well be due to an early call depressing the price. One exception to the likelihood of a call are equity preferred stocks. These securities are considered perpetual stock issues much like common stock. Although they are generally callable anytime, that risk is not factored into the pricing unless they have an extraordinarily high dividend rate.

A call provision can sometimes be an investor's friend. Investors seeking protection against a rise in interest rates may use the call feature of a security to protect against a price decline. They can also use the call feature to achieve a higher rate of return than they can get on money market or two-year securities. Here's how. Suppose you hold a security that has a 7 percent coupon with 20 years to maturity, is callable in two years, and trades at $25.50 versus a $25 call price. Your yield to call is more like 6 percent, which is the coupon rate of new issues coming out today with the equivalent rating. Now, look forward two years and suppose the refinancing interest rate is still 6 percent. In that case, the issue will most likely be called, and your reinvestment rate will also be 6 percent, but the security will trade at the $25 par. But suppose interest rates have moved up to 7 percent. Then this issue most likely won't be called, and you now have a 7 percent yield going forward and a market price of $25. Hence, you are better off today buying the 7 percent security selling at $25.50 than buying a 6 percent security selling at $25, since it will be selling for less in two years. Of course, rates could also jump to 8 percent in two years, so an issue with a 7 percent coupon would protect you for the first 1 percent rate hike. Note that the call likelihood increases the higher the coupon rate of the bond you're buying, and they also sell for a larger premium above par. A key to making this strategy work is not accepting a yield to call that is significantly below the yield on new two-year issues coming out today. This way, you have no downside if the issue is called.

When buying trust preferreds created by a brokerage firm (i.e., third-party trust preferreds), look at the coupon rate of the underlying corporate bond. For example, the 8.375 percent Motorola CBTCS (ticker XFJ) created by Lehman Brothers has an underlying 6.5 percent noncallable bond. Lehman will call this issue unless the underlying bond trades at a price below what it paid for the bonds when it set up the trust, since Lehman stands to pocket the difference between that price and the price in July 2007. Motorola is not a party to the refinancing decision. In other instances, however, the underlying bond may trigger a call. Be aware of a call's point of origin.

Investors seeking a higher return on short-term investments can consider the call date as their yield to maturity for the period from now until that call date. This should not be done for calls beyond about two years, since too many things can change in a longer period. Of course, a call is never certain, but the yield difference is significant enough to make the risk worthwhile. For example, while one-year Treasuries yield 1.28 percent, you can buy a 7.88 percent 9/30/2048 American General Capital (AGCpA) trust preferred rated Aa1/AA with a 1.8 percent yield to call in one year. If it's not called, you accrue interest at 7.4 percent from then on. That's huge for AA paper. It's a heads-you-win, tails-you-win-even-more scenario.

Some call provisions are designed for the protection of the security holder. The most common is a change of control provision whereby the company is taken over by another company or investment group. This provision is designed to permit debt holders to escape an acquisition situation where the acquiring company may be using an excessive amount of new debt and is thereby jeopardizing the company's future, not to mention the market value of its existing debt. Such a call provision may be required by the underwriters or large investors before they will buy an issue. It may also, however, be something a company puts into its debt agreement voluntarily as a *poison pill defense* against a hostile takeover.

Put Provisions

Debt instruments may also have *put provisions*, whereby the debt holder has the right to present the security to the company for immediate redemption under certain circumstances. Normally, a convertible has a call provision whereby the issuer can call a convertible for redemption into cash at its face value. Almost always, the company invokes this provision only when the value of the shares the debt holder can opt to take is higher than that face value. Likewise, a convertible debt holder generally has a right to put the debt back to the company anytime. Put provisions also exist to protect the market value of a debt security. A common provision gives the debt holder the right to put the security back to the issuer if it does not reset the coupon rate to a market yield (i.e., the company brings the market price of the debt issue up to par value).

Money Market Accounts and Funds

Money market accounts can be opened with a bank or made a feature of your brokerage account so that any cash coming in from trades, dividends, or interest payments are automatically swept into a money market mutual fund. These are also alternatives with any of the mutual fund families that offer the option of switching money between funds without a fee. The money put in such an account is invested in short-term Treasury bills, commercial paper (which are corporate short-term debt), or bank debt such as CDs. There is little or no credit risk and the rate of return is closely tied to the Fed discount rate. A money market fund invests in such short-term instruments so that its share value is always $1. It should not normally be viewed as an investment, but rather as a parking place for money between investments or awaiting some major expenditure. It may become an investment alternative in a period such as exists today, when the yield curve is flat or inverted. Then you may decide to park your money there until the interest rate picture clarifies. This can take a year or more.

Money market accounts often come with check-writing privileges and debit cards, so you need never feel an ounce of spending constraint. No withdrawal penalties, no ex-dividend dates to look out for, and only a minimal fee that is netted against your interest income so you need never feel outraged. While most investors opt for a fund that invests in Treasuries or CDs, others exist that invest in munis to generate tax-free income. There are also funds that invest in short-term bonds, but here you have some risk that the principal will rise or fall with interest rates.

If you're adventurous and decide you will invest directly with one of the money market mutual funds, don't worry about comparing Morningstar ratings for them. Go for the one with the lowest fees.

Certificates of Deposit

Better known as CDs, certificates of deposit are IOUs issued by a bank for a fixed period of time at a fixed interest rate. They can run from 30 days to five years. They differ from bank bonds by virtue of the fact that they are insured by the Federal Deposit Insurance Corporation (FDIC). As a result of the insurance, you don't need to worry about the strength of the bank. The yield on CDs depends on the size of the purchase and length of time. The purchase time is important because, unlike most other investment instruments, this one carries a penalty if you withdraw your money early. Many conservative investors love CDs because they are so simple. Say you build a CD ladder of maturities going out two years, with a certificate coming due every month. What they don't spend, they plow back, knowing another issue is coming up next month. If you've saved enough that you can live comfortably on the income such a program generates, then God has surely blessed you and you need read no further in this book.

And where do you buy these CDs? Well, your local banker or most brokerage houses will help. You can even shop for them on the Internet.

Duration

I thought long and hard about including duration in a book that promised to include only the minimum you need to know in order to invest in income securities. I decided to include it despite its complexity because some readers like to be challenged occasionally, and others like terms they can drop at their next social gathering to impress their fellow guests. *Duration* relates to factors that tell you how severely the price of your bond or preferred will be affected by a change in interest rates. It is a rough measure of how many years it will take you to get back your original investment. Thus, a 7 percent coupon bond currently valued at par with a 20-year maturity will return your money in 14.2 years (100% ÷ 7% = 14.2 years). The reason you want to know this is that if interest rates rise by, say, 1 percent, the price of your bond will drop by 14.2 percent (1% × 14.2 years = 14.2%). Note that, since the duration is 14.2 years for this 7 percent bond, all bonds with a maturity of 15 years or longer have the same duration. Pretty simple so far? Good, because it really doesn't get much worse.

The reason you want to understand duration is because, if the general consensus of opinion in any given year is that interest rates will rise, there is something you can do to avoid this drop in price: You can shorten your duration. The easiest way to do this is to buy a bond with a shorter maturity date. Note, however, that you must buy a maturity date of less than 14.2 years before there is any benefit. Buy a 10-year bond and you cut the price-drop risk to 10 percent; buy a 5-year bond and cut your exposure to 5 percent. So, you say, why not just buy nothing other than 5-year or lesser-maturity bonds? The answer, of course, is that in a normal world, a 5-year bond will yield less than a 10- or 20-year bond precisely because it has less interest rate risk. As I am writing this, however, we are in the midst of what is termed a *negative yield curve* (i.e., the yield on a 5-year bond is greater than on 10-, 20-, and 30-year bonds). Since this is not a normal state of the world, what should you do? Well, the short-term rates are set by bureaucrats (i.e., the Fed), and the long-term rates are set by the market. Who do you trust? For my money, I trust the market.

The example here is oversimplified because I did not address how you can also shorten duration by buying a bond with a higher coupon rate (e.g., an 8 percent bond has only a 12.5-year duration). The bond math becomes trickier now since you would have to pay a higher price for the 8 percent bond than for a 7 percent—so, in order not to lose you, I will leave well enough alone. I should add that when interest rates fall, the effect is a price rise, so you want to hold longer maturities if rates are likely to fall (another reason why buying only 5-year maturities doesn't pay). Another point about duration and coupon rate is that securities with a high coupon rate, and therefore lower vulnerability to interest rate rises, also tend to be predominately junk bonds. Because of their shorter duration, junk bonds tend to be much more stable when rates rise. And yet, because of their high coupon, they do much better when rates fall, especially if they have a long maturity. These dual factors make junk bonds attractive to many large institutions and individual investors alike.

Questions to Ask When Buying a Corporate Bond

Most brokers will feel quite challenged by having to provide answers to the following questions and may never want to sell you a bond again. Then again, maybe they were unaware that they were trying to sell you distressed goods and charging you too much (to give them the benefit of the doubt). It's up to you to find out. Try asking these questions.

- *What is the coupon rate for the bond?* The coupon rate determines how much the periodic interest payments are going to be. If that rate is above the current market rate for this quality of bond, then you will have to pay above the par value of the bond, so a portion of the periodic interest payment will be a return of capital, because, over time, the price of a bond migrates down to its face value.
- *What is the maturity date?* The maturity date is the longest date the bond can remain outstanding. It is also a key to calculating a bond's duration, which is a measure of how sensitive the bond will be to interest rate swings. The longer the duration, the more its price is likely to react to interest rate changes.
- *What is the quality rating of this bond?* The quality rating is a measure of safety from default risk. Investment-grade issues (ratings of AAA, AA, A, BBB) have extremely low default rates (below 1 percent, on average) while below-investment-grade issues (ratings of BB, B, CCC) have default risks from 1.5 percent for BB, 30 percent for B, and 60 percent for CCC. A key question here is, what was the issue originally rated, and is the current rating below that? An issue that has declined recently or a number of times is much more likely to default than one that has been stable.
- *Does the company have other, higher rated issues?* Its hard to judge a company's bond in isolation or by its nominal description (e.g., "Senior Secured Bond" may be secured by real assets or by only a promise of the parent company). If the company has other debt issues with a higher letter rating, chances are that it's unsecured debt behind other, more senior, issues.

- *How much and when are the interest payments?* If you are trying to build an income portfolio with steady monthly income, it's nice to know in which months this bond makes its interest payments and how much.
- *When is the bond callable and at what price?* Bond calls are the bane of income investors because it is always the best issues that are called away. When you are buying a bond well below its call price, you can bet it won't be called. On the other hand, if you are paying a price well above the call price, you face the real possibility of a capital loss if the bond is called, especially if it is called within a year or two.
- *What is the current yield?* Because bond coupons, ratings, and maturities vary so widely, the current yield is one apples-to-apples yardstick you can apply to determine whether the bond is fairly priced. This yield should compare favorably to similarly rated issues or provide an explanation of why it does not. Another comparative measure here is the *yield to maturity*. This is what your annual yield would be if the issue is held and not redeemed until its maturity date.
- *What is the yield to call?* This is another apples-to-apples yardstick you need to know to ensure that the current yield is not misleading you. Another measure is called *yield to worst*, which is the yield for a bond with a variety of call dates and prices. It measures the worst-case scenario.
- *What is the total cost to buy—principal, accrued interest, and commissions?* The price you are quoted for a bond is augmented by the amount of interest accruing to the date of the purchase plus any commission. Note that commissions on bond trades can be per bond (typically $5 per $1,000 bond) or a flat minimum fee (e.g., $40). The flat fee will be charged if you are buying less than 10 bonds, which is why you don't want to buy in such small quantities.
- *Is your firm acting as an agent or a principal in this trade?* When a broker is initiating the purchase offer, chances are he is trying to sell you a bond his firm has in inventory. In that case, he may be acting as a principal in the transaction, (i.e., he is the seller). Or he can act as your agent and have his firm be the principal in which he charges you a commission. In any case, the brokerage house will make a markup over its cost of the bond, so you should ask that the transaction be commission-free.

Questions to Ask When Buying a Muni

- *Is the bond insured, and by whom?* This may seem like a strange lead question, but the fact is that over 80 percent of municipal bonds are insured by a monoline bond insurance company or by another third party. (See under "Insured Municipal Bonds" in this chapter.) This question is necessary because some types of so-called insurance are inferior or limited in what they cover.

- *What type of bond is it?* If a bond is not insured, you need to know a little more about who is actually backing the bonds and the source of their revenue stream. General-obligation state bonds backed by the full faith and credit of the state are very strong. Not necessarily so if it's a city or county, in which case you would feel more secure if they are backed by local sales or property taxes.
- *What is the bond's rating?* Credit ratings for uninsured municipal bonds are very, very important. Often you have no other indication of an issue's financial strength, since municipalities are not entities that issue regular, audited financial statements. Hence, when you buy an unrated muni, you are flying blind.
- *Who is the bond issuer?* The bond issuer name can provide some comfort, especially if it is a large or well-known and prosperous municipality. For example, Palm Beach, Florida, issues only unrated bonds, but that is because it is so well known that it doesn't need ratings or insurance to sell its bonds. Also, be sure that a government entity is the obligor on the issue and not some private developer who is merely using the municipality as a financing conduit. (See under "Conduit Bonds.")
- *What is the coupon rate?* The coupon rate is the stated rate of interest, which determines how much the periodic interest payments are going to be. If the coupon rate is 5 percent, then the semiannual interest payments on a $5,000 bond will total $250 a year.
- *What is the maturity date?* The maturity date is the longest date the bond can remain outstanding. It is also a key to calculating a bond's duration, which is a measure of how sensitive the bond will be to interest rate swings. The longer the duration, the more its price will react to interest rate changes.
- *What is the current yield?* Because bond coupons, ratings, and maturities vary so widely, the current yield is an apples-to-apples yardstick you can apply to determine whether the bond is fairly priced. This yield should compare favorably to similarly rated issues or provide an explanation of why it does not.
- *What is the yield to call?* This is another apples-to-apples yardstick you need to know to ensure that the current yield is not misleading you. Another measure is called *yield to worst*, which is the yield for a bond with different call dates and call prices and which measures the worst-case scenario.
- *When is the bond callable, and at what price?* Bond calls are the bane of income investors because it is always the best issues that are called away. When you are buying a bond well below its call price, you can bet it won't be called. On the other hand, if you are paying a price well above the call price, you face the real possibility of a capital loss if the bond is called, especially if the call is within a year or two. Munis sometimes have partial calls whereby they redeem, say, $150 of your $5,000 principal in a given year. This leaves you with a $4,850 bond. In this case, plan to hold it to maturity.
- *Is the bond exempt from the AMT calculation?* Certain municipal bonds are exempt from inclusion in the alternative minimum tax (AMT) calculation. Such bonds are clearly more desirable than those that are not.

- *Is the bond exempt from my state income tax?* The answer here is almost always yes if the issuer is an in-state municipality and usually no if it's an out-of-state issuer. If your state has very low taxes, this should not be a primary consideration, especially if the issue is not very liquid (i.e., the issue is too small to be widely held or known).
- *What is the total cost to buy—principal, accrued interest, and commissions?* The price you are quoted for a bond is augmented by the amount of interest accruing to the date of the purchase plus any commission. Note that commissions on bond trades can be per bond (typically $25 per $5,000 bond for a high-quality bond to as much as $200 for unrated and illiquid bonds) or a flat minimum fee. The flat fee will be charged if you are buying less than five bonds, which is why you don't want to buy in small quantities. Since most municipal brokers are selling from their inventory and charging you a markup, commissions are more an issue when you want to sell your bonds.
- *Are you (the broker) acting as my agent or as a principal in this trade?* When a broker is initiating the purchase offer, chances are she is trying to sell you a bond her firm has in inventory. In that case she may be acting as a principal in the transaction (i.e., she is the seller). Or she can act as your agent and have her firm be the principal in which she charges you a commission. In any case, the brokerage house will charge a markup over its cost of the bond, so you should ask that the transaction be commission-free.

4

PREFERREDS AND HYBRIDS

General Features

Prior to a revolutionary change in 1993, corporations owned most of the preferred stocks in the market. Utilities and banks were the dominant issuers, and corporate investors, who could deduct 85 percent of the dividends received from their taxable income, were the main buyers. This Dividend Received Deduction (DRD) advantage allowed issuers to sell them with a lower dividend rate than they would otherwise have had to pay. Individual investors avoided preferreds because of these low yields and because they were very illiquid.

The preferred market changed dramatically in 1993 with the invention of a new type of hybrid security that allowed issuers to treat them as debt for tax purposes, thus allowing them to deduct the interest expense from their taxes. These hybrids were aimed at the rapidly growing mutual fund and pension fund markets, and today they make up over 65 percent of the nonconvertible preferred universe.

To help to understand today's universe of preferreds, I have classified them into nine logical groupings dubbed *families*. There are seven nonconvertible and two convertible families. The convertibles will be covered in the next section.

Hybrids: Bonds/Indirect Bonds

The following three families of preferreds are either pure bonds or represent an indirect ownership in a bond. They come in a multitude of different structures and carry a variety of acronyms, but all have several things in common: They pay interest, not dividends; they have a maturity date; and they trade on the New York Stock Exchange. For individual investors they offer the opportunity to buy a bond in $10 or $25 par share value increments versus the $1,000 par value of a typical bond. Hence, a 100-share trade represents only a $1,000 to $2,500 investment (versus the $25,000 considered a minimum lot size for a bond trade at a reasonable commission cost).

Preferred Equity Traded (PET) Bonds

This family of preferreds are actual bonds in $25 denomination rather than the typical $1,000. They may pay interest monthly, quarterly, or semiannually. They differ from conventional bond trading not only because they are exchange traded, but also because they trade without accrued interest. For this reason, these securities have a designated ex-dividend date prior to each interest payment date. This is the first day the security trades without a claim on the latest interest payment. The previous day's price is thus reset to the actual closing price less the amount of the dividend for purposes of measuring the normal price movement for that day. This is particularly important when semiannual interest payments are made, since the amount can be $1 or more on a $25 security. Investors should be aware of the next ex-dividend date when buying a preferred that pays semiannually in order to avoid buying into a taxable event just days after their purchase. Likewise, if you prefer capital gains over interest income, a strategy of selling such a preferred before the ex-date and buying it back right after should be kept in mind as an option. More on this in Chapter 9 under "Tax Strategy."

Trust Preferreds

Beginning in 1992 both foreign and domestic companies began raising capital through a new-style preferred that allowed them to pay the interest or dividend with pretax money. In effect, the reduced tax benefit previously accruing to the preferred holder now passes back to the issuer. In addition, the credit rating agencies counted such preferred issues as equity rather than debt, thus enhancing the company's credit standing and debt capacity. The general structure of these issues involves the parent company creating a vehicle (grantor trust) that issues a hybrid preferred, which then lends the funds to the parent company by purchasing a bond. In some cases, the parent company issues the bonds or debt directly (i.e., without a grantor trust entity) as a hybrid preferred. Trust preferreds are senior to common and preferred stock and are considered debt, not equity.

Today, the majority of new issues of nonconvertible preferreds are trust preferreds (hybrid preferreds). They typically yield more than the equivalent bonds and have five-year call protection. Because they trade on a stock exchange, most on the NYSE, they are very liquid and easy to follow. The issues trade under the company's name followed by the brokerage house acronym that defines common features of such issues. Some of the acronyms are as follows:

MIPS
MIDS
QUIBS
QUIPS
TOPRS
SQUIDS

Trust preferred shareholders are paid before regular preferred holders or those who hold common stock. One difference between these trust preferreds and bonds is that most have a deferred interest clause that may last up to five years. During such a deferral period the interest accrues and is taxable to the holder. I have seen very few instances of this clause being invoked, since the issues are generally not substantial enough in the overall financial structure of a company. When a company gets to the point where it can't pay these issues, it is generally only months away from a bankruptcy, and then it doesn't have to pay anybody.

Third-Party Trust Preferreds

These are similar to trust preferreds except they are issued by a third party. A *depositor* corporation, usually a wholly owned subsidiary of a large brokerage firm, will buy a block of bonds of a particular company on the open market, generally below their par or face value. These bonds are deposited into a trust, which then issues $25 par value preferreds representing a pro rata interest in the bonds. Each of the major brokerage houses that creates these preferreds markets them under a proprietary acronym that stands for a name you should have no interest in knowing, since they are contrived to be catchy acronyms. Some of these acronyms are as follows:

CABCO

CBTCS

CorTs

PPLUS

SATURNS

TRUCS

TRUPS

Since these acronyms are the brand names used by the brokerage houses to market the preferreds, when you see the daily prices of the securities in the paper, it is difficult to identify the underlying corporate issuer. These third-party trusts are subject to the call provisions of the underlying bond, but also generally have a five-year call provision for the trust.

Such preferreds began coming out in great quantity about five years ago, as brokerage firms saw an opportunity to buy up blocks of bonds at below their face value, repackage them as preferreds, and sell them to their retail clients. Aside from the commissions they could earn from marketing these new securities, they had a long-term compensation incentive in that the appreciation in the price of the bonds held in trust would accrue not to the preferred holders, but rather to the brokerage house that created them. Most of these trust preferreds have a provision allowing them to be called in five years. In five years, most of the bonds in these trusts have increased in value to par or above. As you might expect, they are being called in as quickly as the call dates come up. Worse still, few bonds in the market are selling at significant discounts from their face value. Since there is no residual profit for the brokerage houses when creating a trust preferred out of par or above par bonds, there is little new product coming onto the market these days.

One vulnerability of these third-party trusts is that they can be terminated if the company goes into bankruptcy. This means your claim against the company will be sold at the worst-possible time, pricewise, since its being sold when many others are selling and there is no good information yet available on what their recovery value is likely to be. Hence, these preferreds are not the place to be if bankruptcy looms.

Foreign Preferreds

These preferreds are issued by foreign-based corporations in U.S. dollars. There are several types of these securities, most being issued as American Depository Receipts (ADR), alternatively known as American Depository Shares (ADS). The attraction of these preferreds is that they offer a higher dividend rate than a comparably rated U.S. corporation and their dividends are usually eligible for the 15 percent dividend tax treatment. While generally of high quality, such issues may be noncumulative (i.e., unpaid dividends don't accrue). Note that these issues may be subject to foreign withholding tax for U.S. holders; however, this is recoverable from the IRS by filing a Form 1116 with your annual income tax return. More on this in Chapter 9 under "Income Taxes."

Partnerships

This family of preferreds is issued by entities using a limited liability company (LLC) or a limited partnership (LP) structure rather than the corporate structure. In most cases, a parent company establishes the LLC and becomes the general partner. Oil and natural gas producers are frequent users of this structure because of the tax benefits in the form of depletion allowances that they can pass on to the preferred holders. For income tax reporting purposes the investor receives an IRS Schedule K-1 rather than a Form 1099. Since your broker creates your 1099 and the company provides the Schedule K-1 directly to you, you will have to augment the amounts reported on the 1099.

Perpetual Preferred Stock

This family of securities is senior to common equity but junior to all debt. Perpetual preferreds have no maturity, like common stock, and pay a fixed dividend amount that is cumulative (i.e., accrues as an obligation of the corporation and must be paid before any payments to the common shareholders). The failure by a company to make a preferred dividend payment does not constitute an event of default and thus give cause for a bankruptcy filing. Credit rating agencies, however, do view a failure to make such payments as a default on a company's financial obligations and may downgrade a company's debt ratings as a result. In practice, a company that fails to make its preferred payments and has substantial debt outstanding is not far from a debt default and bankruptcy. Hence, it is not a step a company takes lightly. The most vulnerable perpetual preferreds are those of companies whose only loan liabilities are bank debt. When they stop their preferred dividends, it is at the insistence of their bankers.

Most perpetuals are callable sometime in the future and are DRD-eligible for qualified corporate investors. For individuals, the dividends are subject to the 15 percent dividend tax rate. Note that if the dividend is not earned by the company, the payments may qualify as a return of capital in which case the tax rate is zero. Your annual Form 1099 report from your broker should break out the nature of any dividends that represent such a return of capital.

Buying Preferreds

Preferreds trade much like common stocks, with symbols to designate each issue. Preferreds are frequently coded with the issuers symbol plus a series code. For example, IBM A and IBM D designate two different IBM preferreds. If these are the only IBM preferreds outstanding, it generally means the series B and C series have been called in or have matured. Symbols for hybrid preferreds generally have an unrelated code. For example, the General Motors PET bonds use such symbols at HGM, GMS, or GOM, while the third-party trust preferreds use symbols that have no identity other than the fact that issues starting with the letter *C* are CBTCS issued by Lehman Brothers and those starting with the letter *K* are PreferredPlus issues by Merrill Lynch.

One annoying aspect of trading preferreds is the lack of agreement between brokerage houses and quotation services on a standardized preferred designator. The preferred designator is the space between a company's symbol and the preferred series being requested. In the preceding IBM example, depending on the quotation system you are accessing, the symbol to type in for a quote could be IBM A, IBMpA, IBM+A, IBM_pA, IBMPRA, and IBM-A. This is confusing at best, especially when a brokerage house uses one designator to make quotation inquiries, but requires another designator to enter an order. Most annoying is when a company's preferred symbol is the stock symbol followed by a designator only. This happens when a company has only one preferred issue and fails to designate a series letter for it. This has led to countless purchases of common stock when the objective was to buy the preferreds.

Buying and selling preferreds is a little different from trading in common stocks. *Preferreds are attractive because they offer relatively higher yields than bonds.* This is because the average preferred issue is often no more than 1 or 2 million shares. This keeps out the large institutional investors, but it also means trading can often be spotty and the pricing erratic. Many of the third-party trust preferreds can go for days with no shares traded, and quoted bid and ask prices are often 20 to 50 cents apart. When you are buying these shares, it is often useful to look at a price graph of where the shares traded over the past month or two in order to establish a reasonable price. You will often see a bid and an ask price for 100 or 200 shares. These are put up by market makers to provide buyers and sellers a reference point. Should you enter an order to buy, say, 1,000 shares, you can get an execution for the 100 shares at the quoted price followed by a new offering, this time by a true seller for, say, 500 shares at a price that may be 20 cents higher. If you buy these, the next increment may again be 20 cents higher before you get your 1,000 shares. The same can happen on the sell side. Hence, when buying and selling these preferreds, set your price and make it a good-til-canceled order. It may take several days for the entire order to be filled, but if you're making a fair bid, chances are it will fill. Note that if such an order is filled over a number of days, you will be charged a commission for each day's transactions. If you are using a discount broker, however, this should still be less than chasing the price in order to complete the order the same day. One way to avoid too many fills is to specify a minimum quantity in the order. You can specify "all or none" if you want the entire 1,000 shares in one execution, or you can specify a minimum fill quantity of, say, 300 shares in order to avoid more than three or four commissions. However, all such order limitations do is reduce your chances of getting the shares you want when you want them.

The date when you want your shares is important because trust preferreds do not trade with accrued interest. Hence, an issue that pays dividends only twice a year entitles the holders to receive six months' worth of interest, even if they buy it the day before the ex-dividend date. For this reason, the price pattern of most preferreds is a gradually rising price up to the ex-dividend date. On that date, the price will drop by as much as a dollar if it pays semiannually and the coupon rate is 8 percent, or a 50 cent drop if it pays quarterly dividends. When buying a preferred, it is important to know how many days it is until the next ex-dividend date, since it is assumed you are buying a certain amount of accrued dividend in the purchase price. When using good-til-canceled orders, you should know that your target price will automatically be reduced by the amount of the dividend on the ex-dividend date. Hence, you don't need to worry that you get your order executed on that day when the price drops by the amount of the dividend. You might, however, want to set a new price on the ex-dividend date, since there is often a bit more trading just after the dividend, and you could catch an interday low well below your target price.

Note that a favorite game of fixed-income investors is what is called *scalping dividends*. This is where you buy a preferred just before a large dividend payment, on the theory that the price will not drop by the full amount of the dividend or will look relatively cheap after the dividend and thus will recover a disproportionate amount of the price drop in the first week or two after the ex-dividend date. As someone who has played this game, I can tell you it does work more often than not, especially for securities that pay only twice a year. You do have to be selective in the securities you target and look at the price history for the security to see what has happened after previous dividends. You can go wrong here if an institutional investor decides to sell its position after collecting the latest dividend, in which case the price will drop by more than the dividend—sometimes much more. Aside from this, you do pick up taxable income when you play this game, so restrict it to your tax-free account. Scalping dividends is one way to satisfy the day-trading instinct in you with a greater likelihood of making money.

Two other caveats in trading preferreds: Never place market orders, and never use stop-loss orders. As I indicated, the market for preferreds can be quite thin on any given day. If you place a 1,000-share market order seeking an ask price of, say, $24.50 for 300 shares, you could quickly find out the next 700 shares cost you $24.80. When trading is thin, you are in a position to make the market come to you. Don't chase it, whether you're buying or selling. As for stop-loss orders, this is where you put in an automatic sell order if the price goes below a certain level. Don't use these on preferreds. Brokerage houses can trigger such orders by executing a below-market trade, knowing they can make it all back by then executing your trade. Remember, they can see these orders waiting and are trading for their own account.

5

CONVERTIBLES AND ADJUSTABLE-RATE DEBT

Convertible Bonds

Convertible bonds have long been popular with investors and companies alike. Investors like the possibility that they might participate in the growth of the company and are willing to forego some current yield and some credit quality for the privilege. Companies like this cheaper way of issuing more stock, and they like the looser debt restrictions. Even a company's bankers love convertibles, since they provide an extra cushion for their loans. Some people will argue that original-issue junk bonds, especially of the single-B and CCC variety, are actually disguised convertible bonds since so many end up being redeemed with stock after a default. I take exception to this contention. Lots of CCC and even single-B bonds never get a single share of stock; in fact, they never get any payoff, but this is a story for later in this book (see Chapter 9).

Most conversion clauses specify a fixed number of shares into which the bond will convert. At the time the bonds were issued, this is usually set at a price level about 20 percent above where the stock is then trading. This price remains fixed except for any adjustments for stock dividends or stock splits. On occasion, the conversion privilege will be based on the market price of the common stock at some future date or at some future event. Such conversion privileges are extremely attractive for the bondholder, but can be catastrophic for the company. The Mirant Corporation bankruptcy was the direct result of such a market conversion clause that threatened to give control of the corporation to the convertible bondholders through massive dilution of the shareholders equity. A classic lose-lose situation. General Motors has a similar convertible bond packaged as a preferred (GXM), where bondholders have the right to put the bonds back to the company in March 2007 for cash or the $25 market equivalent in GM stock. Here, bondholders of one of the lowest-rated GM debt issues hold a piece of paper paying 4.5 percent interest and selling at a price of $24, while higher-rated GM debt with long maturities paying 7.25 percent sells at $18. Sometimes the value is in the details.

Most convertible bonds can be converted to stock at any time by the holder. The bond issuer will also have this privilege, but only after a few years and generally will not exercise it until the value of the stock exceeds the par value of the bond—and maybe not even then if the coupon rate makes it a cheap borrowing. At that point, all holders will take the stock rather than accept the lower cash amount. As the price of a company's stock rises, the convertible bond will also rise, but always maintaining a premium to its conversion value. Once the stock conversion equivalent equals or exceeds the par value of the bond, the bond price will move dollar for dollar with the stock at or near its conversion equivalent. The conversion premium disappears as the stock price reaches its conversion equivalent if the issuer can call the bond anytime after that.

Frequently, a company falls on hard times, and the likelihood of the stock ever recovering to a level where the conversion privilege is at full value is remote. In such an instance, the bond will trade at a price based on its yield and credit rating. I say conversion at full value may be out of the question, but conversion will still play a role. Say you have a junior, 4 percent, 20-year $1,000 bond issue with a conversion privilege into 50 shares of common, and the price of the stock drops to $10. If that same company has 8 percent, 20-year senior bonds trading at 90, you would expect the junior bond to trade somewhere below 50. However, the junior convertible bond will trade based on its coupon yield only down to a price of 50, since below that price, its share equivalent value (50 shares times $10 a share) is greater than its value as a bond. Hence, the current yield on the lower-rated debt will actually be lower than on the senior bonds, although the yield to call will be higher.

Convertible Preferreds

Convertible preferreds have characteristics similar to their bond cousins. They differ mainly in that a convertible preferred can pay either interest or a dividend that may or may not be qualified dividend income (QDI). They also differ in that the conversion privilege may be optional or mandatory.

Whether a convertible preferred pays interest or a dividend is determined at the time of issue. The issuer may decide to define the preferred as a debt instrument in order to take an interest expense deduction for the costs of the issue. If the company pays a high dividend rate on its common stock, this may actually represent a lower cash cost, since common dividends come out of after-tax income. A company may elect to issue a convertible preferred as a capital stock rather than as debt. This may be done because the company can get a better credit rating, since the preferred would be considered as equity by the rating agencies. It may also issue equity if it is a REIT, since it pays no taxes anyway. In fact, using convertible preferreds is a popular way for REITS to raise capital.

Optional convertibles may have a maturity date or may be perpetual. Those with maturities are debt issues and pay interest; those that are perpetual pay dividends. This tax difference is clearly important for those interested in low taxable income and is one of the advantages of convertible preferreds over convertible bonds.

As with optional convertible bonds, the pricing of the security is dependent on the relationship of the conversion privilege to the interest rate and the call date. This means there can be significant divergence between stock price and the conversion equivalent price of the convertible. The normal situation is as follows: When the bond is issued, the number of shares into which it converts is set at about 20 percent below the par value selling price of the bond. If the preferred has a maturity or call date, that premium will shrink over the life of the convertible as long as the value of the common stock equivalent rises and exceeds the face value of the convertible. If the common stock rises from a price of $10 to $12, the preferred would rise from $25 to $30. From there, the convertible would continue to rise, dollar for dollar, with the common, except that the 20 percent premium would shrink to almost zero by the time you reach the first call date. Note, a call will normally take place only if the value of the stock is greater than the par call price, since the issuer really does not want to pay the convertible off in cash but rather in stock. When the price of the common stock falls, however, it's altogether another story. Since the issuer pays a much lower rate on convertibles, the conversion premium quickly shrinks to nothing as the price of the convertible plunges with the stock price until the yield on the convertible is near that of similarly rated nonconvertible securities. Here it will remain no matter how low the common stock goes. An extreme example of this is a $500 million Ford 6.5 percent convertible preferred (ticker F S) issued in January 2002 at $50 a share and convertible until January 15, 2032. At the time, Ford stock was at $13.70 a share. The conversion value was set at 2.8249 shares of common, or a 22.5 percent premium over the stock value at that time. As Ford's prospects dimmed, the common sank to $7, or 50 percent, by early 2006. The preferreds followed the common down by 42 percent to a price of $29, but held up further decline from there, since the 6.5 percent coupon was now yielding 11 percent, which was in line with the yield of other Ford debt. Risk aside, this convertible is attractive because the conversion privilege is totally free (i.e., you no longer are giving up any yield over comparable debt issues) and still have 26 years to go. I don't know whether or when Ford will turn around, but a 26-year window at no cost should prove rewarding the minute Ford stock begins showing recovery. Also, if you purchase the convertible at $29 a share, you participate in that turnaround, dollar for dollar, even before the stock crosses its $10.26 equivalent ($29 divided by 2.8249 shares.) In Wall Street parlance, this one is a keeper.

Mandatory convertibles are different from all other convertibles because the ultimate conversion date is fixed in the future, usually five years or so from the date of issue. This mandatory conversion aspect significantly increases the risk to the buyer, and therefore certain additional features are thrown in. The yield on such convertibles is closer to that of the straight debt of the company, and the number of shares into which the issue converts is dependent on the market value of the shares at the time of conversion. The typical structure is that if the price of the common stock at the time of conversion is between, say, $20 and $25, the conversion rate is the par value of the convertible ($25). If the price of the common is above $25, the convertible holder gets one share of common stock. If the common stock price is below $20, the convertible holder gets 1.2 shares of common stock. Hence, you have 20 percent downside price cushion and you collect a higher yield than the common shareholder. On the upside, you participate dollar for dollar with any price appreciation of the common except for the 20 percent or so premium over the common price that was the benchmark price set when the convertible was first sold. *This downside protection makes these preferreds a worthwhile alternative to buying the common stock, assuming the stock pays little or no dividends*. But note, you should not buy these preferreds for income unless you find the underlying stock attractive.

When buying a mandatory convertible, you need to make an evaluation about the fairness of the purchase price relative to the stock performance and the remaining time and conversion premium. Let's say you are considering buying a mandatory convertible selling at $33 with a conversion into 1.14 shares of common stock and presently selling at $25.50. In this instance, the preferred is selling at a 12 percent premium ($25.50 times 1.14 divided by $33) to its stock value. The conversion is still two years off, and the stock is attractive, so the 12 percent premium is way below what you would pay for a long-term option to buy the stock. In this case, the premium is fair because it can be measured against the price charged for an option that would give a similar outcome. In most cases, the price of a mandatory preferred is very near its conversion value and will fluctuate accordingly. This is why such securities provide a diversification away from interest rate—sensitive securities.

One aspect of mandatory convertibles that most investors find very confusing is the tax treatment when a convertible comes due. In order to allow the issuer of the convertible to take the tax benefits of paying interest and at the same time enhance its credit standing with the rating agencies, the convertible is made up of two documents: a debt instrument and a purchase contract for the company's stock. At maturity, the debt is repaid, and at the same time, the repayment proceeds are used to purchase the common stock. This means that, from an IRS point of view, two separate events have taken place. The redemption of the debt was the first transaction. See Chapter 9 for a discussion of the different income tax scenarios this can create.

Adjustable-Rate Debt

The biggest fear of most income investors is that interest rates will rise, thereby eroding the value of their fixed-income holdings. Preventing this through diversification is, of course, the main theme of this book. Nevertheless, it doesn't hurt to have other options for protecting against a rate rise if one looks imminent. *Fortunately, in today's markets you have options that allow you to benefit from rate rises, not just protect against them.*

The best-known options for protecting against inflation-driven rate rises are issued by the U.S. Treasury, called *Treasury inflation-protected securities* (TIPS). These securities adjust the value of the underlying security semiannually based on the consumer price index (CPI) and then pay the stated coupon rate on that adjusted value. Values adjust only upward, so you are protected against deflation. These securities currently pay about 2.44 percent in interest, which is about 2.5 percent below the coupon rate of a 10-year Treasury bond. Hence, you are losing ground unless annual inflation averages higher than 2.5 percent. Note, one added drawback here is that you pay taxes on the value adjustment and not just on the cash interest received.

Another semi-government-backed security that offers protection of another sort is an issue by Freddie Mac, the home mortgage provider. It has an adjustable perpetual preferred tied to a five-year Treasury yield index (ticker FRE L), but its pay rate resets only every five years, or not until December 31, 2009. The current pay rate is 3.58 percent, but at its price of 38 for a $50 par preferred, this gives a current yield of 4.7 percent, taxable as QDI. Since the five-year Treasury rate is 4.92 percent currently, this security should migrate close to its par price between now and 2009. That's 12 points, or 31 percent, a handsome sweetener even if it migrates up only halfway. It's like getting the TIPS value adjustment without having to pay taxes on it until you sell, and then it's a long-term capital gain, not interest income.

In choosing an adjustable-rate security, the index or benchmark to which it is tied is often the most important consideration. The current rise in interest rates in the United States is driven in large part by international factors such as world interest rates in general, the strength of the dollar, and the huge amount of dollar-denominated reserves held by foreign governments. The free flow of international capital under the current world trade system is bringing interest rates around the world in line. Hence, debt securities that are tied to an international index such as the London Interbank Offered Rate (LIBOR) may be a better benchmark than any measure of historical U.S. rates or inflation. LIBOR interest rates are set daily by the British Bankers Association for a range of short-term maturities of from one week to one year. They are the principal benchmark interest rates outside the United States. You can follow LIBOR rate changes at www.bloomberg.com/markets/rates/index.html.

Freddie Mac also has a perpetual $50 bond (ticker FRE N), rated AA−, tied to LIBOR minus 20 basis points with a reset once a year on April 1 (no pun intended). The current rate is 5.05 percent, but since rates have risen, the issue trades at $45 and yields 5.7 percent. Clearly the LIBOR index did not provide adequate rate protection in the past, but at the current price, it is a good buy for the future. If you are willing to assume a little more risk, there is the SLM Corporation, the student loan people (Sallie Mae, ticker SLM B), which has an issue rated BBB+ that is linked to three-month LIBOR plus 70 basis points. It's reset every three months, so in a rapidly changing rate environment, you have much less volatility because of the frequency of the payment rate adjustments. The added benefit is that its income is qualified dividend income subject to only a 15 percent tax rate.

Other corporate issues would be Goldman Sachs Group Capital I perpetual preferreds (ticker GS A or GS B), which are adjusted quarterly based on the three-month LIBOR rate plus 75 basis points. They also have a floor, or minimum rates, of 3.25 percent and 4 percent, respectively, and the dividend is QDI. If you need an adjustable security for a tax-sheltered account, then buy one of Goldman's interest-paying preferreds (ticker GYB). Since Goldman Sachs receives the tax benefits, it pays a more generous three-month LIBOR plus 85 basis points and yields even more since it sells at a greater discount to par than the QDI issues.

Floor rates are common in adjustable issues, as are ceiling or maximum rates. It's important to be aware of the floor rates when shopping for an adjustable issue. It is not uncommon for issues to have high floor rates and therefore look more attractive than other adjustable issues. They may, however, have an adjustment factor that is far below current market rates. Hence, rates may have to rise 1 or 2 percent before any yield increases kick in. Not much protection there.

6

INCOME STOCKS

Overview

Common stocks have historically had a limited role in income portfolios. This has meant buying mainly utility stocks and REITS. Figure 6.1 demonstrates how poorly, on average, stocks serve as income producers. The reduction of the tax on dividends to 15 percent seems to have inspired significant dividend increases since 2004, broadening the range of companies that appeal to income investors. Although many of these stocks pay only 2 or 3 percent in dividend yield, they offer growth in dividend payouts as well as price appreciation over time. Others offer immediate high payouts in the 10 to 12 percent range, but are more volatile in price and need to be purchased very selectively. Investing in income common stocks is an attractive, and I believe necessary, way to diversify to achieve a more balanced income flow.

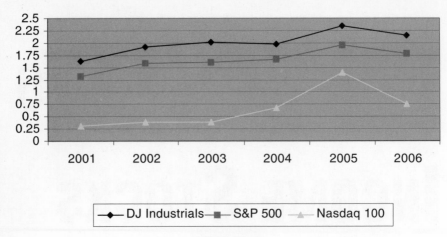

Figure 6.1
Equity Dividend Yields 2001–2006, Percentage Returns

Canadian Energy and Royalty Trusts

Mention royalty trusts to most investors and you get mixed reactions. They are not for the "keep it simple" crowd, but their double-digit, tax-advantaged yields make them a serious contender for the next three minutes of your attention.

First, let's explain what they are. In the United States, a *royalty trust* is a tax-exempt entity that holds the extraction rights for natural resources but does not own the property itself. The most common are oil and gas trusts, but timber and coal trusts also exist. As the oil and gas are extracted, the revenues are paid out to the trust holders, usually monthly. Because you hold only the rights to the extraction of a proven reserve of resources, and because the trust cannot acquire new reserves by issuing more debt or equity, the value of your investment is constantly declining. For this reason, a portion of each year's distributions is considered a return of capital and is not subject to any federal income tax and is a reduction of your cost basis in the shares you hold. Additional tax complications occur because oil and gas are subject to state taxes. Also, you have to deal with depletion allowances, which are calculated by the individual properties owned. These tax complications make most U.S.-based trusts unattractive unless you can afford to make a large investment—to offset your accountants' bill. There is an alternative, however.

Canadian energy trusts are more attractive, both tax- and incomewise. First of all, the income is usually eligible for the 15 percent dividend tax treatment rather than being fully taxable as is a U.S.-based trust. Also, the 15 percent Canadian tax paid on the dividends can be used as an offset to your U.S. income tax. Hence, the monthly cash dividends are essentially tax free in the United States. This is ideal for investors who live off their dividend income. The best news is, those dividends amount to 9 to 14 percent a year. Your risk here is that energy prices continue to stay high, since your payout is directly tied to them. If prices drop, so will your dividend. The flip side to this is that if interest rates rise, neither your yield nor share price is affected. *Hence, these trusts represent an attractive risk diversification away from interest rate-sensitive investments.* Unlike their U.S. cousins, Canadian trusts can issue more shares and use debt to acquire producing properties. Thus, well-managed trusts can exist in perpetuity. Also, they can be operating and development companies, not just passive royalty trusts.

Many energy trusts are listed on Canadian exchanges and sold over-the-counter (pink sheets) in the United States. I won't make specific recommendations here, because these trusts are ever changing, and their relative outlook changes along with the price of oil and natural gas and the years of reserve life left. While most are yielding 10 percent or more, selection of trusts that will be able to sustain their payouts depends on such variables as the number of years of reserve life they have, the amount of probable reserves they have, the amount of current excess cash flow being paid out in dividends, and the amount held in reserve for further development. Also, most of these trusts produce both oil and natural gas, the prices of which move in very different ways. Certain trusts like PrimeWest Energy are 73 percent gas and 27 percent oil, while Penn West Energy Trust is 48 percent gas and 52 percent oil. The location of their resources is important, too; for example, Provident Energy Trust produces the majority of its natural gas from U.S. fields only a few hundred pipeline miles from a Midwestern market. I do make specific fund recommendations in my monthly newsletter based on the then-current outlook for each fund.

At the end of October 2006, the new Conservative government shocked everyone by proposing to begin taxing trusts beginning in 2011. Whether this change is enacted by the Canadian Parliament is uncertain as of this writing. The four-year grace period before the tax change goes into effect does, however, provide existing trusts time to adjust their operations to mitigate the tax effect and to lobby Parliament for a longer extension period. The major effect of the proposed change in taxation is that investors can expect little growth in dividend payouts over the next four years as these trusts use their growth in cash flow to expand the earnings base. The stronger trusts can be expected to grow their way out of this tax increase, in part by acquisition of weaker trusts. In any case, current double-digit dividend yields will likely continue for the next four years, and if you hold the right trusts, for many years thereafter.

Current energy prices are expected to fluctuate, and the price of these securities reflects much of this, so timing of a purchase is important. In any case, with interruption of energy supplies being a major concern, it's comforting to know this energy source is only a pipeline away.

Other Canadian Trusts

The trust structure is used in Canada for more than just the energy business. It has become quite popular for mature business entities that generate positive cash flow and don't have a need to finance high growth. Some of these are energy-related, such as electric and hydropower producers and coal, timber, and paper companies. Others are business trusts as diverse as breweries, food wholesalers, transportation, and even yellow pages. Yields range from 6 to 14 percent, but payouts are subject to normal economic forces in the industry for that company. Still, they do come with the 15 percent tax status, so they are worth a look versus similarly situated businesses in the United States that pay little or nothing. Note that many of these trusts trade only on the Canadian exchange and must be bought via the pink sheets in the United States. Hence they are hard to trade here and expensive to buy in Canada, since commissions for a U.S. buyer are exorbitant. A good source for information about the whole range of Canadian trusts is a publication called Roger Conrad's Canadian Edge, which is sold at www.canadianedge.com.

With regard to the previously mentioned proposed tax law change, trusts other than REITs and energy-related trusts will lose much of their past appeal. If the proposed changes are enacted, there will be little difference between these business trusts and normal Canadian corporations. While these business trusts were attractive for mature businesses, this may no longer be the case. For now, hold off making any acquisitions in this sector until the tax changes are clear.

Real Estate Investment Trusts (REITs)

REITs are trusts authorized by Congress as tax-exempt vehicles for investing in real estate. Up to 90 percent of their income must be distributed to shareholders each year in order to maintain their tax-free status. Those dividends are fully taxable to the shareholder at ordinary income rates except to the extent that the distributions are considered either capital gains or a return of capital. The intent of Congress was to give small investors the opportunity to participate in the commercial real estate market, which previously had been only for wealthy investors who could make large commitments for long periods of time. Today more than 100 REITs trade on the major exchanges, and thousands more exist as private investment vehicles. These entities can be quite sizable, as evidenced by the fact that 11 of the S&P 500 Index companies are REITs.

A REIT may invest in property mortgages or it may be an operating company that buys, sells, and operates properties in a range of industries. Generally, a REIT will specialize in one type of property in which it is knowledgeable. Properties include hotels, apartment houses, office buildings, industrial buildings, retail malls, storage buildings, and health care facilities. Dividend yields run from 3 to 12 percent, but are vulnerable to interest rates and general economic conditions. With the diversity of properties, however, you can imagine that performances vary according to the cycles in different industries. For example, when the economy is good, commercial properties do well; when the economy is bad, apartments do well.

One way to participate in REITs and still get a steady income is to buy the convertible preferreds of a REIT. These pay a higher interest rate than the common shares and yet give you the opportunity to convert to common when the common dividend begins to exceed the preferred payout. But even the straight preferred stocks of a REIT are attractive because of the strong collateral value their property or mortgage holdings provide.

Other Common Stocks

Generally speaking, any common stock is a candidate for consideration by an income investor if it pays a high dividend now or is on a track to pay ever-increasing dividends in the future. Today, companies in the natural resource extraction industries are prime candidates. The evolution of China and India as world-class economic powers with huge populations is putting permanent pressure on natural raw materials of all sorts. I'm not just talking about oil and natural gas, but also copper, coal, bauxite, gold, silver, and so forth—a range of a dozen or more in all. What makes natural resources different is that, unlike agricultural or manufactured products, you can't just build a new factory or plant a new field to increase production. For natural resources, you have to find a new source that is, more often than not, located in a remote or politically unstable region. Hence you need to build infrastructure and relocate workers to bring the materials to market. Keep in mind that over the centuries, all the low-hanging fruit in natural resources exploitation has taken place or is spoken for, so additional resources are bound to be much more expensive to produce. This means that the price increases we have been seeing in most of these materials are, here to stay. While few natural resource companies have histories of high dividend payouts, this is likely to change in the future. Companies with existing properties are currently enjoying tremendous profits with low development expenditures. Only those with soon-to-be-depleted properties will be in a hurry to spend significant amounts of this wealth on new exploration and development. More likely, they will engage in a round of takeovers first, thereby postponing internal growth.

Another area of common stock interest is in financial institutions such as banks. Current Fed policy has limited their ability to make money through loans and through playing the spread between the short and long rates. As a result, their prices are depressed, but they have maintained their dividend payouts, which run 3 to 4 percent. As the Fed has ended its policy of short-term rate increases, these institutions are expected to benefit, provided the Fed has not already killed off economic growth, as the inverted yield curve would suggest. Here again, as with REITs, Canadian trusts, and natural resources companies, choices about what to buy will be different today than in the future. My objective is simply to have you open your investment horizons to opportunities in these various sectors.

7

MUTUAL FUNDS

Overview

Mutual funds are far and away the most popular investment vehicle in America, with some 13,000 funds having amassed $16 trillion in assets. Did the industry achieve this phenomenal success by providing superior performance and careful attention to their customers' best interests? Not at all. *The mutual fund industry succeeds through astute marketing that recognizes that the vast majority of investors are scared to death of losing their capital and not up to the challenge of learning how to invest their money themselves.* Wall Street reinforces this fear and actively encourages clients to invest in mutual funds for one reason: *fees.*

Many of the people you meet who represent themselves to be financial advisors are not licensed or qualified to do anything but sell you mutual funds or annuities. Many brokerage firms try to sell you *wrap* accounts, where they charge you a flat percentage to manage your account and then put you into a selection of mutual funds. That way, they can charge you a fee on top of any revenue sharing they get from the mutual funds they promote.

Now 2 to 4.5 percent in fees, or *load*, may sound like a small price to pay to have your money managed by a professional. However, if the definition of a *professional* is defined as someone who can equal or exceed a total market index such as the S&P 500 or the Dow Jones Industrial Average, then fewer than half the fund managers can meet this test. As to whether they are adequately paid for their efforts, consider that 2 percent of $16 trillion equals an industry that takes in $320 billion in revenues a year. That makes mutual funds one of the top 10 industries in the nation.

Not all investors are so easily swayed about which fund to buy. So they rely on services such as Morningstar or the quarterly performance tables in the more popular business magazines and newspapers to select last quarter's or last year's best performers. And they think they are doing research! This is about as effective as picking the horse in the race that won its last time out or that had the most wins. Many firms in the fund industry have managed to reduce this fund shopping by, in effect, allowing you to invest in the entire stable. That is, once you join their family of funds (some numbering in the hundreds), they allow you to switch from one fund to the next without any transfer or withdrawal fees. Some people consider this fund switching to be the equivalent of investment decision making. In fact, it is patronization.

Despite all the platitudes found in the typical sales literature about the investment goals of the fund, there is reason for skepticism. Typical fund managers are in their thirties, while the typical fund clients are in their fifties. These people see the world differently, and their concepts of risk are quite different. The number one priority of a fund manager is attracting new investors, and the best way to do this is by superior short-term performance. This means lots of trading, and it can entail taking additional risks when performance lags. Recent scandals involving funds that permitted hedge funds to buy after-hours is a sad example of how some managers will bend the rules to attract capital and fees. And don't look to the fund's board of directors to exercise oversight. A mutual fund's board of directors is often just a rubber stamp.

Fixed-income investors who look to profit through investing in bond funds or other income funds have a particularly difficult task making a decent return, because even a 1 percent fee and expenses load can add up to 14 percent of the fund's total return if that return is only 7 percent before fees. Such funds can offset this disadvantage by using leverage, or low-cost short-term borrowings, to boost the overall yield. If their guidelines permit, they can also buy lower-quality debt and hope for the best, or they can churn the portfolio to pick up short-term capital gains or to scalp dividend payments. The problem with these strategies is that they leave the fund investors with sizable interest income and realized capital gains, even in years when the total return was a loss. There is nothing more frustrating than paying taxes on an investment that lost money. I recall a recent performance tabulation for high-yield bond funds where the top performer had a 63 percent total return for the year. When you looked at its performance the year before, however, you see it lost over 50 percent. Statistics being the fine art that it is, this fund's cumulative performance for the two years was not +13 percent, it was— 19 percent. This fund is for those with masochistic personalities, which might just describe this fund's managers.

Bond Funds

If you are one of those investors who is not comfortable investing in anything other than traditional bonds, and you don't have $1 or $2 million to invest, then a bond fund may be your most practical alternative. Such funds come in many flavors and many fee structures. Funds define whether they invest in short-, medium-, or long-term bonds. They tell you whether they use leverage or other means to boost the return and whether they buy foreign bonds or foreign currency–designated bonds. They also break down whether they invest in U.S. Treasuries, corporate bonds, or municipal bonds. Municipals break down even further into general, state-specific, and insured/uninsured. They also break down by quality levels, with junk or unrated issues being considered a separate category. It obviously takes some studying to see where you fit in here.

There is little reason to accept a low return in a bond fund simply because you want safety. If you want the safety of U.S. Treasuries or insured munis, you don't need a bond fund to buy them for you. You buy them directly. For all the rest, a bond fund should give you a better return, better diversification, and lower interest rate risk.

One of the biggest problems faced by bond funds is their size. Many such funds have assets of $5 billion or more. This size acts as a constraint on what they can buy (e.g., bond issues of at least $250 million or more in size where they can buy or sell $5 million positions without moving the market). In the investment-grade market, this means yields of 4.5 to 6 percent before fees. To boost this return, the managers will trade in various derivative products, thereby introducing a whole new set of risks beyond defaults or interest rate spikes. In short, they increase your risk in order to earn enough extra income so that their performance looks competitive. Only the fund investors see from their year-end distributions and Form 1099 how much additional taxes they will have to pay for this game playing. If only Morningstar would compare fund performance on an after-tax basis and flush out the cowboys.

Another tax inefficiency of bond fund arises from the fact that they typically turn their portfolios more than once per year. This means any decrease in interest rates will be reflected in a more sizable capital gain at year-end. If rates rise, however, you'll see the value of your holdings shrink, but worse yet, you won't get any tax relief for the capital losses the fund incurs, since a fund cannot pass these on. In fact, these losses are carried forward by the fund until they can be offset with gains. The problem with this is that you share your carryforward losses with new shareholders coming in after the loss year, since all such offsets are shared pro rata in the year they can be used. Carryforward losses are an unrecognized asset in a bond fund because they provide the means for creating future tax-free income. Too bad they have to be shared with new fund investors. Not fair, you say? If you think this, then my whole criticism of the industry so far has been lost on you.

Fees are very important in selecting a bond fund, because we are talking about investing in something that earns only 5 to 7 percent a year. If a fund has a front-end load of 2.5 percent, a management fee and expense ratio totaling 1 percent a year, and a back-end fee of 1 percent, then your first year's earnings are pretty much spoken for. And that 1 percent a year, for 6 percent earnings, is 16.6 percent of each year's earnings. It's your call, but I thought I should let you know. You can save some of this by buying a no-load fund. Also, funds have A, B, and

C shares, which offer different fees depending on how long you intend to stay. Note the annual expense level of whichever fund you select, because no-load doesn't mean cheap.

Investors who buy and hold their own bonds and preferreds for monthly income would ignore fluctuations in interest rates. And guess what? Their monthly income is unchanged and they have no capital gains. Even better, if they need capital losses to offset gains elsewhere, they can sell some of their bonds, save some taxes, and reinvest the funds in new bonds paying out pretty much the same amount as the old ones.

Junk Bond Funds

Junk bond funds, including some of the international bond funds, provide a different set of challenges. They compete in a market where almost all the other competitors are also large funds—institutions that all have a Bloomberg terminal on their desks. This means that when a particular security becomes questionable, all the market participants know it at the same time. Result: no buyers. The same problem comes when you have a periodic flight to quality (when world events give new meaning to the words *investment grade*). The last such flight to quality was the onset of Gulf War II (the previous one was Gulf War I), and the result was no buyers. Hence, such bond funds are frozen in place with their holdings and no one sells, because that would dramatically drop the price at which they must price out their remaining holdings. This situation can last for months, made no easier by the fact that astute fund shareholders, who know what is happening, will bail out at inflated valuations, thereby putting a cash demand on the fund that can force a sell-off of holdings. Closed-end junk bond funds have it somewhat easier since they don't have to sell to meet share liquidations. In that case, too, the smart investors are early sellers, as the shares quickly drop in price to a discount from the shares' net asset value. Timing is key as the exit at or near NAV, for a closed-end fund closes a lot faster.

In fixed-income funds, unlike stock funds, portfolio managers can actually buy short-term performance. Just lower the credit quality a bit, extend maturities, and increase the portfolio's leverage, and chances are performance will excel. Long term, you will most likely lag in performance, but who's watching long term? A fixed-income fund manager who achieves a 7 percent annual growth by putting together four quarters that are up 5 percent, down 10 percent, down 5 percent, and up 19 percent is much happier than one who achieves the same result by growing a steady 1.75 percent a quarter, because in two out of the four quarters that fund manager looks like a star. Never mind the added risks taken—the fund holders will never know. And the more the fund falls behind, the more scrambling goes on in the background to regain lost ground in the next quarter. So, when you see a fixed-income fund falling behind, hold off new purchases unless you are prepared for a high risk/reward play.

Municipal Bond Funds

Municipal bond funds are strictly for individuals in the top tax brackets and in high state income tax states. They provide diversification over a number of in-state issues, which would be difficult for an individual to put together and would probably be an illiquid portfolio. The most popular funds are state-specific for the high tax states like New York, California, and New Jersey. A key consideration here is that the fund's portfolio have a high component of holdings not subject to the federal alternative minimum tax limitation.

Note that there are also municipal funds with low-rated and unrated munis paying fairly attractive yields. Such funds should be avoided by all but the highest-risk investors. There have been some serious disasters with such funds, and future ones are likely because of structural vulnerabilities in many such bond issues.

The long-term outlook for municipal finances, and therefore their bond ratings, is not promising. The problems we see on a national scale with Social Security may be small compared to the funding shortfalls faced by most states due to years of overpromising and underfunding for state and municipal employees' pension funds. This problem has not received the attention that Social Security has drawn, but collectively, it represents a huge burden on state finances. Just another reason to buy insured AAA munis and avoid a possible downgrade cycle for these bonds.

International Bond Funds

These funds can be in investment-grade companies or junk. They offer investors an opportunity to earn a higher total return through investing in debt securities denominated in a foreign currency (although dollar-denominated issues are also included here if the issuer is foreign). These funds often offer a higher nominal rate of return. The debt may be from overseas companies or may be sovereign debt (i.e., issued by a governmental entity). *Sovereign debt appears to be safe; after all, governments don't go bankrupt. That's right, they don't go bankrupt; they simply stop paying.* Sovereign debt got a bad reputation in the 1970s when oil price hikes caused many countries to incur debts they could not repay. What the world found out from that exercise is that creditors have little legal recourse unless the U.S. government or the IMF gets involved. Much of the British empire was built in the 1800s by sending in the fleet to collect on debts due British bankers. This history has given such collection practices a bad name and made national governments immune to collection efforts except when trade pressures or refinancing alternatives can be brought to bear. As for debt issues by private foreign companies, the hazard is that bankruptcy laws are haphazard in most developing countries and will tend to favor a national company over foreign creditors. Still, if you have an adventurous spirit and want to play the currency angles, the international bond funds are definitely safer than going it alone, but examine their management fees, which tend to run much higher than those for domestic bond funds.

Exchange-Traded Funds (ETFs)

Exchange-traded funds are the best investment idea to come along in the past generation. The origins of ETFs can be found in academic studies, which support the idea that all managed mutual funds, over time, will underperform an indexed fund representing a broad cross section of the market. The fact that some funds may have outperformed the market average for 10 or 20 years does not necessarily attest to their superior performance. With some 13,000 funds in existence, the law of averages, combined with luck, can easily account for a handful of funds having a string of superior results. As Nassim Taleb points out in his book, *Fooled by Randomness: The Hidden Role of Chance in Life and in the Markets*, never underestimate the importance of luck.

ETFs are designed to give you the average results for a particular market or sector, nothing more and nothing less. They buy a basket of securities representing a cross-section of a particular market. Most important, they make very few changes to that basket. The fund sponsor creates new fund shares as demand requires. Sellers can either sell their shares on the open market or turn them in to the fund sponsor, who will give them the equivalent in underlying securities. This feature ensures that, unlike closed-end funds, the fund will never vary much from the underlying net asset value of its holdings. Shares within the basket are bought and sold only if a new security is added or removed from the index being tracked or if a merger/acquisition makes a share disappear. Over time, such an ETF will outperform all but the most fortunate conventional/open-end funds because it has a number of factors working in its favor:

- There is a minimal management fee since there is minimal intellectual input, minimal trading, and minimal administrative requirements (e.g., no need for shareholder accounting at the fund level).
- There are no 12b-1 fees for distribution costs, advertising, or trailing commissions to the selling brokers.
- There is a minimum of capital gains distributions, since the fund hardly trades. Hence, there are no unexpected year-end tax consequences.
- The typical mutual fund holds up to 5 or 10 percent of its assets in cash to meet share redemptions, whereas the ETF holds virtually none. This money is not working for you.
- For a long-term holder, there is no cost for the portfolio turnover so common to all conventional mutual funds, nor do you share the

costs in buying and selling holdings to accommodate new investors or those who are liquidating.

- Your cost basis in the fund is what you paid for your shares. You don't inherit unrealized gains and losses accumulated from prior years or prior holders and distributed to those who hold the shares at year-end. You also don't end up with taxable gains in years when your fund has declined in value.

- Shares can be bought and sold anytime of the day during trading hours. Hence, you don't have to wait until 4:00 p.m. or the next day to find out what you paid for the shares. This can be important in unstable markets.

- You are not exposed to the trading styles, personal agenda, and human fallibility of the fund manager.

- ETF shares can be bought and sold anytime with limit, stop, and market-if-touched orders. Mutual funds can be bought only at day's end and at end-of-market prices (unless you're a friend of the management, in which case the books may be kept open a little longer, per Elliot Spitzer).

- Many ETFs have put and call options, as well as being able to be bought on margin and sold short. These financial instruments allow investors to hedge their exposure in a fund holding rather than buy or sell their holdings and thereby generate long-term or short-term capital gains.

- The investor always knows what the fund holds. Conventional fund holdings are not transparent, being reported only quarterly at most. When a Merck-Vioxx type situation comes up, you may not know your exposure for three months. Also, you aren't exposed to short-term portfolio style changes a manager may make between reporting periods to try to catch up for performance shortfalls.

Even if you have avoided mutual funds and made your own selection of individual securities in the past, ETFs still provide instant diversification through one purchase versus the cumulative commissions for the purchase of multiple positions.

The ETF product is currently pretty much only for equity investors. However, this is changing and, given the number of new ETFs coming out each month, there will likely be an array of fixed income choices shortly. The first ETF offerings for fixed-income investors were in U.S. Treasury securities. Their attraction is mainly in the convenience of moving in and out versus a TreasuryDirect account. More recently, an outfit called Wisdom Tree has begun offering a series of ETFs focused on high-dividend-paying stocks. Its approach sounds logical, but we will have to see if regression analysis as a way of picking income stocks really works.

Closed-End Funds (CEFs)

Closed-end funds (CEFs) are also exchange-traded funds; however, their shares are not redeemed, so must be resold to another buyer. This means that at any point in time, they can sell at sizable discounts or premiums from their net asset value (NAV). These funds charge a management fee more like that charged by mutual funds, but they don't have the same expense level, since they don't have to keep track of share ownership or handle continuous share liquidations and new share sales or incur marketing expenses.

When a new closed-end fund is launched, you pay the underwriting costs in your purchase, so you immediately begin with a NAV that is about 4 percent below your purchase price. Historically, you can expect the shares to lag the NAV by 5 to 10 percent within six months. The reason for this dismal performance is not known, but I suspect it's due to the fact that once the shares are all sold, there is no incentive by the management company or underwriter to continue promoting the fund. Hence, when investors look to sell, there are few buyers familiar or interested in the stock. Those funds that have a niche, such as the India Fund (ticker IFN) at this writing, sell at huge premiums because they represent a high-growth area that no other funds are focused on and for which no ETFs currently exist. This is likely to change, in which case you can expect the India Fund's premium to shrink very quickly.

The advantage of closed-end funds is that they offer a variety of income-producing funds following different investment strategies. They differ from mutual funds in that the closed-end structure allows them to use as much as 30 percent leverage to enhance the yield. They do turn their portfolios over at a high rate, but less so than mutual funds, because they don't have to be concerned with seasonal redemptions or inflows of new monies. What is particularly attractive here is that these funds can sell at sizable discounts to their NAV. We are currently in this market state because the Fed interest rate policy has created a flat yield curve. Hence, these funds cannot boost earnings by employing leverage and have therefore had to cut their dividends. While their returns are still decent, any time you cut dividends you get selling. Since a flat yield curve is not normal, such funds become attractive because, as the yield curve steepens, you foresee the benefits of leverage kicking back in. In fact, these closed-end funds constitute a good way to anticipate a rise in long-term interest rates since, as rates rise, their use of leverage once again provides a boost to earnings. Meanwhile, selling at a discount to NAV cushions the value decline of existing holdings that a rise in long-term rates will bring—a value decline that will also take place in a bond mutual fund, but with no offset.

Closed-end funds exist for junk bonds or investment-grade bonds, preferred stocks, convertibles, and municipal bonds. Those seeking 15 percent tax qualified income (QDI) can also find preferred CEFs that have a high percentage of their distributions so qualified.

Closed-End Bond Funds

Closed-end bond funds, like their open-end cousins, come in all varieties. They have the advantage of being exchange traded and the disadvantage that their price may be more or less than their net asset value. What may be different also is that these funds tend to use more leverage and more exotic hedging techniques to boost earnings. This is something more readily done in an environment where cash flow is predictable, because there are no share additions or liquidations. These funds do suffer in their performance when short-term interest rates rise and flatten the yield curve, because this means they cannot boost earnings through using leverage. In that situation, dividends are cut and shares get dumped, causing them to sell at significant discounts from net asset value. Since we are currently in this situation, many of these funds are indeed selling at a discount, which means it is the best time to buy them.

Closed-End Preferred Funds

You probably haven't read much about closed-end preferred funds because, before 2004, only a handful were available. However, the search for yield has made this investment vehicle quite popular. There are now some 20 new funds, with over $20 billion in assets. The attraction of these funds is the high level of monthly cash income that they generate. They can offer these returns, in part, because preferred yields are traditionally 100 to 150 basis points higher than bonds. These funds also magnify returns by using leverage. In effect, they are taking advantage of the very low short-term interest rates to borrow and invest in longer-term higher-rate issues. Risky, yes, but that's why the closed-end fund structure is so important. Unlike open-end funds, which must change their investment strategy in reaction to investors cashing out when rates start to rise, the closed-end funds are under no such pressure. Barring interest rate hikes of over 200 basis points, their leverage should still produce favorable results. Another positive is that preferreds have historically been much less volatile to interest rate changes than bonds. This is due in part to the fact that the bond market is dominated by open-end funds. When rates change and investors withdraw, open-end funds need to sell holdings into a market, where most of the other participants need to do the same thing. Hence, prices overreact. There are no open-end preferred funds, so this market is not subject to this selling pressure when rates rise.

These closed-end preferred funds invest primarily in investment-grade securities, but the type of instruments varies. The range of investments includes bonds, trust preferreds (de facto bonds), foreign bonds, and REIT shares. Also, because they are closed-end funds, they can hold less-liquid, but higher-yielding securities. The use of leverage up to 30 percent seems to be the most common. While they will produce some income subject to only the 15 percent dividend tax, tax savings is not a principal goal. Shares in these funds can be purchased on the New York Stock Exchange at a price that closely tracks the net asset value of the fund. Unlike open-end funds, shares can trade at a premium or discount to the daily net asset value. Also, the management fees and operating costs of these funds are lower because they are not engaged in trying to market more shares.

Buy-Write Funds

The shrinking universe of traditional fixed-income securities requires a constant search for new products that can provide steady income, capital growth, and a different risk profile. Unfortunately, most of these are equity-based products, so I look for elements that will diminish the volatility and unpredictability that goes with stocks. A recent new product, buy-write closed-end indexed funds, seems to offer all of these features and tax benefits to boot. They offer high income, portfolio diversification, and stock market exposure beyond those of convertible preferreds.

A buy-write index fund holds a portfolio of stocks that may be tied to or track a popular stock index, thereby providing a less volatile stock investment. They become income vehicles because they also write call and index options to generate income beyond the 2 to 3 percent dividend payouts they earn on their holdings. Their option-writing strategy creates distributable income above what the stock portfolio would yield and also reduces the volatility of the fund's share price. Note, other closed-end funds that achieve a higher dividend payout do so using leverage, whereas these funds do not.

What makes these funds interesting from a tax perspective is that, due to a quirk in the tax law, the premiums earned from writing stock index call options are treated as 60 percent long-term gains and 40 percent short-term gains. This means that in a flat or declining stock market, you get dividends that are roughly 50 percent long-term capital gains. In a rising stock market, however, where the option writing may lose money while the portfolio of holdings appreciates, the fund's distributions are treated as a return of capital and thus not taxable at all. If you have tax loss carryforwards, this security offers an opportunity to use up some of those losses, so you will pay little or no taxes, whether the distributions are capital gains or a return of capital. Any appreciation in the value of the portfolio will remain mostly unrealized, since trading actual stock is secondary in the fund's strategy.

SECURITIES AND OTHER INVESTMENTS TO AVOID

Unit Investment Trusts (UITs)

*O*ne of the worst investment products ever devised by Wall Street are *UITs*. These trusts are an unmanaged pool of fixed-income securities that are put in trust for a fixed amount of time (e.g., 20 years), without being traded. At the conclusion of that period, any remaining securities will be sold and the proceeds distributed to the holders. I say "remaining," because during those 20 years, securities will be called, in which case the cash proceeds will be paid out to the holders along with the interest income. The reasons investors buy UITs are the low fees and the high payout rates, which, because of frequent returns of principal, will run in the double digits with lower taxes, because a portion of the payments is a return of capital.

What UIT investors fail to appreciate is that at the end of the life of the UIT, very little residual value remains. Many were sold on the idea that this was like buying an annuity, only much cheaper, and if you died before maturity, unlike an annuity, you still had a residual value. The fact is that if a UIT is a major source of your income, you need to be sure that you and your spouse don't outlive it, because little is left at the end. You also need to adjust for the erratic cash flow generated by early calls. This money is merely a return of capital and means future payouts must necessarily by smaller. Too many UIT investors forget these small subtleties over the years, or worse, don't alert their spouse before they punch out.

A basic problem with these trusts is conceptual. While you can build a trust with investment-grade securities, over the course of 20 years some obvious sell candidates will appear. Very few securities should be bought and held blindly, just to save fees. In fact, over time, the good stuff tends to be called away, leaving an ever-deteriorating residual. Second, there is no market for these securities, since it is an exercise to value them at any given point in time. The sponsoring brokerage houses will buy a client's position, but expect to take a haircut. Also, you can't transfer this holding to another broker if you decide to move, so be sure of the relationship. But the worst thing about UITs is that they can be the dumping ground for any bond underwriting that didn't sell or any other holdings the firm may own and would rather not. Not exactly the kind of securities an investor would want put into an unmanaged trust, but a great way for a brokerage firm to hide its mistakes.

Derivatives

You have probably read about derivatives and wondered what they were about. The term *derivatives*, in a broad sense, encompasses any security that derives its value from another security. Hence, stock options, commodity contracts, collateralized mortgage obligations (CMOs), and trust preferreds can all be defined as derivatives. However, when used by the media, it most often refers to a class of securities that are really not securities. It has gained prominence because it has grown into a trillion-dollar market, so massive that it will some day jeopardize our entire financial system. It is also an unregulated market in which only large institutions should be participating. But don't think this will stop Wall Street from trying to come up with new ways to let Main Street investors lose money as well (see the following section, "SEQUINS and ELKS").

The derivative market came about to allow large institutions to hedge their portfolios against adverse events in interest rates, currencies, commodities, or credit defaults. The market came about precisely because funds have grown too large to move quickly in reaction to the events they are hedging against. This is done not by trading securities, but simply by making a contract with a counterparty where, for a specified fee, one party will agree to settle a certain amount of contract value at a specific date in the future at the then-existing market prices. It's much the same as a stock option, but is more like an option on the economy itself. The risks come about because the counterparty with whom you are dealing may not be as financially strong as it appears, or may it be overextended in money-losing arrangements. The 1998 blowup of Long-Term Capital Management was such a situation. That firm had leveraged its capital base some 300 times, so when things went bad, its contractual promises became worthless. In that instance, the Federal Reserve Bank had to step in to stop a market panic, since the counterparties to LTCM's contracts were banking institutions that were suddenly in violation of their capital requirements. Today, exposures are many times greater than back then, making a successful Fed intervention more problematic. One difficulty in overseeing the level of systemic risk caused by derivatives is that there is no relationship between the level of contracts and the risks being insured. By way of example, when GM began its ratings downgrade cycle, credit default swaps against GM debt became a popular speculation. The problem is that although GM has only $30 billion in outstanding debt, credit derivative contracts totaled $100 billion. This is probably not a problem if GM never defaults. However, it could be a major problem if it does, since it is generally the weaker party, such as a hedge fund, that takes the higher-risk side of such contracts. This market can also be a direct influence on events. For example, when Mirant

Corporation tried to restructure its debt outside of bankruptcy, it tried to force its bank lenders into sharing some of the asset collateral. One bank held out and forced the bankruptcy filing. It turns out that bank had insured itself in the credit default swap market and so had every reason to say no (sort of like when the baseball team owners insured themselves against a player strike and then precipitated one).

SEQUINS and ELKS

Underwriters sometimes create securities that look good on the surface, but they reserve the really big payoff for themselves. With a resurging stock market, these folks are once again busy creating derivative investment instruments with more promise than is likely to be achieved. Two examples deserve recognition. The first example is a Citigroup Global Markets 7 percent security called SEQUINS, an interesting acronym for something that's all glitter but has little value. The acronym was concocted from the term "Select EQUity Indexed NoteS," but a more appropriate concoction would be "Senseless EQuities for Uninformed InvestorS." The issue is rated investment grade and matures in two years, but is callable in one. Its redemption value is tied to the share price of Comcast Class A common stock. Well, yes, but not really. It's tied to Comcast stock only to the extent that it drops in value. If it should rise, your redemption value is capped at a call price that limits your upside to a 13 percent return. Hence, if Comcast does well, even in just one year, the underwriter can call the security and pay you a total return of 13 percent. If Comcast does poorly, they can wait two years and hand you a fixed number of shares of stock guaranteed to be worth less than you paid for your SEQUINS. While the offering statement clearly discloses all the risks, it fails to explain why anyone interested in owning Comcast stock would seek out such a lose-lose way to buy them.

My second candidate for dubious investment honors is also a Citigroup product. Its called Citigroup Global Markets 11 percent 12/29/04 ELKS. These Equity LinKed Securities (ELKS) promise a bigger payoff by sporting an 11 percent coupon rate and an investment-grade rating, but that's all show. The fun here is in speculating how much of your principal you can you expect back at maturity. This is based on a formula tied to the price of five high-visibility stocks in five different industries: high-tech, retail, pharmaceutical, banking, and beverage. Your principal recovery is the lesser of what you paid in or the value of the worst performing of the five stocks less the first 10 percent of price decline. What are the odds that all five of these industries, as well as all five of the players in these industries, will have a good year? It's like putting five apples in a barrel and giving you the pick of the most rotten one after a year.

These securities are designed for hedge funds and others for whom they are just one card in a poker hand. Investors seeking high-yield short-term investments may see a virtue in the apparent high-yield from these securities, but in fact the risk here is much greater than the inflation risk they may be trying to avoid. In no way should they be considered as growth or income investments. The biggest redeeming quality of these securities is that they do not sully the term *preferred* stocks or bonds by using it in their name, although they are listed and trade in the preferred market. They are strictly equity hedge plays, much like selling puts or calls.

The preceding evaluations of these two types of securities were written in December 2003. When these securities subsequently matured, the SEQUINS, which sold for $10, returned a total of $9.63 in 2005. The ELKS matured in 2004 and returned only $7.27. Clearly, you should avoid these types of securities.

PARRS

Investors looking for protection against interest rate fluctuations may be tempted by a security called Putable Automatic Rate Reset Securities (PARRS) created by Morgan Stanley. The Tennessee Valley Authority (TVA), an AAA-rated government agency, put out such an issue in 1998 with a 6.75 percent interest rate that resets annually after the first five years at the index rate for 30-year Treasuries plus 98 basis points. If the reset is downward, you have the option of putting the issue back to the TVA at par. Sounds great until you read the fine print. Rates are reset *only* downward, hence you suffer every rate decline and never get back to your starting rate. Worse still, once a rate bottom is reached, all future resets would be at a higher rate, so they never reset, which means you can't exercise your put option. The TVA issue reset to a low of 5.49 percent in 2005, after which rates rose. Hence, future downward resets are unlikely, which means invoking the put provision will not occur. For this reason, a security that should be trading near its $25 par is trading closer to $23. This security was put out at an attractive initial interest rate to suck in investors with an apparent promise of protection against rate fluctuations. In fact, however, the only fluctuations it "protects" against are rate declines, normally a positive event for investors. But couldn't investors have put the issue back to the TVA in 2005, when the rate was reduced to 5.49 percent? Yes, and 19 percent of holders did. The rest were apparently asleep at the wheel or did not realize the long-term implications of a low reset price.

Hedge Funds

Over the past three years the media has developed an infatuation with hedge funds as if they were something new. What's new is that some very smart people have figured out a way to siphon off even more fees from clueless investors by convincing them that an illiquid fund that does not have to meet SEC requirements or scrutiny must somehow be a better way to invest. What's new is that some less smart people have also jumped on this same bandwagon for fundamentally the same reason. Hence we now have a whole new industry with thousands of funds and an estimated $1.5 trillion in resources. I am not exaggerating when I say that rarely has so much money been entrusted to so few people with such limited talent. Your typical hedge fund management has one or two name partners who, likely as not, made lots of money for themselves by various means and now tell you they can do the same thing for you, for a mere 1.5 percent a year plus 20 percent of any gains if you lock your money up with them for five years and promise to stay out of the way. With those kind of rewards, you can bet the risks they take with your money can't stand up to close scrutiny.

The days of making 25 percent a year through traditional investing are over. Today's hotshot managers play currency markets, derivatives, natural resources, option strategies, and lots of foreign markets where stock manipulation is still easy to do. Investing with these managers is an act of faith, since few of their investors do so with any degree of understanding.

Of more concern to me is that much of this vast pool of money will be going to help company managements take their companies private with a view to a relaunch in three to five years at a big profit. What's wrong with that, you say? Company managements don't just decide suddenly to take a company private; it's something that takes lots of planning, planning that takes place while they are being paid to run the company in the best interest of shareholders. To take a company private, you have to line up a cooperative board; you have to line up the financing; but most of all, you have to run the company for a year or two in such a way that the stock price is cheap and shareholders are ready to throw in the towel. That means investing loads of money in development projects that won't pay off in the short run; it means running down margins and running up expenses in areas that can be cut back in short order after privatization. In short, much of the value creation derived from taking a company private actually takes place before the company was privatized. If not, then there might actually be substantial risk for the buyout team, and who needs that?! Dishonest, yes; illegal, try to prove it; being done today, you bet.

Surely he exaggerates, you say, but you need look no further than the bankruptcy courts to see the same kind of financial manipulations I describe. In bankruptcy, you don't buy out the shareholders, you wipe them out. You don't line up new lenders, you stiff the parties already on the hook. Proof of what I am saying lies in comparing the price of a company's stock used for settling the bankruptcy claims with the price, say, one year later. The media may praise these as highly successful turnarounds. In fact, they are often highly successful con jobs.

Hedge funds promise to make these type of mismanagements profitable with little risk and without having to pay off a large contingent of bankruptcy attorneys or risking someone spoiling the game. No, not all bankruptcies are suspect; in fact, most are not. All management teams taking companies private, however, *are*. There is no place here for serious income investors. In fact, I believe abuses in this area will lead to tighter regulation, the education of media pundits, and the eventual decline in popularity of these funds. Unfortunately, this may take 20 years!

Commercial Paper, Bankers Acceptances, and Repos

Commercial paper is short-term (mainly 30- to 90-day) corporate debt issued by investment-grade companies to cover their day-to-day cash needs (they both buy and sell such paper). Transactions are for large amounts and offer no significant yield advantage over money market funds for individual investors. The same goes for bankers acceptances and repurchase agreements, or repos. If these really interest you, you have way too much money to be reading this book.

Collateralized Debt

All the following securities are derivate securities created out of pools of mortgages, bonds, or other forms of debt.

Collateralized Mortgage Obligations (CMOs)
Collateralized Bond Obligations (CBOs)
Collateralized Debt Obligations (CDOs)
Collateralized Loan Obligations (CLOs)

What makes them dangerous is the fact that all participants are not treated equally. By way of an example, a pool of mortgages may be put together and then carved up into several distinct securities, called *tranches*. The first tranche may be entitled to, say, a 5 percent rate of return, be the first to receive the proceeds from early liquidations, and be the last to suffer any loss from defaults. The second tranche may get a 6 percent rate of return, receive all proceeds from early liquidations after the first tranche has been fully paid off, and have to absorb default losses only after they reach a defined level. A third tranche may specify an 8 percent rate of return, but be obligated to absorb all default losses and required to fund the interest payments to the first two tranches if the portfolio's rate of return drops due to having adjustable rate mortgages.

Alternatively, any additional interest income, because rates rise, would accrue to this tranche. So, which tranche do you buy? The answer is, the only one left for retail buyers, since these CMOs are put together with large institutional investors in mind. Therefore, you can assume the best tranches will be tailor-made for those institutions and fully subscribed. This tranche structure provides for one group of holders to make money at the expense of other participants and not just at a cost to the borrowers. If you are seriously tempted by one of these securities, just assume Warren Buffett is holding one of the other tranches. Now, how lucky do you feel?

9

OTHER TOPICS OF INTEREST

Bankruptcy

Ask investors what risk they fear most in their investments and they will reply default or bankruptcy. But what is bankruptcy, really? We see today hundreds of companies that have gone into bankruptcy and emerged as ongoing enterprises with little aftereffect from the experience. We see companies like USG and Armstrong World Industries still in bankruptcy after many years and their stocks trading at record prices. We see people like Donald Trump use bankruptcy like a reset button on a videogame to wipe out past mistakes and begin again. In short, bankruptcy is a vehicle for reorganizing a company, not just to put it out of its misery.

Bankruptcies are rarely a surprise to the financial community, and no individual investor who keeps up with events should be caught unaware. This is because bankruptcy is normally the end of an erosionary process I like to compare to metal rusting. It can be due to poor management, sudden changes in the business, legal issues, industry-wide problems, labor problems, creditor problems, or just plain bad luck. We see entire industries where a large number, if not all, of the participants have gone through bankruptcy. Recent examples are the airlines, asbestos companies, movie house chains, auto parts manufacturers, telecoms, and steel companies. More frequent, however, are companies that accumulate too much debt, either through failed acquisitions or years of negative operating results. Such defaults are easy to predict, even down to when they will occur. This is because the decision to go into bankruptcy is generally not made by the company, but rather is in the hands of the senior lenders (i.e., the banks).

Banks take a very simple approach to the decision of how long to let a company go on failing. They do periodic reviews of the balance sheet of a company and determine the going-concern value of the enterprise. As long as that value is greater than the value of their loans to the company, they will allow it to continue and will even fund the losses, even when a portion of such loans goes to paying interest to less-senior creditors or bondholders. Crunch time generally comes when the economy slows down or the industry goes into a slump. This is because, once a downturn occurs, the banks find that the going-concern value of the business has suddenly dropped to where a portion of their loan is now in jeopardy. They were willing to go along with the company before because maybe the business would turn around, but when the accumulation of losses and an economic downturn finally forces the issue, they pull the plug.

Note that bank-precipitated bankruptcies (described less harshly by the media as "banks tightening credit" or "raising loan standards") are also the reason why bankruptcy comes in waves, where suddenly dozens of companies are filing bankruptcy at the same time (i.e., a time when the economy or industry is slowing). It has the unfortunate side effect of creating a perception that risk has suddenly increased, causing interest rates on high-yield bonds to jump to levels that effectively close the new-issue market for such debt to be refinanced. It is also believed by some that the effect exacerbates the economic conditions that triggered the defaults and makes the economic downturn more prolonged.

If the banks have done their homework accurately, then little in the way of recovery will be obtained by the lowly bond or preferred investors. This is because, in bankruptcy, a strict rule of priority is observed in satisfying the claims of banks, bondholders, general creditors, employ-ees, the IRS, preferred holders, and shareholders. Since banks are the most hands-on lenders, they make sure they write themselves in as the senior claimants. This not only ensures they get fully paid, it also gives them a position on the creditors' committees where they can block any reorganization plan not to their liking. They are also in a position to insist the company be liquidated if they are not confident the business or the company management can succeed. It was not always this way, but over the years, the bankruptcy rules have become more and more pro-bank.

A sure sign that there may be value for the bondholder who is caught in a bankruptcy situation is when a *vulture fund* or *vulture investor* is reported to be buying up bonds of the company. Such investors often will approach the bank creditors first and buy out the bank debt at some discounted value. Then they buy as much of the more senior bond debt as they feel will allow them to be major participants in the reorganiza-tion plan. As a bondholder, it may well be worth your while to hold on to your bonds if you are at the same seniority level as the bonds being bought by the vulture investors. You definitely don't want to hold bonds that are junior to their claim, since they have little desire to see you get anything. They are playing a zero-sum game, where you and everyone behind you are zeros. In fact, they will work hard to show that the com-pany is worth only as much as their claims and not a dime more. The recent exit from bankruptcy by Kmart is a clear example of this. The stock, which went to the senior group, was valued at only $14 a share for purposes of squeezing out the junior creditors. Within seven weeks of the bankruptcy being settled, those shares were trading at $22 a share and reached $130 a share within two years. Value perceptions like that did not just begin the day after the bankruptcy was settled.

To get technical for a moment, most bankruptcies are filed by a company and are filed as Chapter 11 bankruptcies in one of 92 federal bankruptcy courts. A creditor can also file a bankruptcy on behalf of a company as a means of trying to force payment, but this generally pre-cipitates the company filing, which is the filing the court is more likely to accept. The company management is left in place to conduct business as usual, provided the company has arranged a debtor-in-possession line of credit (which takes priority over all other debts of the company except the bankruptcy attorneys' fees). If a company's management is considered incompetent or is suspected of illegalities, the court may appoint a trustee to run the company instead. A Chapter 11 proceeding may go on for years, as long as the court grants the company continuous *exclusivity periods*, during which no one except the company can propose a plan of reorganization. Recent legislation has sought to cap this exclusivity period to 16 months. If the court decides the company cannot achieve a workable plan, the exclusivity period can be allowed to end and any creditor groups can propose a plan instead. Often, that plan is to liquidate the company (i.e., turn the bankruptcy into a Chapter 7 bankruptcy). If this happens, the court appoints a trustee who then, if the company is big enough, has a job for life. Or at least that is what most creditors perceive. As such, they will agree to almost any plan rather than face this solution. Some companies file for a Chapter 7 bankruptcy from the start, but this is mostly for smaller companies or those that cannot obtain a credit line.

If you are involved with a bankruptcy as a creditor, it is worthwhile knowing the stages a bankruptcy goes through, since it affects the valuation of the debt security you are holding. When a bankruptcy is first filed, the U.S. Attorney for the district in which the filing takes place will determine how many creditor committees will be allowed and who will sit on them. Typically, there is a committee for the banks and all senior secured lenders. Next is the committee for the unsecured lenders—these are the unsecured bondholders and trade creditors. There may also be a junior creditors' committee if enough such debt exists. Preferred stockholders may have a committee and common shareholders may have a committee. Some of the more junior creditors and shareholders may not have a committee until later in the process if it is determined they may have *standing* in the bankruptcy (meaning there is enough possible value in the company to satisfy everyone ahead of them and still leave them a claim of some sort). If there is any doubt of this, a valuation hearing will be held some time before a final reorganization plan is finalized and approved. At that hearing, shareholders will be allowed to present arguments that there is value left for them. The appearance of such a valuation battle is good news for bondholders since, by implication, there first has to be recognition of full value for their claims for shareholders to get anything beyond nuisance value (i.e., a token amount offered in lieu of a protracted valuation fight).

Once the creditor committees are formed, the fun begins. The company will report to these committees on the finances of the company and on what is happening regarding the formulation of a reorganization plan. Issues such as lease terminations, contract renegotiations with workers, contract settlements with customers and suppliers, and facility closings must be addressed. In short, the company must first address what the ongoing business is going to look like. This generally takes one to two years to achieve. Out of this, however, comes a business operating projection from which a new company balance sheet can be constructed. This is necessary in order to determine how much debt the new company can carry and also what the projected value of the shareholders' equity might be. It is this new debt and new shareholders' value that is the currency for settling all prebankruptcy claims. In short, can all bank claims continue to be serviced by the new entity, or will the banks have to take some shares of stock? Then how much stock is left to satisfy all junior claims? This is the crux of the claims' settlement portion of the reorganization plan, and also the most contentious part. The more important decision of how the business will look going forward is pretty much left to management to determine. Since these are often the same people who were in charge before bankruptcy, it is not surprising that a second bankruptcy filing within five years is no longer uncommon.

As a bond investor, you should know that as a matter of law, not only do interest and principal payments on all debt cease the day the company files, but no interest accrues on such debt from that day forward. This does not mean you won't get such interest amounts, only that such recoveries are very unlikely. One exception to this rule is that if you hold a mortgage obligation of the company and there is no question that the collateral value is higher than your claim value, then you can continue to receive interest payments while the bankruptcy is ongoing. Another exception to the interest rule is when you hold a municipal bond that is backed by lease payments on a store or airport gate, for example. In these cases, if the company decides it wants to continue to operate that store or gate, it must continue the lease payments. To you it is interest; to the bankruptcy court it is rent. Once a company files bankruptcy, bonds trade without accrued interest, or *flat*. They may begin trading flat even before a bankruptcy filing if they previously failed to make any interest payment on time or if bankruptcy is seen as inevitable.

Understanding the bankruptcy cycle is important for determining when to sell your bonds or preferreds. Most bankrupt securities reach their lowest valuation in the weeks before the actual filing. This is because many institutions have a fiduciary liability that could make them responsible for any losses on an investment due to bankruptcy, but no responsibility if they sell before a bankruptcy filing. On the buy side, just before a filing, there is great uncertainty and little information of how things will turn out. Hence, many sellers, few buyers. Once bankruptcy takes place, your vulture investors move in and start buying, but these people are in no hurry, so don't expect prices to bounce up. Any bounce is generally based on back-of-the-envelope calculations of what the value of the reorganized company might be. Also, certain vulture investors will draw followers based on their reputation for past success. Here, too, if the company's failure was for technical reasons and the underlying business is sound, significant recovery may be anticipated even when a final settlement plan is far off (e.g., USG).

In making a judgment about how much of a recovery you might achieve by holding on, take a look at the balance sheet of the company. Assume all the intangible assets of the company such as for goodwill will be written off. Assume also that unfunded costs such as pension, health care, lease termination, and plant closings will all have creditor claims on par with your bonds. To keep the balance sheet balanced, all such write-offs and cost accruals will first reduce the shareholders equity to zero and then the preferred stock equity to zero and then the junior debt, such as convertible bonds, to zero. To the extent these amounts exceed all these values, bondholders will take a reduction in their pro rata claim amount. However, keep in mind that the reorganized company's stock, if the business is viable, may be significantly more valuable than the previous shareholders' equity. Yes, it's very much a finger-in-the-air exercise, but you'd be amazed to know that many of the plans put together by corporations before and after a bankruptcy have little more substance than this.

I have spent over 20 years tracking all corporate bankruptcies involving bond debt and have served on numerous creditor committees in the process. The only disappointments I suffered were when the underlying books of account turned out to be massive works of fiction. In this respect, the Sarbanes-Oxley legislation may have improved matters. As a demonstration of the value of what I am advocating here, I will go out on a limb and make a prediction: *Should General Motors file for bankruptcy sometime during the next few years (something I do not believe will happen), bondholders will recover substantially more than the 60 to 70 cents on the dollar, the level at which their debt is currently trading.* Hence, for me, this represents a speculation with little downside and a huge upside. This is what vulture investors see and why they exist.

The message you should come away with from this narrative is that bankruptcy is a tool for companies to improve their business at the expense of *all* stakeholders, not just the shareholders. As a fixed-income investor, you will be dragged into the process, but this does not mean you will lose everything. It is a period of uncertainty and a lot of false alarms and false information. Read everything, question everything, and don't act in haste or on emotion.

Endgame Strategies

Despite your best efforts, you may find after retirement that you are going to outlive your investment assets. Such a blessing should not become a burden. Here are some strategies to consider, keeping in mind that the longer you wait to implement them, the more of a payout they will yield.

I have not discussed annuities so far because, for the most part, they are really not an investment. They can be ideal for someone over 70 who is in good health and who wants to exchange a low certain payout for the higher risk of the securities market. This is also a good option if you have been doing all the investment management so far and fear leaving your spouse to the mercies of strangers.

Selection and features of an annuity plan are quite complex, almost worthy of a book of their own. Since the payouts are based on your age, the longer you wait before signing on, the greater your monthly payments for any given principal amount. You can buy an annuity from a multitude of agents, including accountants, banks, brokers, and insurance companies. Ask around among friends to find a knowledgeable agent. Decide ahead of time not to make a decision in less than a week, because this is not a decision you can reverse without heavy penalties. Also, make sure the insurer is highly rated, creditwise, and will outlive you.

If you own a home free and clear, you may want to consider a *reverse mortgage*, whereby the lender pays you a monthly amount until your death or until you vacate the house. At that point, you will have to sell the property and pay off the mortgage. The fees and interest rates are quite high for such a mortgage, and the lender will participate in any gain on the sale. Such mortgages do, however, provide a means for continuing to live in your home after you run out of funds.

A third strategy to consider is selling your life insurance policy to a third party. This strategy requires some preplanning, since the policy must have been in place for a number of years to qualify. With proper planning, an insurance policy can serve as a safety valve, should you need it, and still be the source of a residual estate if you don't.

Tax Strategies

Your tax return should be an integral part of your investment program for the simple reason that it can make money for you. With even a minimum of planning, you should be able to generate the $3,000 a year in capital losses the IRS allows you as an offset against ordinary income, unless you are one of those who will still be working off your tax loss carryforward from the year 2000 into the next decade. Even then, I have a strategy for you to use those losses more quickly. The point is that if you carefully plan your year-end trading so that you achieve $3,000 in losses, and you successfully do this for 15 out of the next 20 years (you need not lose money in each of these years to achieve this), the cash tax savings, using a 24 percent tax rate, could be $10,800, before counting what you could have earned on that savings. This is a heck of a return for a few hours of tax planning and a handful of additional brokerage trades at the end of each year.

While there is little you can do about the interest income and dividends you receive each year, you can certainly do something about capital gains. If you have a diversified portfolio, you will generally have losers and winners each year. At year-end, unload the short-term losers first and realize those losses. Sell long-term losers next until you get to the $3,000 mark. Make sure each loss is large enough to warrant the commissions to sell, and then reinvest the funds. Also, if you want to get back into the same security, wait at least 30 days. If you own a mutual fund or closed-end fund, look at their year-end dividend distribution policy and the likely payout for this year. Many pay out sizable capital gains to holders of record on a specific year-end date. If you don't want that distribution, sell before the ex-date. If you do want capital gains, you can buy into such distributions by buying closed-end funds. Now you may ask, "Doesn't the distribution just reduce my purchase price so I'm exchanging a realized gain for an unrealized loss?" The answer is, only sometimes. I have noted that closed-end funds that make large year-end capital gains distributions often suffer sizable discounts from NAV in the month or so before that distribution and then recover quite nicely in the following month. This is because more investors are trying to avoid these year-end distributions by selling in November and repurchasing in January (this may in fact account for a good deal of the "January effect" debated in the media at the start of each year). With a little luck, you pick up a realized gain you need for the current tax year and a realizable gain for next year to boot. Once you become comfortable with this year-end strategy, you can graduate to the next level by doing such short-term buy-ins using margin to enhance the tax effect two or three times.

If you do have significant tax loss carryforwards, you should read "Buy-Write Funds" in Chapter 7, as these offer you predictable capital gains rather than interest or dividend income.

Dividend Strategies

Trust preferreds and preferred stocks provide an opportunity for you to change the character of your gains according to your tax needs. This is because preferreds trade with accrued income embedded in their price. Hence, on their ex-dividend date, they start again at zero, since all dividends or interest up to that point go to the holder of the security on the previous day. Since we are talking here about three or six months' worth of interest or dividends, the amounts could be a dollar or more per share. If you have tax-loss carryforwards, it may be advantageous to sell a holding the day before the ex-date, recognize a capital gain, and then buy it back on the ex-date when the price is generally lower by the amount of the dividend. If you deal with a discount broker, the commissions are minimal and, as often as not, you can repurchase the shares at a price even lower than the previous day's, less the dividend, since many investors tend to sell the day after they collect their dividend.

Taxation and Mandatory Convertible Preferreds

Mandatory convertible preferred securities have always been controversial. This is, in part, because they more closely tie the fixed-income investor's fortunes to the performance of the stock than do optional preferreds. In short, if the common stock price happens to be depressed at the point in time when the conversion date is reached, you may get, say, 20 percent more stock than if the stock had appreciated. However, there are serious adverse tax consequences to mandatory convertibles when they convert below the par value equivalent. This is because most of these convertible preferreds consist of two elements: a bond and a purchase contract. For tax purposes, when the preferred is converted to stock, it is looked upon as two transactions: a redemption of the bonds at par and the exercise of your purchase contract to buy the common shares at the conversion price. To illustrate just how adverse this can be, take a Duke Energy 8.25 percent convertible preferred that converted on May 18, 2006. Assume you bought the preferred share for $20 a year earlier. With Duke common stock at $21.60, you got 0.6414 share of stock worth $13.85. This would be a $6.15 long-term capital loss, right? Wrong—for tax purposes, Uncle Sam will assume you got $25 cash and used this to buy 0.6414 share of stock, which you can assign a cost basis of $25 (equal to a $38.98 share price, or 25.00 divided by 0.6414). Hence, you will have a long-term taxable gain of $5 per preferred share. If you turn around and sell the 0.6414 common share at the same $21.60 market value, you will receive $13.85. Now you have a short-term capital loss of $11.15 per share. Add these two together and you get the $6.15 loss you would expect if this had been treated as one transaction, but the gain would be long term and the loss short term.

This complicated tax treatment is something an investor must take into consideration before the actual conversion date. If you want to avoid this gain/loss scenario, you can opt to sell the preferred shares before the redemption date and have a long-term capital loss of $6.15. However, if you can't use the gain in the current year to offset other losses, you may wish to hold the shares over to next year and then decide when to take the then-existing gain or loss.

Unfortunately, if the common stock is worth less than you paid for the convertible, the tax consequences work in reverse. Then the IRS rules are that you redeemed the convertible loan contract at face value, even if you bought it at, say, 80 cents on the dollar, or worse, paid a dollar and the common stock you get is worth only 80 cents. In that case, you have the unfortunate situation of having a 20 cents per share loss, which the IRS considers as 20 cents of income instead. Only by selling the stock before that year-end can you be assured of getting your true loss recognized. While these tax treatment matters seem incidental, they give you one of the few ways in which you can create taxable losses or gains legitimately, as and when needed, without assuming any additional risk. For that reason alone, they are worth your attention.

For the really clever investor, you may even consider buying such a security as a vehicle for moving capital gains or losses from one tax period to another and for changing their nature. Keep in mind, also, that when such a security is at a premium to par value, the tax consequences are the reverse. Hence you can play this tax game both ways. However, as I have cautioned before, consult your tax advisor beforehand.

Tax Reporting

At year-end, most investors are being inundated with special statements from brokerage houses and mutual funds. Lately, I've found that the array of reports is greater than ever due to the new tax treatment accorded dividend payments. I also find that the extent of misinformation is at an all-time high. *For those who prepare their own tax returns,*

I commend you for your pluck. But then, you have probably been doing this for a number of years and know by now that it's mainly an exercise of fill in the blanks—not unlike doing a crossword puzzle without an answer page. The advantage here, however, is that the IRS often has no answer page, either. The main report you receive will be a Form 1099 from your broker. This provides a daunting array of numbers, broken down into sections: a 1099-DIV, 1099-INT, 1099-B, and various summary sections. To add to the complication, for some reason, Form 1099-OID (original issue discount) merits a separate form and mailing. While no tax expert, I offer some advice, based strictly on personal experiences, that could help you at tax time.

- Paid tax return preparers diligently itemize every buy and sell transaction in order to report capital gains and losses. I've found, over 30 years, that giving the IRS only the account number, the total cost and proceeds for all transactions and the net gain or loss for the year in one number works just as well as reporting the minutia of every trade, as called for by the form, and it has saved me a whole lot of time and preparation fees.Your accountant won't recommend this, but then, accountants bill by the hour.
- If you've had foreign tax withheld on your dividend or interest on a taxable account, it's quite easy to get a tax credit against your U.S. tax bill. When filing your Form 1040, you simply attach a Form 1166 based on the tax withholding numbers reported to you by your broker on the 1099. You'll find it's quite easy to prepare, and it gives you a really nice feeling because it directly reduces the tax to be paid or, better yet, increases your tax refund.
- A major problem arises each year in distinguishing preferred dividends that are eligible for taxation at the reduced 15 percent rate (QDI) from those that are not. This has not yet been sorted out completely. Brokers have been relying on a study they commissioned by a big four accounting firm to identify the proper tax treatment of all outstanding issues. The problem is that when the accountants weren't sure, they treated the dividend as fully taxable. You can check the eligibility of your dividends on our Web

site, www.incomesecurities.com, to identify issues where tax treatment advice differs. You can then try to argue the point with your
broker, but be prepared to waste a lot of time. A second, more
serious error encountered on the Form 1099 is the treatment of the
dividends on the Canadian oil and gas trusts. These are fully eligible for the 15 percent tax treatment. The Web sites of the various
trusts clearly tell you this. Trying to convince your brokerage firm
of this is often a waste of time. Ameritrade, Scottrade, and Schwab
seem to have it right. Some others are reportedly refusing to budge.

- You want to closely examine your 1099 for an item called "Payments in lieu of Dividends." This represents payments made to
you by the brokerage house because it lent out your shares to a
short-seller during a dividend payment period. It cannot credit you
that dividend because it did not receive it, hence the "payment in
lieu of." The problem with these payments is that they are considered ordinary income, not dividends eligible for the 15 percent tax
rate. Your brokerage firm is aware of this and should be crediting
you with the dividend amount plus the tax difference amount. You
want to check and be sure, since there are no hard-and-fast rules
on this. There is an additional problem with in-lieu-of payments as
they pertain to Canadian oil and gas trust dividends—the brokerage firm will credit you back the net amount after the Canadian
withholding tax of 15 percent, thus you lose your right to recover
the 15 percent tax on your U.S. tax return. This is money straight
out of your pocket, and you should demand that your brokerage
reimburse you for this loss.

- Another issue regarding the Canadian trusts is the fact that a portion of your distribution is considered a return of capital and therefore not subject to income tax until you sell your shares (i.e., it is
an adjustment of your cost basis). Granted, this is complicated and
may require you to have a tax accountant, but your savings can be
significant. Check each trusts' Web site for the details each year.

- If you received a slew of 1099-OID forms from your broker, you
have a special headache. You will have to report these amounts as
interest income or expect a brief note and bill from the IRS in the

late fall. To avoid this problem, report the OID as a one-line entry under the brokerage firm name as interest income and deduct that amount from the capital gain (as described in the first bulleted item) if the security has been sold.

Original Issue Discount

One of the most annoying features any security can have is a requirement to pay taxes on income you never received. Such phantom income is called *original issue discount* (OID). The amount of such OID is calculated at year-end by the brokerage firms and diligently reported to the IRS. It is one of the things the IRS can check for all taxpayers because it can match it to your return electronically; hence, it is not something you want to overlook.

There are at least three ways OID can happen. The most common is when a bond is issued at a discount from its face value. This includes all zero-coupon bonds, but also many others that were issued at a discount and that only began paying after a number of years (step-up bonds). You must report the OID as interest income, but you are allowed to add the same amount to your cost basis for the security, because it is only when you sell or redeem the security that you actually collect this interest.

A second, and most annoying, type of OID is on unpaid preferred stock dividends, also known as *dividends in arrears* or *arrearage*. Here the IRS adds insult to injury by taxing you on a dividend you were supposed to get but didn't because it was postponed. The IRS looks only at the fact that you are entitled to a dividend and not whether you actually received it. The problem is that if you sell the security before the arrearage is finally paid, you add the dividends to your cost basis and thereby increase your capital loss. This is because when you sell the stock, the arrearage becomes the property of the new holder, who has the happy circumstance that when the dividends in arrears are finally paid, it is only a return of that holder's capital and not considered income. You should therefore be aware of this tax treatment when a dividend arrearage occurs, since it may be better for you taxwise to sell the preferred while the loss is still short term. Note that when payment of the dividend looks imminent or was never seriously in doubt, the price of the security will often reflect the back arrearage well before it is paid.

A third source of OID comes with convertible preferreds. These securities usually consist of a note and a purchase contract for the conversion privilege. This structure leads the IRS to require the holder to use the accrual rather than the cash basis for recognizing income. This means that the brokerage firm reports your accrued income based on the daily dividend accrual rate times the number of days you held the security. Unfortunately, it also reports the dividends actually received, so you want to make sure you don't report the same income twice. In fact, if you purchased the security just before an ex-dividend date, your income received may exceed the OID accrual. I question whether the IRS computers can keep this situation straight, so check with your tax advisor on what to do to avoid a deficiency letter.

Another of the unhappy consequences of the OID rules is that most brokerage houses do not recognize when a company has filed for bankruptcy. Hence, they will report OID income on the bonds and preferreds of such companies, ignoring the fact that, by law, interest ceases to accrue the day bankruptcy is filed. Getting a big tax bill for income you never received is bad enough; getting it on income you will never get is maddening. So keep your records in order, and when a dispute arises, try to find someone in the IRS knowledgeable enough to understand this specific problem.

10

SUMMING UP

A Long-Term Strategy for Income Investing

If you managed to get through this book to this point, congratulations. You will recognize most of what I am summarizing here and find this a convenience only. If you're like my wife and skipped to the end halfway through, you'll find this section provides an overview of the portfolio management approach I am advocating.

My basic premise is that the key to building a steady, growth-oriented income portfolio is to diversify over a variety of securities that depend on different drivers (i.e., portfolios that are not vulnerable to any one specific economic factor such as interest rates). This is not unlike the approach used by most stock investors or mutual fund managers. We live in uncertain and rapidly changing times. It follows that, for income investors, the drivers for a diversified portfolio will change, so a buy and hold strategy will no longer suffice.

To help new subscribers to my *Forbes/Lehmann Income Securities Investor* newsletter, I begin each year with a model portfolio of low-, medium-, high-risk, and convertible securities. New and old subscribers are free to buy these portfolios (they are put together in $100,000 incre-ments) or use them as a starting point for building one of their own. Fig-ure 10.1 demonstrates how well each of these portfolios performed over the past five years. It also includes a diversified portfolio representing the performance if someone bought all four portfolios. While this is only an approximate reflection of the diversification I am advocating in this book, it nevertheless provided an attractive rate of return. Just how good a return can best be seen from Figure 10.2, in which I compare the diversified portfolio to the performance of the three major stock indexes (the S&P 500, the Dow Jones Industrials, and the Nasdaq Composite), adjusted for dividend income. So as not to skew the results by including the disaster year of 2000, the comparison is made based on a dollar invested at year-end 2000. Nevertheless, we can clearly see that over the past six years, a diversified income portfolio handily outperformed all three stock indexes. It would seem that the concept that it takes high risk to achieve high rewards could use some reexamination. If you've been out of stocks over the past six years, you haven't missed a thing.

Learning how to manage your investments well is not an easy task, especially at a late stage of life. It is, however, one of the most impor-tant things you can spend your time on if you want your retirement to be financially carefree. Hiring a financial advisor is certainly a safeguard

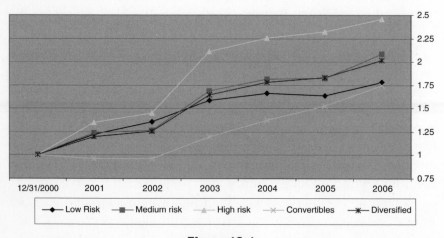

Figure 10.1
Six-Year Model Portfolios Performance, Growth per $1 Invested

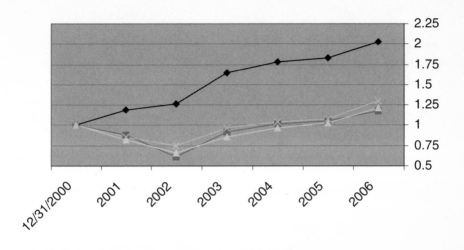

Figure 10.2
Stock versus Income Securities, Growth per $1 Invested

for those with the resources to do so, but you should still know enough about the securities markets to understand the strategy your advisor is following and to ask the right questions. Too often, I am faced with investors who say they want a conservative portfolio and also want an 8 percent rate of return, after fees!

It is important to understand what are and what are not realistic expectations. To construct your own portfolio, go to my Web site and download the Excel spreadsheet. Put in what you hold now and then decide where you need to rearrange holdings to achieve a better balance of income and risk. Following is a recap of the allocations I currently recommend.

Begin by deciding how much you want to allocate to income securities and how much to growth stocks. Also, build two different accounts, one for your tax-free investments and one for your taxable. Keep in mind that you want to have your income tax return work for you as much as possible, so where you hold an investment is important. Generally speaking, your taxable account should be where you hold the growth-oriented securities such as convertibles and special-situation investments that have downside risk (i.e., more than just the risk that they will do nothing). Also, here you would hold the QDI-eligible securities and municipal bonds if you are in a high tax bracket and hold any Canadian energy trusts (so you can recover the 15 percent withholding tax). Your tax-free account should hold mostly interest rate-sensitive securities and high-yield special situations (e.g., GM or Ford preferreds at 60 cents per dollar of face value that offer high yields and low price-decline risk).

Let's revisit the allocations first proposed in Chapter 1 (under "Diversification"). As an overall guide, I currently recommend the following allocations for the amount you decide to allocate to income investing (see also Figure 10.3). (Specific security selections change from month to month, so look to my monthly newsletter for individual picks.)

- *A 40 percent allocation to interest rate-sensitive issues, mostly in the BBB- and BB-quality levels.* Look for issues with coupon rates near current interest levels to minimize calls. Avoid issues selling at premiums of 5 percent or more over their face value, because they will generate capital losses. Look instead for issues trading well below their par value, since they offer the chance of capital appreciation and will decline less if interest rates rise. (One precaution here:

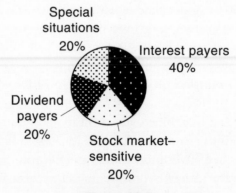

Figure 10.3
A Diversified Income Portfolio

Know why it's selling below par before you buy. Markets tend to be very good at pricing risks). Calculate how much you stand to benefit from buying QDI preferreds and municipal bonds. If the tax savings (after the AMT calculation) are significant, then a healthy portion of this allocation should be in QDI preferreds and municipal bonds. Include here REITs and closed-end income funds.

- *A 20 percent allocation to stock market–sensitive issues (convertible bonds and preferreds).* Returns here are in part dependent on the performance of the stock market. This allocation may be in specific issues or in closed-end convertible funds. You may also consider an allocation here to some long-shot convertibles such as those for GM and Ford.

- *A 20 percent allocation to high-dividend-paying companies.* Returns here are dependent on the performance of various industry sectors or specific high-dividend-paying companies. Today, U.S. and Canadian energy trusts offer double-digit returns. Tomorrow, public utilities and financial services companies may again be the stars. Investments here offer growth, high income, and favorable tax treatment, a combination that's hard to beat.

- *A 20 percent allocation to special situations.* This category is the most dynamic because returns are dependent on issuer-specific variables rather than on market-driven factors. At year-end 2005, I focused on GM and Ford because they are the most attractive special situations at that moment, and not just because they are priced as though the companies are likely to file bankruptcy. Their finance subsidiaries, GMAC and Ford Credit, were also beaten down and yet faced far lesser risks. Hence, a lower risk, but still a rewarding special situation. At year-end 2006, the uncertainties created by the Canadian government regarding the taxation of Canadian oil and gas trusts (see Chapter 6) caused massive selling and drove yields as high as 17 percent. Other such opportunities will come along. You need to stay tuned to the financial markets to spot them. Subscribing to my newsletter would also help alert you. Many opportunities last only a few days, so you often need to be quick to act.

There are some guidelines for your allocation of stocks as well. I have been merciless in my criticism of open-end mutual funds as the vehicle for investing in stocks or bonds. Get to know exchange-traded funds (ETFs) and closed-end funds (CEFs) as alternative vehicles. In making your allocation decision between stocks and income securities, consider that the preceding income securities allocation has a significant stock market exposure already embedded. Also, as discussed in Chapter 1, you want to have the flexibility to shift allocations between the two should major market movements make you over- or underweight in either.

I leave you with this final thought: As you approach retirement, become as knowledgeable about securities as you do about staying healthy, and both your health and finances will benefit.

APPENDIX

INTERNET INVESTMENT INFORMATION SOURCES

The Internet provides today's investor with unlimited resources to become informed on investment opportunities and stay informed on new developments. Most people are probably familiar with the hard-copy stalwarts of the financial and investment news such as the *Wall Street Journal*, *Forbes*, and *BusinessWeek*, all of which provide comprehensive financial news reporting. In addition to these big names, a niche industry of sector-specific information resources has emerged. These publications are good sources for ideas. The Internet is the resource for following up on those ideas.

Information sources now abound that focus on specific investment sectors like ETFs, preferreds and convertibles, tech investing, distressed company investing, developing markets, and so on. The expanded coverage of the investment world has led to the creation of very specialized reporting to go along with the traditional broad analysis. In short, if you have a question or a curiosity, you should be able to find the answer or information you're looking for without having to consult a professional.

If you are going to be your own investment manager, you need to put in the time both to educate yourself and to monitor the investments you have. While this may be dreary work at first, many investors find it gradually becomes less so, and eventually it can even prove fun. It takes determination and persistence, but the end result may just be a more valuable investment portfolio.

Newsletters or other periodical publications are a smart decision for anyone looking to take a hands-on approach with their investments. Don't be afraid to spend some money on a subscription to a publication that provides commentary on the specific securities you hold. I don't say this as newsletter publisher, but as an investor. It's always beneficial to have outside opinions, especially expert opinions, and the people providing the analysis are paid to spend their time researching and analyzing so you don't have to. Unless you have access to extraordinary information, these analysts, in most cases, are very likely to be much more knowledgeable on the specific investments. It's not just looking for good ideas on what to buy, but also advice on when and what to sell. Many times, just one timely tip a year can more than offset the cost of a subscription. In addition, printed investment news periodicals often have corresponding Web sites accessible to subscribers or provide the option to subscribe to the electronic version of the newsletter. If you have regular access to the Internet, this can be an especially attractive offer, as rates for the electronic format are often cheaper due to lower production costs and provide updated information not included in the printed versions.

Following, I list some investment information and analysis sources on the Web that are important for any investor to be aware of. Because they are constantly updated with the latest information, unlike paper information sources such as books, newspapers, magazines, or newsletters, they are places you should visit routinely. Some sites are interactive, allowing you to construct a virtual portfolio of your holdings (or holdings you might be thinking of purchasing), and the site will track the securities within the portfolio as well as offer news and analysis specific to those securities.

There are numerous sites, and the list grows daily. I have selected a few of my favorites that are easy to navigate and provide much of the essential information investors will need. To access all the features generally requires a free registration, which requires you to provide certain information such as an e-mail address, mailing address, and other nonfinancial data. But this takes only a minute and is well worth it.

American Stock Exchange (www.amex.com)
Home page for the AMEX. Allows you to search conveniently for listed companies by sector. Very efficient search options that allow you to find exactly the security you're looking for. Good source of ETF market news and prices. *Free.*

Bloomberg (www.bloomberg.com)
Perhaps the most comprehensive global investment news site there is. Tracks and graphs, updated currency, stock, index futures, and just about any other relevant market. In-depth analysis. Live audio and video streams to Bloomberg radio and television. *Free.*

BondsOnline (www.bondsonline.com)
More of a clearinghouse for information than an analysis provider. Has links to other information sources that are quite informative. It also has an interesting bond tutorial section accessible without charge. Most of the information requires a subscription that varies from source to source. A good place to look for comprehensive bond information sources.

Bond Desk (www.bonddesk.com)
A Web site for shopping for municipal and corporate bonds that are currently available. Individuals can shop here and compare prices before placing an order with their current broker.

Breifing.com (www.breifing.com)
Good day-to-day market recaps and summaries of what's going on with securities markets. Half-hour updates. Excellent for equity investment.

Very informative. *Free section*. Also offers $10 and $25 subscription packages that provide live market information and are geared more toward day traders. Subscription prices are based on frequency of anticipated trades.

Closed-end Funds (www.cefa.com)

Good source for shopping closed-end funds based on current discounts or premiums from net asset value. Good histories and holding information.

Clearstation (clearstation.etrade.com)

Great investment education section with terms and ideas easily explained. Keeps track of trends and market patterns. Great graphics and graphing visuals if you're into that sort of thing. *Free*.

CNET INVESTOR (investor.news.com)

Tech-heavy investment news. Up-to-the-minute Nasdaq reports. Quick access to daily price charts. Not the most comprehensive site, but great for tech investors. *Free*.

EDGAR Online (www.edgar-online.com)

Huge database of companies' SEC filings. Great way to access detailed reports on companies' financials and fundamentals (available for a fee). Detailed and extensive data of foreign firms' financial information. Also provides market quotes and charts updated every 15 minutes. A bit pricey (unlimited access for $1,200 annually, limited access for $59.85 per quarter).

ETF Connect (www.etfconnect.com)

A comprehensive site where you can search for ETF info by security class, region, or asset holdings. An ETF education section as well. *Free*.

ETF Investor Newsletter (www.Etfinvestornewsletter.com)

This is the Web site that supports the *ETF Investor Newsletter*, a monthly advisory on what's new in exchange-traded funds (ETFs) and closed-end funds (CEFs), with specific monthly buy recommendations. Subscription to the newsletter is $195 yearly and $345 for two years.

Financial Times (www.ft.com)
Same dependable and extensive news source as the printed daily. Excellent international financial news reporting. Plus, the site has detailed sections devoted to individual investment types likes bonds, commodities, equities, and so forth. Great general market news source. *Free.*

Hoover's (www.hoovers.com)
Provides extremely in-depth coverage of companies. Has a massive database of over 43,000 businesses spanning over 600 industries. Detailed company profiles are accessible for *free.* Individual access to the database starts at $69.95 per month. Highly detailed reports also available for a fee.

Income Securities Advisor (www.incomesecurities.com)
This is the support site for the *Forbes/Lehmann Income Securities Investor* newsletter. The newsletter is unique in that its advice is geared toward individual income investors. And, if I failed to mention it, I am its publisher. The newsletter is $195 per year, $345 for two years. The site also provides an investor alert service for time-sensitive news affecting past recommendations. Most Web site functions require a subscription to the newsletter.

InterNotes (www.internotes.com)
This site lets you track weekly price updates of InterNotes, provides access to prospectuses of all the InterNotes offered, posts fact sheets of all InterNote issuers, offers a laddering option, and has a laddering feature that allows you to construct sample portfolios of new and secondary notes. *Free.*

Investopedia (www.investopedia.com)
Outstanding glossary and dictionary of investing terms. One of the best educational sites for investors there is. If you have an investment question, you'll find the answer here. *Free.*

Morningstar.com (www.morningstar.com)
Another great investment news site. Started out as a mutual fund advice site but now has comprehensive coverage of all types of investing news.

Great in-depth analysis, with 90 equity analysts on staff. Very good tutorial and education section. Well-balanced. Extensive access to free information. There's a 14-day *free trial*, after which you can purchase a $14.95 month-to-month subscription, a $135 annual subscription, a $225 two-year subscription, or a $320 three-year subscription.

MSNBC (www.msnbc.com)
Attractive site that provides broad range of financial and business news. A lot of fluff to sift through, but broad analysis is provided. Access to all the major markets and updated prices information. Impressive collection of news stories and sources. Similar to Yahoo!'s *Finance* but a little more Hollywood than *Wall Street*. *Free*.

MSRB (www.Investinginbonds.com)
The Municipal Securities Rulemaking Board is the SEC of municipal bonds. This Web site provides the latest trading information on all municipal and corporate bonds. It is as good as transparency in bond pricing gets.

MuniBond (www.munibond.com)
A Web site for shopping for municipal bonds that are currently available. Individuals can shop here and compare prices before placing an order with their current broker.

NASD (www.nasdbondinfo.com/asp/bond_search.asp)
This Web site of the National Association of Securities Dealers (NASD) contains transaction information on investment-grade, non-investment-grade, and convertible corporate bonds as reported to NASD's Trade Reporting and Compliance Engine (TRACE). In addition, basic descriptive information and credit ratings on individual corporate bonds are available. The transaction data are updated and available on a real-time basis, except for certain transactions in new issues and large transactions ($1 million or more) in less active high-yield bonds. The information delays can be 2, 4, or 10 business days. *Free*.

NASD Bond Info (www.nasdbondinfo.com)
Best and most comprehensive online source for checking corporate bond prices. Uses NASD TRACE system. Is the most widely quoted bond

pricing source. Lists the most current trading prices for nearly every corporate bond imaginable. Also has an in-depth bond investing educational section. *Free.*

Nasdaq (www.nasdaq.com)
All the bells and whistles and investor tools you can imagine. Very comprehensive information source for equities and ETFs. Helpful interactive tools like *screeners*, which allow you to compare securities' performances over chronological intervals. *Free.*

New York Mercantile Exchange (www.nymex.com)
Everything you ever wanted, or didn't want to know, about the NYMEX. Up-to-the-minute commodities futures pricing and market information. Allows you to trade futures online with an account. Provides helpful price charts, market profiles, and tutorial sections. Heavy on trading mechanics and execution, but not really a news and analysis site. *Free.*

New York Stock Exchange (www.nyse.com)
Home page of the NYSE. Great glossary of trading terms and acronyms. Good source for pricing of foreign companies' stock listed on the NYSE. Good for NYSE-specific info, but other general sites like Yahoo! or MSN offer more information and track the stock market just as well. *Free.*

OTC Bulletin Board (www.otcbb.com)
A wealth of charts and tables that make market information easy to understand. Run-of-the-mill information site with news and market information. *Free.* Company reports can be purchased for $26.00 apiece.

Pinksheets (www.pinksheets.com)
Extensive company news provider. Great place to find details about specific security issues. Allows you to search and graph stock price histories of up to five years. Keeps a database of companies' SEC filings. Links to online trading sites. *Free.*

Preferred Stock Guide (www.preferredstockguide.com)
Complete database listing of preferred stock offerings. Provides detailed security profiles. Has a very thorough section on preferred stock invest-

ing and glossary of trading terms. Convenient tax treatment information is a real bonus. *Free.*

Quantum Online (www.quantumonline.com/)
This Web site contains the most comprehensive source of information on preferred stocks, including summary descriptions and links to the full prospectus. It also provides good search and lookup capabilities. *Free.*

U.S. Securities and Exchange Commission (www.sec.gov)
Complete listing of every SEC filing on record. Uses EDGAR database but without the fee. No frills, but it has all the filing information if you know to look for it. Provides helpful tutorial on how to search the database. Premier site to search for SEC filings. *Free.*

Reuters (www.investor.reuters.com)
Along the lines of Yahoo! but has fewer advertising distractions. Very easy-to-use layout. Quick and easy. All the investor information you need. News links and analysis aren't quite as comprehensive as Yahoo! but market information is easier to access.

RiskGrades (www.riskgrades.com)
Has devised its own formula for risk analysis and assigns each company a quantifiable risk element. Lets you plug in your virtual portfolio and run experimental what-if scenarios to help you improve on your risk/return and diversification. Very interesting to play around with. *Free.*

Shop 4 Bonds (www.shop4bonds.com)
As the name implies, this site allows you to see what is currently available in the market and current pricing.

ValuBond (www.valubond.com)
A Web site for shopping for municipal and corporate bonds that are currently available. Individuals can shop here and compare prices before placing an order with their current broker.

Yahoo! Finance (finance.yahoo.com)

Good all-around site. Postings from a large collection of well-established news sources. Extremely accessible and well-organized. Good investing section. Easy-to-access market and company information. Very comprehensive, one-stop investment site. MSN money has similar content, but Yahoo! is easier to use and provides more relevant info.

GLOSSARY

Most glossaries are an accumulation of terms that one can get from any of a hundred Web sites or publications. I have tried to include here only those terms with which an income investor should be familiar in order to get a fuller understanding from the financial things he or she will be reading in the future. Hence, you should read this section and not just use it as a lookup guide.

Acronym   A word or term made up from the initial letters of a name or parts of a series of words, such as "QUIDS" for *Qu*arterly *I*ncome *D*ebt *S*ecurities. These are used to describe, in an abbreviated fashion, securities with similar features. Most of the preferred acronyms are trademarked identifiers that represent certain types of hybrid preferreds created by specific Wall Street firms. Therefore, a security with the same features, but issued by different brokerage houses, can be called TIGRS, CATS, LYONS, or STRIPS.

Accrued interest   The amount of interest accumulated but not paid between the last payment date and the buy or sell date. When purchasing *bonds* on the secondary market, this is the interest the former owner earned but has not been paid. It will be added to the buy price of a bond and returned to the seller. The new buyer will receive a full interest payment on the next pay date. Preferreds also accrue interest, but trade *flat*, without the participants having to account for the accrued interest. Instead, preferreds have an ex-dividend date and the accrued interest is bundled into the price of the preferred. For example, a quarterly pay preferred that is going to go ex-dividend tomorrow will generally trade at a higher price today because the purchaser will receive three months' worth of accrued interest. The next day, the preferred will drop in price by the amount of the payment.

Adjustable-rate securities   These are securities with a variable interest or dividend rate. Their rate is usually related to the yield of another security (Treasury bills, notes, bonds) or to indexed lending rates such as the prime rate or LIBOR. The amount they pay will rise or fall in concert with the rate or yield they are related to. Thus, these securities are ideal for principal protection when rates are rising.

American Depository Receipt (ADR)   A share of stock, issued by an American bank, that is backed by foreign securities held in deposit. All dividends on the foreign shares pass through to the ADR holder.

Alternative minimum tax (AMT)   A second tax calculation, intended for wealthy individuals, under which certain tax-exempt interest and charitable contributions are limited for individuals earning incomes above specified limits.

Annual report   A yearly report on the financial operations of a company that is required for all publicly listed companies. The report includes a variety of financial statements that must be certified by an independent accounting firm.

Arrearage   Refers to the past-due dividends on cumulative preferred and preference stock. This obligation must be satisfied before common stock dividends can be paid. Arrearage payments, when finally made, are to the current holders of the stock issue being paid off, not to holders of the stock when the dividends were missed.

Ask price   The lowest price anyone who owns a security will accept for a specific quantity of a security at a specific point in time. Also known as the *offer price*. See also **Bid price**.

Balance sheet   A financial statement that details a company's assets and the claims against them. The left or upper side details all assets in the order of their liquidity (i.e., cash, accounts receivable, and inventories first). The right side or lower part details the claims against the company in the time order in which they will have to be met. Hence, trade payables and current loans are followed by longer-term debt, pension claims, and deferred taxes. Shareholders' equity is the final section and is adjusted to make the assets balance with the claims against them.

Bankruptcy   A legal process under which a company files a declaration of bankruptcy with a regional federal bankruptcy court. The filing of bankruptcy stops all accrual and payment of interest or debt except as approved by a judge. Most bankruptcy filings are under Chapter 11 of the Federal Bankruptcy Code, which allows the company to continue in operation. A bankruptcy can also be filed under Chapter 7, which calls for the liquidation of the company. In that case, a company ceases operations and a trustee is appointed by the court to administer liquidation of the company's assets and settlement of all claims. Creditors' recovery in a bankruptcy have varied from 0 to 100 percent plus interest, but payment is often made in stock of a newly reorganized company.

Barbell strategy   An income investing strategy whereby a portfolio is balanced between short-term and long-term maturities to balance the interest rate exposure.

Basis point   The smallest measure used when quoting yields on bonds and preferred stocks: 100 basis points = 1 percent. Example: An increase of 60 basis points to a yield of 7.00 percent would make it 7.60 percent. Also called "beps" in Street jargon.

Bid price   The highest price at which a willing buyer is prepared to immediately buy a specific security in a specified quantity.

Bid/ask spread   The difference between the highest bid price and the lowest ask price for a security.

Bond   An IOU of a corporation that usually requires the issuer to pay the holder an agreed-upon interest rate for a set period of time and to repay the IOU at maturity. Corporate bonds are usually issued in $1,000 denominations. The holder of a bond is a creditor of the corporation, not a part owner like a shareholder.

> **Secured bonds**   are backed by collateral, which can be sold to satisfy the debt.

> **Debentures**   are noncollateralized bonds backed only by the full faith and credit of the company.

Bond insurer   This term refers to anyone other than the borrower who provides a payment guarantee for a bond issue. It is most commonly found in municipal bonds. A bank may do this for a fee by issuing a letter of credit. A government agency such as the FDIC,

HUD, or FHA may also do this. Most municipal bonds are insured, and that insurance is provided by one of four monoline bond insurance companies who are all AAA rated: MBIA, AMBAC, FIGIC, and FSHA.

Call date　The first date an issuer can redeem a bond or preferred before maturity. In most cases, the issue can be called anytime after this date at a defined price. The issuer, however, is not obligated to call the security.

Call premium　The value above the par value that an issuer will pay the holder if the issuer wants to retire the security before its maturity date.

Call price　The price at which a bond or preferred stock with a call provision will be redeemed. In most cases, this price will be the par value. Some securities have a call price schedule, which begins at a premium to par value, then declines annually to eventually settle at the par value.

Calls　Most bonds and preferreds have a clause that permits the issuing company to redeem or retire all or part of the shares outstanding at defined prices for specific dates in the future. There are several types of call provisions:

Continuous calls　These are the most common redemption plans in use by companies. This type of call allows the company to redeem its bonds and preferreds at any time, usually with 30 days' notice. Most bonds and preferreds have a schedule of annual redemption prices with beginning dates (Example: 6/1/91 @$52, 6/1/92 @$51, etc.). In this example, the issuer can redeem these shares at $52 anytime between 6/1/91 and 6/1/92 and at $51 anytime between 6/1/92 and 6/1/93.

Discrete calls　These will list specific days and prices the issue can be called. In some cases, it may indicate that the issue can be called only on a dividend pay date.

Soft calls　A provision that can be attached to a convertible bond or preferred that determines the callablity of the security by triggers in the common stock price. Example: ABC's bonds or preferreds will become callable if the underlying security trades at or above a price of $20 for a 30-day period.

Closed-end mutual fund (CEF)   These funds have a fixed number of shares, which are traded on the secondary markets similarly to stocks. The market price may exceed the net asset value per share, in which case it is considered at a *premium*. When the market price falls below the net asset value per share, it is at a *discount*.

Collar   Bonds and preferreds (floaters, adjustables, etc.) with this feature have upper and lower limits within which the dividend rate can be reset. These limits are frequently referred to as the *ceiling* and *floor*.

Collateral   Specific hard assets that are pledged as guarantees of payment for a debt. Such assets are protected from other creditor claims in case of a bankruptcy, except to the extent that the collateral value exceeds the debt and interest amounts due the collateral holder.

Collateralized mortgage obligation (CMO)   A security created from a pool of mortgage obligations. The pool of obligations is divided up into pieces called *tranches*, which have different risk or volatility characteristics.

Collateralized debt obligation (CDO)   A security created from a pool of bonds and notes from different issuers. The pool of obligations is divided up into pieces called *tranches*, which have different risk or volatility characteristics.

Commercial paper   Short-term corporate debt obligations issued by investment-grade-rated issuers with maturities from 2 to 270 days. Such debt is used to finance day-to-day cash needs and is bought mainly by banks and corporations with their short-term surplus cash.

Convertible   A bond or preferred that can be converted or exchanged into common stock, usually from the same company. Income Securities Advisor, Inc., has created two Families of Preferreds: (1) *Mandatory*, in which case the security will automatically exchange into common stock on the maturity date. These preferreds are usually created and issued by a third party such as an investment banker or broker-dealer and usually have a variable conversion ratio based on the common stock price. (2) *Optional*, in which case the holder has the right to convert at any time. The issuer will often force conversion by calling the issue at par when the conversion value is greater than par.

Conversion Parity   The price at which a convertible bond or preferred must sell for it to equal the current market value of the common shares to be received upon conversion.

Conversion Premium   The value of the common stock one would receive if converted immediately compared to the current market price of the convertible. This number is usually expressed as a percent. For example, if the security is convertible into common stock with a value of $885.96 (conversion value), and the current market price of the security is $1,050.00, then the premium would be $164.04. To get the conversion premium, divide the premium $164.04 by the market price $1,050.00 times 100. This gives a conversion premium of 15.62 percent.

Conversion Price   The dollar price at which convertible bonds or preferred stock will be converted into common stock. The conversion price is established at the time of the issue of the convertible.

Conversion Rate   Same as *conversion ratio*.

Conversion Ratio   The number of shares into which each convertible bond or preferred can be converted. For example, if one convertible bond can be converted into 50 shares of common stock, then the conversion ratio is 50 : 01, or 50.0000. The conversion ratio is established at the time of issue of the convertible.

Conversion Value   The value of the number of shares into which a convertible security can be converted. Multiply the conversion ratio by the common stock price. Note: Sometimes referred to as *conversion parity*.

Convexity   A measure of how sensitive a debt instrument is to interest rate movements. When interest rates are rising, an adjustable-rate security is said to have *positive* (low) convexity. A zero-coupon security then has *negative* (high) convexity. When interest rates are falling, however, the reverse is true.

Coupon rate   Annual interest in percent based on par value $1,000.00 (e.g., 8.00% = $80.00).

Credit rating   Credit ratings are evaluations by independent agencies recognized by the SEC of a debt issuer's financial strength based on subjective or objective criteria.

Ratings are standardized with letters that denote levels of risk. Rating categories run from a high of AAA through D (for defaulted). Ratings are broadly categorized as investment grade and below investment grade, also called *junk*.

Cumulative dividend Almost all preferred stocks are designated as cumulative; thus an issuer must declare and pay all current and unpaid past dividends (arrears) before it can pay common share dividends. An issuer can pay current dividends and still be in arrears from past dividends. Missed payments on noncumulative issues are usually not covered. Note that the board of directors must declare dividends on preferreds each quarter. Hence, such dividends do not accrue and are not added to the purchase price, as with bonds.

Currency risk The risk associated with a rise or fall in the value of a foreign currency against the U.S. dollar, where a debt instrument is not denominated in dollars.

Current price The price of a bond is traditionally shown at 10 percent of the par value ($1,000.00). Example: A bond trading at 98.5 is actually priced at $985.00.

Current yield The annual rate of return (stated as a percent) an investor will be paid on a specific bond or preferred based on the current price.

>   **Bonds** To calculate current yield for bonds, divide the coupon rate by the number shown as current price and multiply by 100. Example: (9.60% coupon ÷ 95 current price = 0.1010) × 100 = 10.10% current yield.

>   **Preferreds** To calculate current yield for preferreds, you must first convert the dividend (issue) into dollars. To do this, divide the percent by 100, then multiply the results by the par value. Example: (8.25% ÷ 100 = 0.0825) × $25.00 = $2.063. To complete the calculation for current yield, divide the dollar dividend by the current price of the security, then multiply by 100. Example: ($2.063 ÷ current price $24.00 = 0.0859) × 100 = 8.59% current yield. Note: some preferreds show dividends in dollars.

CUSIP Acronym for Committee on Uniform Securities Identification Procedure, a unique identifier assigned to a security. No two are alike (similar to an individual's Social Security number). CUSIPs can be numeric (for stocks) or alphanumeric (for bonds and preferreds). CUSIPs consist of eight digits, with a ninth, *check digit*, that guards against typographical errors.

Debt maturity The date the underlying bond of a trust preferred or a third-party trust preferred matures. The preferred will expire on this date and return to the holder par value plus any accrued interest/ dividend. Bonds will mature on this date and return to holder's par value plus accrued interest.

Debenture An unsecured bond whose holder has the claim of a general creditor on all assets that are not specifically pledged to secure other debt.

Default The failure of a borrower to pay interest or repay principal in a timely manner. For bond issuers, additional nonpayment conditions constituting an event of default are defined in a legal document called a *bond indenture*.

Deferral of distributions This is when a preferred or underlying bond has a feature allowing the issuer to defer interest payments, under certain circumstances, for up to five years before it can be declared in default. This can be done only if the parent also suspends dividend payments on its common stock. (Distribution on the preferreds will continue to accrue during any deferral period, and investors must pay tax on the accrued but unpaid interest. Dividends on the common and preferred stock cannot resume until all unpaid interest has been paid.)

Depletion allowance A designation, for tax purposes, of a portion of a stock's dividend payment to the investor as a return of capital rather than dividend income. This is an accounting calculation used by natural resources companies to recognize that the company is using up or *depleting* its source of revenue or asset. This is not unlike a depreciation allowance to corporations to recognize the wear and tear of machinery and equipment.

Deritvatives This is a broadly used term that encompasses dozens of different securities, the common trait being that they all derive their value from some underlying security.

Direct Access Notes (DANs) Debt instruments sold by large investment-grade-rated companies directly to individual investors, without using a broker. Notes can be bought in $1,000 denominations and staggered maturities. Notes usually have a put provision for a sale back to the company if the note holder dies before the issue matures.

Discount   The amount a bond or preferred trades below the face or par value of the security. Note: Such discounts may occur because a security was issued at a price below par or because of a decline in its market price. If the security was issued at a discount, a portion of such a discount (original issue discount, or OID) must be recognized as income by the holder for federal income tax purposes.

Discount bonds   See **Zero-coupon bonds**.

Dividend   The money paid to shareholders. It is usually a fixed amount stated in dollars or a percent of par value. When the dividend amount is stated as a percent of par, the dollar value of the dividend is calculated by multiplying the percentage by the par value. (Example: Widget Co. $25.00 par with a 6.25 percent dividend = $25.00 × 0.0625 = $1.5625.) Sometimes a dividend can be *paid in kind* (PIK) (i.e., with common stock shares of the issuing company or additional preferred shares).

Duration   A measure of the price sensitivity of a bond to interest rate changes. The basis of its calculation is how many years it will take for an investor to get back the cost of a security selling at its face value.

DRD   An acronym for *dividends received deduction*, a tax advantage that allows certain corporations to deduct 70 percent of the dividends they receive from DRD-eligible preferreds.

Earnings before interest, taxes, depreciation, and amortization (EBITDA)   This amount represents operating results before certain expenses, which can make year-to-year or company-to-company comparisons more difficult. It allows an analyst to get a better feel for how a company's day-to-day operations are doing without the distortion from known variables that are measured by a different standard.

Equipment trust certificate   A type of debt instrument issued by an airline, railroad, or shipping line whereby the debt is secured by a specific piece of equipment (e.g., an airplane, a railcar, or a shipping container). Title to the equipment is held in the name of a bank trustee until the debt obligation is paid.

Equity-linked security (ELS)   A bond or preferred that is potentially convertible into shares of another company's security. The ELS typically pays interest or dividends, and its price will move with the price of the linked security.

   Commodity-linked security   A hybrid similar to equity-linked; however, this security is dependent on a commodity, price, or index.

Escrowed to maturity   When a debt issuer has the funds to pay off a debt issue that has no early call provision, it may put all the money needed to make all future interest and principal payments into a trust, thereby escrowing the debt to maturity. The issuer does this because such debt need not then be shown on its financial statements. Such debt issues are extremely low risk.

Euro bonds   Bonds denominated in U.S. dollars or other currencies for sale to investors outside the country whose currency is being used.

Eurodollar bonds   Bonds denominated in U.S. dollars for sale outside the United States (i.e., outside the jurisdiction and registration requirements of the SEC).

Ex-date, ex-dividend date   The date on which a security trades without the dividend. Investors purchasing a preferred or stock on or after the ex-dividend date will not receive the declared dividend. Opening price ex-dividend date is usually down an amount roughly equal to the dividend.

Exchange-traded fund (ETF)   Represents shares made up of an index or basket of shares that track a popular stock index, a geographic sector, an industry sector, or a commodity. ETFs are similar to an index mutual fund except that they trade continuously. The two most popular ETFs are the Standard & Poor's depositary receipt (SPDR) launched in 1993, which tracks the S&P 500 stock index, and the Nasdaq 100 Index Tracking Stock (QQQQ), which was launched in 1999 and tracks the Nasdaq 100 index. These vehicles are popular for hedging as well as investment.

Face value   This is the principal amount of a bond, usually $1,000.00. Commonly used synonymously with the term *par value*.

Fallen angel   A bond issue that was investment grade when issued and has since been downgraded to below investment grade, or junk. Such issues can suffer a large price decline at the time of the downgrade because many institutional investors must sell any they hold.

Family One reason preferreds remain a secret is that they are harder to understand than common stocks or even bonds. Hence, to feel comfortable with them you need to invest some serious time studying their features. To ease this process, we have broken up the preferred universe into nine logical groupings, which we have dubbed *families*. The members of each family have similar characteristics.

For the *nonconvertible preferreds*, we have created seven families. We use the term *preferreds* instead of *preferred stock* because many of the securities are bonds or represent indirect ownership of a bond:

Foreign These preferred stocks are issued by a foreign corporation in U.S. dollars. The legal rights of the holder are dictated by the rules of the issuer's country.

Partnerships These preferred stocks are issued by a partnership, which has its distributions reported on an IRS K-1 form. The tax treatment of payment on such preferreds may differ.

Perpetuals These preferred stocks have no maturity date and have tax preference for corporate buyers (i.e., they are DRD-eligible).

Trust preferreds These preferreds are backed by a bond held in trust; hence, they represent a creditor claim rather than a shareholder claim against the company.

Third-party trust preferreds These are trust preferreds created by an investment banker or broker-dealer, not the issuer of the underlying bond. They go by trade names such as CorTS, CABCO, SATURNS, PPLUS, and so forth.

Preferred equity-traded (PET) bonds These are preferreds that are in fact bonds, usually $25 par, traded on the NYSE.

REIT These are preferred stocks issued by a real estate investment trust (REIT).

Convertible preferreds have only two families, which may or may not have a bond as the underlying security:

Mandatory The preferred will automatically exchange into common stock on the maturity date. These preferreds are usually created and issued by a third party such as an investment banker or broker-dealer and usually have a variable conversion ratio based on the common stock price.

Optional These preferreds give the holder the right to convert into common stock at any time. Note: The issuer will often force conversion by calling the issue at par when the conversion value is greater than par.

Fitch One of the major three independent credit rating agencies recognized by the SEC.

Flat trading A bond traded without separate accrued interest. The price paid or received is deemed to include the accrued interest. Issuers in default and income bonds commonly trade flat.

Floating-rate securities (floaters) These are securities with a variable interest or dividend rate. Their rate is usually indexed to the yield of another security (U.S. Treasury bills, notes, bonds) or to another lending rates such as the prime rate or LIBOR. The amount they pay will rise or fall in concert with the rate or yield they are related to. Thus, these securities are ideal for principal protection when rates are rising.

Foreign This family of preferred securities is issued by foreign-based companies in U.S. dollars. There are several types of securities in this family. They are often issued as American Depository Receipts (ADRs), also called American Depository Shares (ADS). Some of these preferreds are subject to foreign withholding taxes. Those issued by banks usually have noncumulative dividends.

Funds from operations (FFO) FFO is the most commonly accepted and reported measure of a REIT's operating performance. It is equal to a REIT's net income, excluding gains or losses from sales of property and adding back real estate depreciation. This alternative measure is preferable to traditional profit measures because REITs are principally tax shelter vehicles and, as such, are designed to minimize taxable income.

General obligation bond A type of municipal bond that is backed by the full faith, credit, and taxing power of the issuing governmental authority.

Hedge funds Private investment funds for qualified investors that are exempt from SEC registration. They can invest in anything and everything and, for this reason, are the focus of SEC concern since they can disrupt otherwise orderly markets.

High-yield (junk) bonds   In some cases, the term *junk bonds* is used to refer to all high-yield bonds (i.e., those that are rated below investment grade or are not rated). In other cases, the term refers to the lower tiers of high-yield bonds in credit quality.

Hybrid preferreds   Corporate securities that have characteristics similar to both preferred stock and corporate bonds. There is a multitude of structures and acronyms for these securities, but several things are common to all of them: The issuers can deduct the payments from their taxes; holders receive interest, not dividends; and they are very liquid, since they trade as stocks on major exchanges. For further details look under **PET bonds**, **Trust preferreds**, and **Third-party trust preferreds**.

Illiquid securities   Securities that have very low daily trading volume. They suffer from wide price fluctuations and large bid/ask price spreads. Such securities are mainly found in the over-the-counter, the pink or yellow sheets, and the Nasdaq debt markets, although many NYSE-traded trust preferreds have the same characteristic.

Income bonds   These bonds pay interest only if the issuer has sufficient earnings. They are usually issued when a company is not sure of its earnings prospects (e.g., frequently issued as part of a bankruptcy settlement).

Income statement   This is the financial statement that summarizes the operating results of a company for a given period of time. It provides the best picture of how well or how poorly a company is performing and thus is the best measure of the likelihood that a company will prosper. The final number, or *net income*, is what is famously termed the *bottom line* and is the starting point for the statement of cash flows.

Indenture   The formal agreement between bondholders and an issuer defining key elements of the bond or debenture, such as maturity, amount issued, redemption rights, and protective covenants. This information is shown in the prospectus.

Institutional investors   Large investors, such as mutual funds, pension funds, and insurance companies.

Institutional trading   Trading done by large institutions, usually in $1 million or higher per-trade amounts.

In-the-money   A term used to denote a convertible security where the underlying stock into which it converts is greater than the face value of the convertible. The price movement of such a security is thus totally determined by the price of the underlying stock as long as it remains in-the-money.

Interest   The agreed-upon payment a borrower pays a lender for the use of money. Bonds are defined in annual interest rates often referred to as *coupon rate*. To convert the percentage into dollars, multiply by 10 (e.g., 9.60% × 10 = $96.00).

Interest rate risk   The price erosion of a fixed-income security in a rising interest rate environment.

InterNotes   Debt instruments sold by large companies directly to individual investors, without using a broker. Notes can be bought in $1,000 denominations and staggered maturities. Notes have a put provision for a sale back to the company if the note holder dies before the issue matures.

Investment grade   Bonds considered suitable for purchase by prudent investors. Bonds rated Baa3 and above by Moody's and BBB and above by Standard & Poor's, Fitch IBCA, and Duff & Phelps are considered investment grade.

Issue   Many firms have multiple preferred issues; thus, it is imperative to correctly identify each issue. Each preferred is identified by the term issue that shows the annual dividend, usually in a percent, and any special-series identifier. (To convert percentage dividends into dollars, divide by 100, then multiply by the par value.)

Issuer   Any authorized legal entity, including governments, agencies, and corporations, that has the power to issue a security.

Junk bonds (high-yield)   In some cases, the term *junk bonds* is used to refer to all high-yield bonds (i.e., those that are rated below investment grade or are nonrated). In other cases, the term refers to the lower tiers of high-yield bonds in credit quality. Many of today's high-yield bonds, particularly those rated Ba by Moody's or BB by other rating agencies, are not considered junk.

Laddering   An income investing strategy where a portfolio is made up of securities that mature in equal amounts each year. This strategy allows the investor to ignore interest rate fluctuations, but requires a large enough portfolio so that nothing need be sold before it matures.

Letter of credit (LC)   A guarantee issued by a bank. An LC is often used as collateral for a debt issue, especially for commercial paper.

London Interbank Offered Rate (LIBOR)   The rate banks charge each other for short-term eurodollar loans (from one week to one year). LIBOR is frequently used as the base for resetting rates on floating-rate securities.

Mandatory   This family of convertible preferreds will automatically convert to common stock on a specific date. Most issues have a variable conversion rate based on the common stock price it relates to. Example: If the common stock of ABC Corporation is at or above the threshold price ($46.93), the conversion ratio will be 0.8314. If the common is at or below the reference price ($34.81) the conversion ratio will be 1.1122. If the price is between the threshold and reference price, the investor will receive the par value of the preferred ($25.00) in common stock. In most cases, these securities are units made up of a purchase contract and a bond or trust preferred. Most convertibles in this family are not callable before the mandatory conversion date and usually *are not convertible by the holder.*

Margin   The use of securities and cash in an account to leverage the rate of return. Brokers will provide about 30 percent and up for every $1 of marginable securities and cash in a brokerage account and even more on U.S. Treasuries.

Margin call   A call for more cash or collateral to support the amount of a margin loan. Various things can trigger a margin call and, if not met, will result in the sale of securities in the account.

Matrix pricing   Debt instruments that are infrequently traded may be assigned a price or value based on comparable issues. This is done to permit daily valuations by mutual funds and others.

Maturity   The date a bond comes due. Principal and any accrued interest must be paid off.

Money market funds   A mutual fund that invests in debt instruments with a maturity of one year or less. Such funds offer only current yield and no capital appreciation. They are used by most investors to park cash while awaiting better investment opportunities. For this reason, growth or decline in the amounts of money held by such funds is considered a good market sentiment indicator.

Moody's   One of the major three independent credit rating agencies recognized by the SEC.

Municipal bonds   Debt obligations issued by a state, county, city, or other municipal governmental entity. Such bonds are generally exempt from federal and state income tax (in the state of issue).

Mutual funds   Pools of money that are managed by an investment company. They offer investors a variety of goals, depending on the fund and its investment charter. Some funds seek to generate income on a regular basis, others to preserve an investor's money or invest in growth stocks. Funds can impose a sales charge, or *load*, on investors when they buy or sell shares. Many funds these days are *no-load* and impose no sales charge, but all have expense charges.

Closed-end mutual fund   These funds have a fixed number of shares, which are traded on the secondary markets similarly to stocks. The market price may exceed the net asset value per share, in which case it is considered at a *premium*. When the market price falls below the net asset value per share, it is at a *discount*.

Open-end mutual fund   An investment fund that stands ready to sell new shares to the public and to redeem its outstanding shares on demand at a price equal to an appropriate share of the value of its portfolio, which is computed daily at the close of the market. This is typical of the majority of mutual funds.

Net asset value   The market value of all the securities held in a mutual fund divided by the number of shares outstanding.

NYSE   Acronym for the New York Stock Exchange, one frequently encountered in financial correspondence.

Noncumulative preferred   Missed dividends do not accrue. Omitted dividends are, as a rule, gone forever.

Open-end mutual fund   An investment fund that stands ready to sell new shares to the public and to redeem its outstanding shares on demand at a price equal to an appropriate share of the value of its portfolio, which is computed daily at the close of the market. This is typical of the majority of mutual funds.

Optional   This family of convertible preferreds are normally convertible at any time by the holder at fixed conversion rates and typically are perpetual or with a long maturity. They are usually callable after five years. Most convertibles in this family *are convertible at the option of the holder into common stock at any time.*

Original issue discount (OID)   A bond that sells at less than its face value at the time of its issuance is said to have OID. This OID amount is amortized, for tax purposes, over the life of the security. Hence, if you owned the security for six months of a year, the brokerage firm will report to the IRS six months' worth of OID as income you received, even if you sold the security at a loss.

Out-of-the-money   A convertible where the value of the stock into which it converts is less than the face value of the convertible. The more out-of-the-money a convertible gets, the more its price is dependent on its yield. A convertible who's price no longer reflects any value for the conversion feature is said to be *busted.*

Par   A shortened term for *par value.*

Par value   The face value of a security. For bonds, it's the principal amount due at maturity. In the case of preferreds, the issuing company sets this value. Par value is often referred to as *liquidation value.*

Parity (conversion)   The price at which a convertible bond or preferred must sell for it to equal the current market value of the common shares to be received upon conversion.

Participating preferreds   These rarely seen preferred issues receive their regular stated dividend plus participate with common stockholders, under specific conditions, for additional distributions of earnings by the issuer.

Partnership   A family of preferred securities issued by a partnership. There are a variety of partnership, the most common of which are *limited liability companies* (LLCs) and *limited partnerships* (LPs). In most cases, a parent company establishes and becomes the general partner of these entities. For the most part these securities are structured like trust preferreds, including the holder having an indirect ownership of a bond. These issues pay interest, not dividends. Note: Investors receive an IRS Schedule K-1 rather that Form 1099. The K-1 is usually sent out much later than 1099s.

Pay chain   The rating of securities is a subjective activity based on both qualitative and quantitative factors involving current business and economic conditions of an industry an of individual issues. Securities of an issuer may vary because of collateralization as well as status in the pay chain, which may appear as follows:

Senior secured debt

Senior unsecured debt

Subordinated debt

Trade creditors, junior subordinated debt

Debt secured hybrid preferreds

Preferred stock

Preference stock

Common stock

Note: Commonly, the preferred stock of an issuer will be rated one level below the issuer's bonds. This is also related to the pay chain. When comparing securities, use either the bond ratings or the preferred ratings; to mix the two will give a disjointed view.

Payment-in-kind (PIK) securities   These securities normally pay dividends or interest in the form of additional securities. However, PIKs can also include securities with payment in common stock, cash, or even the securities of a different company. Because the payment options are so diverse, the dividend amount is usually stated in cash so that holders will know, for example, that they will receive, say, $2.00 worth of securities.

Perpetual   This family of securities consists of capital stock in a company that is senior to common equity but junior to all debt. Perpetual preferreds usually have a fixed cumulative dividend and have no maturity, just like common stock. Most are callable sometime in the future and are DRD-eligible for corporations or qualifying investors.

PET bonds   Pet is an acronym for *preferred equity-traded bonds.* This family of preferreds actually consists of bonds. They are unique in that they are usually $25.00 par and traded on the New York Stock Exchange. (The normal bond is $1,000.00 par and trades over-the-counter). PET bonds are issued directly by a parent company. PET bonds pay interest, not dividends, and can pay either a quarterly or semiannual distribution.

Preference stock   These securities fall between preferred and common stock in their rights to dividends or liquidation payments. It is common for this stock to be rated lower than the preferred stock of a company by the credit agencies.

Preferred designation Many preferreds need a special designator attached to their symbol for identification. Brokerages and online quote systems use different designators; thus it is important for investors to know the designator for the system they are using. Examples: Yahoo! uses _p to denote a preferred; CCJ is the symbol for Cameco Corp.'s common stock and preferred stock. To get the preferred you must type CCJ_p. Household Capital Trust V symbol HI X should be typed HI_pX. ISI brackets preferred symbols that do not require a designator. Example: (DCX).

Preferred stock   This is the senior class of capital stock or equity of a company. Preferred stock must pay its stated dividend amount before preference or common stocks receive dividends. This stock also has priority over the other two in any liquidation distributions, such as bankruptcy. However, all forms of capital stocks, which make up the equity of a company, fall in line behind debt issues (bond, notes, etc.) and all other creditor claims in their right to payments of any sort. Although these equity issues represent part ownership in a company, they normally do not have voting rights.

Premium   The amount that a bond or preferred is selling for above face value (par value). Examples: A $1,000 bond trading at $1,050 has a $50 premium; a $25.00 par preferred trading at $26.00 has a $1 premium.

Premium (convertibles)   The percent of market price the convertible bond is trading at above the value of the common stock a convertible bond could be converted into (conversion value). Example: Market price $1,050.00 "*conversion value* (which is common stock price $20.25 (conversion ratio 43.751 = $885.96) = $164.04. To convert the premium dollars into a percentage, divide the premium $164.04 by the market price $1050.00 and multiply by 100, which equals a *premium* of 15.62 percent.

Principal   The face value or par amount of a debt security that must eventually be repaid.

Prospectus   This is the official selling circular that must be given to purchasers of new bonds or preferreds registered with the Securities and Exchange Commission (SEC). The prospectus contains details of the security. Included are financial details of the issuer as well as management overview, history, experience, competition, and prospects. A preliminary version of this document is called a *red herring*.

Proxy statement An annual statement issued by a company announcing the annual meeting and soliciting the shareholders' votes on director elections and other matters such as the officers' and employees' stock option plan. Certain required disclosures (e.g., officers' and directors' compensation and share ownership) are also reported here. This report and its content are specified by SEC rules, which also provide for minority and dissenting resolutions to be put before the shareholders.

Put bonds Bonds that give the holder the right to require the issuer to purchase the bonds at a set price, usually par, at some date prior to maturity.

Rapid Ratings A global credit and equities rating agency that provides letter-grade ratings on some 15,000 U.S. and foreign companies using objective financial criteria (versus the more subjective approach favored by Moody's and S&P).

Rate of return For bonds or preferreds, see **Current yield**.

Rating agencies Independent companies recognized by the SEC to provide comparative credit risk evaluations of debt issuers and debt issues. The most prominent issuers are Moody's, Standard & Poor's, and Fitch.

Ratings Ratings are based on an evaluation of an issuer's strength to meet its credit obligations. Credit risk concerns both the financial and moral obligations that an issuer of securities will meet its payments as promised.

	Moody's	S&P
Investment Grade		
Highest credit quality	Aaa	AAA
Minimal risk of meeting financial obligations		
Very high credit quality	Aa	AA
Little risk of meeting financial obligations		
High credit quality	A	A
Low risk of meeting financial obligations		
Medium credit quality adequate		
Quality for meeting financial obligations	Baa	BBB

	Moody's	S&P
Below Investment Grade		
Speculative credit quality	Ba	BB
Very thin coverage of meeting financial obligations		
Highly speculative credit quality	B	B
Questionable coverage of meeting financial obligations		
Vulnerable to default	Caa	CCC
Must have improved conditions to meet financial obligations		
Highly vulnerable to default	Ca	CC
Most likely will not meet financial obligations		
Lowest quality	C	C
Avoid—could be in default arrearage		
In default arrearage	C	D
Ratings modifiers (1 is highest)	1, 2, 3	+/−

Redemption   The repayment of a security at or before its maturity date. Redemption values are commonly at par and in some cases can be in the form of another security.

Real estate investment trust (REIT)   This family of preferreds is issued by a special-purpose corporation or trust that raises capital from investors to acquire or provide financing for all forms of income-producing real estate. These properties include shopping centers, hotels, office buildings, apartment complexes, health facilities, industrial properties, and more. Generally, a REIT does not pay corporate income tax if it distributes at least 90 percent of its taxable income to shareholders. To qualify for this tax treatment, at least 75 percent of gross income must come from rents of real property or interest income from mortgages on real property. Some of the preferreds have a clause that requires the REIT to pay the higher of the fixed minimum dividend or the common stock dividend.

Reset   Refers to the next scheduled date for a possible adjustment of the payout rate of a floating-rate or adjustable-rate security. Adjustments are calculated based on a defined index for the specific security.

Revenue bonds   A type of municipal bond backed only by the revenues generated by the project being financed. The bondholders may have a lien against specific assets should the project fail.

Rich   A term used to designate a security that costs more than other securities with similar risk, maturity, and return characteristics. This may come about because of the high-profile name of the company or because it has been generous in its treatment of creditors in the past. It can also come about because it's overpriced.

Rising star Any bond issue that is upgraded from below investment grade to investment grade.

Risk In the context of income securities, risk refers primarily to loss of principal or income because the company was unable to meet its obligations. This is also known as *credit risk* and does not refer to other risks associated with income securities, such as changes in interest rates or market risk.

Sarbanes-Oxley (SARBOX) Refers to reform legislation enacted by Congress following the Enron and WorldCom financial scandals. The legislation makes a company CEO directly responsible for the accuracy and completeness of all financial disclosures and specified criminal penalties for certain acts. It also expands the role of auditors in ensuring financial accuracy.

Savings bonds Bonds sold by the U.S. Treasury through banks at a discount from their face value. There is no secondary market for such bonds, and there is a penalty for early redemption. The most popular of these bonds are EE Series bonds.

Secondary market Once an income security is issued by its underwriters, all subsequent trading is done on a secondary market such as the NYSE, the over-the-counter market,s or the Nasdaq market.

Securities and Exchange Commission (SEC) The government agency charged with regulating the securities markets by promulgating and enforcing securities regulations. Any violations of securities laws, however, are prosecuted by the Department of Justice. All sales of securities in the United States must be registered with the SEC via the disclosure documents, which the SEC reviews and comments on but never approves. Its main concern these days is transparency in financial instruments and dealings.

Sinking fund Money accumulated on a regular basis in a separate custodial account that is used to redeem bonds or preferreds. Some bonds or preferreds have a mandatory retirement clause, which requires the issuer to retire a set number of securities each year for a set time frame. The securities can be purchased in the open market or selected by lot. The redemption date can be a specific date or can extend over a full year.

Soft call   A provision that can be attached to a convertible bond or preferred stock. If such a provision exists and the underlying stock of the convertible reaches a predetermined price for a set period of time, the bonds or preferreds become callable.

Sovereign risk   This term refers to the credit risk associated with a national entity such as a country. Such risk is considered good from the point of view that governments rarely go bankrupt or disappear. It is considered bad from the point of view that countries can rewrite the law or ignore the law with impunity.

Split rating   A debt security that has different levels of ratings, as between two of the three major rating agencies. Such rating differences are significant when one of the agencies rates an issue as below investment grade and the other(s) do not.

Spot price   The current market price or the price of the last trade.

Statement of cash flow   Also known as the *statement of sources and uses of funds*, it is a summary of the cash flows that occurred in a company during a particular reporting period. It reconciles the opening and closing balance sheets and explains how the cash demands from operations affected the closing cash position.

Statement of shareholders' equity   This financial statement reconciles the opening and closing shareholdings and shareholders' equity as reported on the balance sheet. It reports on share sales, share repurchases, exercise of stock options, changes to the balance sheet that did not arise from operations, and dividends.

Standard & Poor's   One of the major three independent credit rating agencies recognized by the SEC.

Step securities (up/down)   These securities have a specific schedule for changing the interest or dividend rate. Commonly called *step-up* or *step-down notes* or *preferreds*.

Subordinated debenture   A type of bond that is junior in claim to another bond by the same issuer. Such subordination is relevant only if the issuer defaults or goes into bankruptcy, since such debt has a lower-priority claim.

Symbol   The letter code used to identify a security on the exchange on which it trades. Note: Also called *ticker* or *stock symbol*.

10-K report   An annual filing with the SEC that is made by all publicly traded companies. The data disclosure requirements go beyond those found in the annual report, which is normally included by reference.

10-Q report A quarterly filing with the SEC made by all publicly traded companies for reporting their financial results for that period and year to date. The data is more abbreviated than in the annual report and requires no audit by an independent accountant.

Tender offer An issuer of a bond or preferred offers to buy back a specific security at a set price and for a set time period. Holders of the security are not obligated to accept the tender offer.

Third-party trust preferreds This family is similar to trust preferreds, except these preferreds are issued by a third party. A *depositor* corporation, usually a wholly owned limited-purpose subsidiary of a large brokerage firm, will buy bonds of a particular company, deposit them into a trust it establishes, which in turn will issue the $25.00 par value preferreds.

30-day wash sale rule The IRS will allow investors to sell a security and take a tax loss as long as they do not purchase the same or a very similar security 30 days before or after the tax loss sales date. You are free, however, to take a taxable gain without restriction.

Tombstone A newspaper advertisement for a new security issue that lists which investment firms are in the offering syndicate, a description of the issue and its size, and a warning that "this is not an offer to sell the security because we all know that can be done only through the offering prospectus."

Total return A measure of an investment's performance, including interest or dividends received, change in price, and any currency exchange gain or loss (for foreign securities).

Trade confirmation A formal memorandum given by a broker to a client detailing all the particulars of a transaction. In the case of a bond transaction, it must also specify whether the broker was acting as an agent or a dealer.

Tranche A portion of a CMO or CBO that has characteristics different from other portions of the total CMO pool of securities. It is sold as a separate security with its own unique CUSIP number.

Trading flat A bond that trades with no accrued interest, such as a bond in default or an income bond. Most bonds trade with accrued interest, meaning the buyer pays the seller the market price of the bond plus the accrued interest since the last payment date.

Treasury bill (T-bill)   Short-term U.S. Treasury obligations sold at a discount from their value at maturity. Maturities are for 91 days, 182 days, and 52 weeks.

Treasury bond   Long-term debt obligations of the U.S. Treasury running from 10 to 30 years in maturity. Interest is paid semiannually.

TreasuryDirect   A program under which individual investors can maintain an account with the U.S. Treasury and make noncompetitive bids on U.S. Treasury securities.

Treasury-indexed performance securities (TIPS)   A U.S. Treasury bond that has its principal value adjusted quarterly based on the consumer price index, thus providing protection against inflation.

Treasury notes   U.S. Treasury obligations with maturities of 2 to 10 years. Interest is paid semiannually.

Trust preferreds   This family of hybrid preferreds has characteristics of both bonds and preferred stocks, but is essentially a bond. These preferreds are issued by a business trust established by a parent company (e.g., ABC Corp. sets up ABC Capital Trust). The trust will issue the $25.00 par value hybrid preferred and lend the proceeds to its parent by purchasing a long-term (usually 30-year) subordinated bond. When the trust receives interest payments on the bond, it passes them directly to the preferred stockholder as monthly, quarterly. or semiannual distributions. Trust preferred shareholders are paid before regular preferred and common stock shareholders. Many trust preferreds have a deferrable interest clause. This means the underlying bond has a feature allowing the issuer to defer interest payments for up to five years. Distribution on the trust preferreds will continue to accrue during any deferral period, and investors must pay tax on the accrued, but unpaid, interest.

Underwriter   The investment banker or brokerage firm that brings a new security issue to market. The underwriter buys the issue from the issuer and then assumes all risk of reselling it. Its fee is made by being able to buy the entire issue at a discount from the issuer.

Unit investment trust   An unmanaged pool of income securities with a finite life designed for income investors. All income and principal from early calls is distributed to holders during the life of the trust and at maturity date, and any remaining securities are sold off and the principal distributed. Because they are unmanaged, the fees for such trusts are extremely low; however, the shares are illiquid.

Variable conversion rate The conversion rate of this type of convertible depends on the price of the common stock. Typically, the higher the common stock price the lower the conversion rate, and vice versa. Mandatory convertibles all have variable conversion rates based on the common stock the security converts into.

Variable rate These are securities with a variable interest or dividend rate. Their rate is usually related to the yield of another security (Treasury bills, notes, bonds) or to indexed lending rates such as the prime or LIBOR. The amount they pay will rise or fall in concert with the rate or yield they are related to. Thus, these securities are ideal for principal protection when rates are rising.

Window dressing When used in reference to a mutual fund, this refers to the practice of selling or buying certain securities before the end of a reporting quarter to dress up the investment portfolio. When used in reference to a corporation, it means accounting gimmickry, both legal and illegal, designed to dress up the financial statements or hide problems. The Enron scandal was all about this.

Wire house A full-service national or international brokerage firm.

Yankee bonds Dollar-denominated bonds sold in the United States by a foreign issuer.

Yield Return on an investor's capital investment, expressed as an annual percentage rate.

>**Current yield** The annual rate of return (stated as a percent) an investor will be paid on a specific bond or preferred based on the current price.

>>**Bonds** To calculate current yield for bonds, divide the coupon rate by the number shown as current price and multiply by 100. Example: (9.60% coupon ÷ 95 current price = 0.1010) × 100 = 10.10 percent current yield.

>>**Preferreds** To calculate current yield for preferreds, you must first get the dividend (issue) into dollars. To do this, divide the percent by 100 then multiply the results by the par value.

Example: (8.25% ÷ 100 = 0.0825) × $25.00 = $2.063. To complete the calculation for current yield, divide the dollar dividend by the current price of the security then multiply by 100. Example: ($2.063 ÷ current price $24.00 = 0.0859) × 100 = 8.59% current yield. Note: some preferreds show dividends in dollars.

Yield to call   The average annual return you would receive to the first call date. This includes any discount or premium to the stated call price.

Yield to maturity   The average annual return an investor would receive if the security is held to maturity. YTM includes total coupon payments to maturity, interest on interest, and any discount or premium to the par value or face value of the bond.

Yield to worst   The lower of yield to call or yield to maturity. The worst combination of all the possible call dates, maturity date, and call or maturity prices.

Yield curve   A graphic display of the yields for benchmark securities (vertical axis) with different maturities (horizontal axis). The benchmark securities are U.S. Treasuries with maturities from 1 to 30 years. The curve normally slopes upward, reflecting the greater yield required for the presumed higher risk of accepting a fixed rate of return over a longer time period. Changes in the slope of the curve are considered an important indicator of inflation and economic outlook.

Zero-coupon bonds   A bond sold at deep discount from its face (par) value that pays no interest until it matures at face value. Although no payments are made, holders of these bonds must pay taxes on the annual accrued interest. These securities are ideal for nontaxable accounts (IRAs).

INDEX

Adjustable rate-debt, 94, 132–134
  floor rates, 134
  mortgages, 164
  tax rate, 133–134
American Depository Receipts
  (ADRs), 121
American Depository Shares (ADS),
  121
Alternative minimum tax (AMT), 96,
  115, 187
American General Capital (AGC),
  109
American Institute of Certified
  Public accountants (AICPA), 78
American Municipal Bond
  Insurance Company (AMBAC),
  97
American Stock Exchange (ASE), 88
Argentina, 30
Armstrong World Industries, 167
Arnott, Robert, 3
Asset allocation, 5–10, 188
  by age groups, 7
  by convertible bonds, 9
  by high-dividend income, 9–10
  by interest-rate sensitivity, 9
  by preferred stock, 9
  by special situations, 10
  defined, 5
Associated Press (AP), 64
AT&T, 74–75

Baby Boomers, 6, 11–12, 54
Balance sheet, 73, 171–172
  book value, 74
  current assets, 73
  current liabilities, 74
  fixed assets, 73
  goodwill, 74, 172
Bank of America, 91
Bankers acceptances, 164–165
Bankruptcy, 10, 45–46, 51–52,
  62–64, 76, 90, 96, 105, 121, 163,
  167–174, 181
  Chapter 7 liquidation, 90, 170
  Chapter 9, 105
  Chapter 11, 105–106, 169–170
  claims, 103
  exclusivity periods, 170
  exit, 94
  international, 149
  prepackaged, 106
  recovery, 45–46
  risk of, 93
  settlement, 25–26
Basis points, 34–35, 45–48, 60, 91,
  133, 154
Bear Sterns & Company, 58, 68
Below-investment-grade bonds, 19,
  35, 46–52, 93–96,
Bernstein, Peter, 3
Bloomberg terminal, 89, 147
Bond funds, 145–149

Bonds, 81–83
  adjustable rate, 94
  acceleration of, 98
  below-investment-grade, 19, 35,
    44–52, 93–96
  broker, 89
  convertible, 9, 25, 33, 88–90, 110,
    127–132
  corporate, 82, 88–90, 113–114
  duration, 111–113
  early/premature redemption, 28,
    84
  flower, 91
  high-yield, 24, 44–46, 68, 107, 145
  indenture, 105–107
  investment grade, 4, 9, 13, 19, 24,
    34–35, 44–52, 154, 93–94
  junk, 24, 44–52, 24, 63, 92–93,
    113, 147–148
  municipal, 82, 96–105, 114–115,
    145, 148–149, 185
  original-issue discount (OID), 25,
    94, 178–181
  pay-in-kind, 94
  PET, 92, 118
  put, 95–96
  redemption, 24–25, 29, 84, 91,
    109, 132, 151, 153, 160,
    176–177
  step-up, 93–94, 180
  trustee, 105–106
  U.S. Treasury, 28, 30, 33–34, 38,
    45, 53, 82–88, 94–95, 109, 112,
    132, 145, 161
  zero-coupon, 25, 82, 84, 87,
    94–95, 180
Brokerage fees, 56–58
Buffet, Warren, 165
Business operating projection,
  171
Buy-write funds, 155, 175

California, the state of, 97, 148
Call:
  date, 23, 107–108
  provision, 106–109
Canadian Edge, 139
Canadian trusts, 9, 136–138, 141,
  179, 186–187
  energy and royalty, 9, 136–138,
    179, 186–187
  other, 138–139
  tax issues, 136–137, 187
Capital gains, 14, 83, 118, 139, 145,
  155, 175–177
Carry trade, 43
Cash flow statement 76–77
Caterpillar Inc., 91
CDs, 4, 6, 17, 33, 110–11
Certificate of deposit. *See* CDs
CIT Group, 91
Citigroup Global Markets,
  160–161
Closed-end funds (CEFs), 150,
  152–154, 175
  bond funds, 153
  preferred funds, 154
Collateralized debt, 164–165
Collateralized bond obligations
  (CBOs), 164
Collateralized debt obligations
  (CDOs), 24, 164
Collateralized loan obligations
  (CLOs), 164
Collateralized mortgage obligations
  (CMOs), 24, 81, 158, 164–165
Comcast, 160
Commercial paper, 164–165
Commissions:
  on bond transactions, 57, 83,
    89–90, 95, 120–121
Conrad, Rodger, Canadian Edge,
  139

Consumer price index (CPI), 86, 132
Convertible bonds, 9, 25, 33, 88–90, 110, 127–132, 176–177
  conversion clauses, 128, 130–132
  convertible preferreds, 129–132
  mandatory, 131
  tax treatment of, 132
Corporate Bonds, 82, 88–90, 113–114
  buying, 113–114
  coupon rate, 113
  current yield, 114
  interest payment, 113–114
  maturity date, 113
  yield to call, 114
Corporate takeover, 41–42
Coupon rates, 27, 85, 114–115, 186
Cramer, Jim, 59–60
Credit default swaps, 159–160
Credit rating agencies, 20, 40, 45–46, 48, 50–51, 62, 119, 122, 129, 132
Credit ratings, 43–52, 75, 79, 93, 149, 159
  changes, 48
  downgrades, 49–52, 75, 79, 93, 149, 159
  upgrades, 93
Current rate of return. *See* Current yield

Daimler-Chrysler, 91
Debt covenants, 62
Default:
  corporate, 46, 49, 63, 113, 159
  municipal, 97–98, 102, 104–106
  risk of, 45–46, 63, 93
  staged, 98
Defaulted Bonds Newsletter, 69
Depositor corporation, 120

Derivatives, 158, 164
Direct access notes (DANs), 90–92
Discretionary assets:
  calculating, 6
  classes, 6
  defined, 5
Diversification, 7–11
  among ratings quality, 8
  defined, 8
  limits on, 7–6
  over different income drivers, 8–9
  traditional mantras on, 7
Dividends, 68, 77, 110, 175–176, 178–179
  common stock, 140
  in arrears, 180–181
  preferred stock, 180
  scalping, 124–125
  strategies, 124–125, 175–176
Dividend Received Deduction (DRD, 117)
Dow Chemical, 91
Dow Jones Industrial Average, 144, 184–185
Duke Energy, 176
Drexel-Burnham Lambert, 92

Earnings, 77–78
  before interest, taxes, deprecation and amortizations (EBITDA), 78
  funds from operations (FFO), 78
EBITDA, 78
EDGAR system, 62–63
ELKS, 160–161
End game strategies, 173–174
Enron Corp., 48, 51, 70, 79
Equipment trust certificates (ETCs), 90
E*Trade, 58
Euro bonds:
  10-year, 34

Exchange-traded funds (ETFs), 149–152
fees, 150
Ex-dividend date, 25, 118, 124, 175–176, 180

Fair value pricing, 38
Fallen angels, 48, 63, 93
Fear:
in investing, 5, 18
Federal Deposit Insurance Corporation (FDIC), 17, 111
Federal Housing Association (FHA), 98
Federal Reserve Bank, the, 10, 17, 28, 52–56, 92, 141, 153, 159
Financial Analysis, example of, 66
Financial Analysts Journal, 3
Financial Guaranty Insurance Company (FGIC), 97
Financial Security Assurance Holdings (FSAH), 97
Financial statements, 71–79
management's discussion, 72–73
Fitch Ratings, 44, 49, 51–52
Fixed income securities:
when to sell, 40–41
Flight to quality, 19, 47, 147
Fooled by Randomness: The Hidden Role of Chance in Life and in the Markets, 150
Forbes/Lehmann Income Securities Investor Newsletter, 34, 183
Ford Motor Company (Ford), 39–40, 51–52, 62, 76, 92–93, 130, 186–187
Franklin, Ben, 3, 83
Fraud. *See* Accounting risk
Freddie Mac, 91, 133

General Electric (GE), 91
General Motors Co (GM) 10, 51–52, 76, 93, 123, 128, 159, 173, 186–187
Generally accepted accounting principals (GAAP), 78–79
GMAC, 187
Goldman Sachs Group, 134
Goodwill. *See* Balance sheet
Greed, 18
Greenspan, Alan, 54
Gulf War I, the, 19, 47, 147
Gulf War II, the, 47, 147

Hedge funds, 162–164
High-yield bonds, 24, 44–46, 68, 107, 145
fund, 145
marketability of, 46–47
Home equity, 11, 13
Housing and Urban Development Agency (HUD), 98
Hybrids, 118

IBM, 91, 123
Income statement, 75
gross profit, 75
net profit/(PAT), 75
operating income, 75
sales, general, and administrative expenses (SG&A), 75
Income stocks, 135–141
India Fund (IFN), the, 152
Individual Retirement Account (IRA), 12, 31, 95
Inflation, 2, 52, 85–86, 132
affect on fixed income securities, 2
versus 10-year treasuries, 30
Insured municipal bonds, 96–99, 114–115, 145, 148–149

Interest, 21
  accrued, 95, 114–115, 172
  calculating, 82
  compound, 31, 84
  payment types, 24–26
  tax treatment of, 27, 95
Interest rates, 21–34, 95, 111–112
  defined, 21
  fluctuation, 161
  long-term, 26, 28, 30, 112
  rise, 32–34, 132–133
  short-term, 26–28, 52, 112, 141
Internal Revenue Service (IRS), 32,
     82, 94, 121–122, 132, 169,
     174–175, 177–181
  Form 1040, 178
  Form 1099, 122, 146, 178–179
  Form 1116, 121, 178
International bond funds, 149
International Monetary Fund (IMF),
     149
InterNotes, 91–92
Investing fees, 56–57, 86
Investment-grade bonds, 4, 9, 13,
     19, 24, 34–35, 44–52, 93–94,154
Investor types
  buy and hold, 4
  desperate, 5
  scared, 4–5
  total return, 4
iShares Lehman TIPS Bond Fund
     (TIP), 86

"January effect," 175
J.C. Penney Company, 93
John Hancock Company, 91
Junior debt, 64, 129, 171–172
Junk bonds, 24, 44–52, 24, 63,
     92–93, 113, 147–148. *See also*
     High yield bonds funds,
     147–148

Kmart, 169
Kodak, 52

Laddering:
  bond maturities, 8, 95, 111
  a portfolio, 90–91
Las Vegas, 32
Lehman Brothers, 86, 109, 123
Leverage, 43
London Interbank Offered Rate
     (LIBOR), 33, 133
Long-Term Capital Management
     (LTCM), 159

Mad Money, 59
Margin, 44
Markets:
  of adverse selection, 88
  secondary, 62, 84, 87, 103
  type of, 24, 81
Maturity date, 23
Mergers, 41–42, 74
Merrill Lynch, 58, 123
Milken, Michael, 92
Mirant Corporation, 96, 159–160
Moody's, 44, 48–49, 52
Money market accounts and funds,
     110–111
Morgan Stanley, 161
Morningstar, 144, 146
Motorola Corp, 109
Municipal Bond Insurance
     Association (MBIA), 97
Municipal bonds, 82, 96–105,
     114–115, 145, 148–149, 185
  bankruptcy, 105
  buying, 103–104
  call date, 115
  conduit, 100
  coupon rate, 115
  default, 97–98, 102, 104–105

Municipal bonds *(Continued)*
  deterioration, 97
  funds, 145–147
  general obligation, 99
  housing, 98
  indenture, 102, 105–107
  insured, 96–99, 114–115, 145,
    148–149
  issuer, 115
  lower-rated, 99
  maturity, 115
  narrow revenue stream, 99
  official statement, 102
  project failure, 98–99, 103
  risk, 101
  secondary market, 103–4
  tax treatment of, 96–97, 99–101,
    103, 115
  taxable, 99–101
  trustees, 104–106
  underwriter, 102–103
  uninsured, 97
  unrated, 99, 101–103
Municipal bond funds, 145–147
Municipal Bonds Rulemaking Board
  (MSRP), 104
Municipal bond tax treatment,
  96–97, 99–101, 103, 115
Mutual funds, 5–7, 11, 47, 57, 110,
  143–155, 162, 188
  fees, 57, 144–146, 149, 162
  open-end, 188

Nasdaq Composite, 184–185
Net asset value (NAV), 11, 151–154,
  175
New Jersey, the state of, 101, 148
New York, the state of, 97, 148
New York Stock Exchange (NYSE),
  69, 88, 118–119, 154
Northern Trust, 58
Notes. *See* Bonds.

Original-issue discount (OID), 25,
  94, 178–181
  accrual, 181
Over-the-counter (OTC) market, 24

Palm Beach, FL, 99, 115
Pari passu, 64
Putable Automatic Rate Reset
  Securities (PARRS), 161–162
Pay-in-kind-securities (PIK), 25
Penn West Energy Trust, 137
Poison pill defense, 109
Preferreds, 23, 35, 117–125, 161
  bankruptcy, 121
  buying, 122–125
  call date, 108
  call provisions, 120
  convertible, 129–132
  defined, 23
  designator, 123
  families, 117–118
  foreign, 121
  mandatory convertible,
    176–177
  partnerships, 121–122
  preferred equity traded (PET)
    bonds, 92, 118
  perpetual preferred stock, 122
  stock, 175–176
  stop-loss orders, 125
  symbol, 122–123
  taxation, 176–177
  third-party trust preferreds,
    120–121
  trust preferreds, 92,119–120,
    175–176
  yields, 35–37
Prime West Energy Trust, 137
Profit after tax (PAT). *See* Income
  statement.
Provident Energy Trust, 137
Prospectus, 60–69, 105

Prudential Financial Inc, 91
Put provision, 107, 109–110

Qualified dividend income (QDI), 35, 129, 133–134, 153, 178, 186–187

Rapid Ratings International Inc., 40
Real estate investment trusts (REITS), 17, 129, 135, 139–140, 187
Repos, 164–165
Retirement planning, 11–13
Reverse mortgage, 174
Rising stars, 48
Risk, 17–21, 46, 50, 93, 148
    accounting, 19–20, 69–71
    flight to quality, 19, 47, 147
    (high) in the future, 17
    objective, 19–20
    of default, 46, 63
    subjective, 18–19
Royalty trust, 136–137

S&P 500 Index, 139, 144, 184–185
Sallie Mae. *See* SLM Corp.
San Diego, CA, 101
Sarbanes Oxley Act (SOX), 65, 69–71, 173
SBC Communications, 74
Schwab, Charles, 58
Scott Trade, 58
Sears Holding Corporation, 93
Securities and Exchange Commission (SEC), 20, 43, 62, 78, 80, 102
Senior debt, 62, 64, 119, 129
SEQUINS, 160–161
Shareholders' equity statement, 77–78
Sinking fund provisions, 29, 62
SLM Corp. (Sallie Mae), 133
Social security, 11, 13, 53–55, 148

Special situation investment, 8, 187
Spitzer, Elliot, 151
Standard & Poor's (S&P), 44, 49, 52
Stocks, income, 135–6

Taleb, Nassim, 150
Tax:
    foreign, 178
    law, 155
    loss carryforward, 174–176
    reporting,177–180
    refund, 178
    return, 177–179
    strategies/planning, 27, 43, 107, 174–180
Taxable income, 15, 27, 117, 125, 129
10-K report, 72
Tennessee Valley Authority (TVA), 161–162
Tranches, 164
TreasuryDirect program, 87–88, 92, 152
Treasury Indexed Performance Securities (TIPS), 27–28, 34, 60, 84–86, 132
    tax treatment of, 85
Trust preferreds, 92,119–120, 175–176

Uncertainty:
    in investing, 20–21
Unit investment trusts (UITs), 157–158
USG Corporation, 167, 172
U.S. Attorney, 170
U.S. energy trusts, 187
U.S. Treasuries, 28, 30, 33–34, 38, 45, 53, 82–88, 94–95, 109, 112, 132, 145, 161
    1-year, 109
    2-year, 84

U.S. Treasuries *(Continued)*
  3-year, 84
  5-year, 84–85, 112
  10-year, 30, 34, 38, 84–6,
    112, 132
  30-year, 85, 112, 161
  series EE bonds, 94–95
  T-bills, 84, 87

Vulture fund/investor, 169, 172
Volatility
  in share price, 155
  in stock returns, 2

Xerox, 52

Wall Street Journal, The, 61, 65
Welch, Jack, 70
William Blair & Co, 57

Yield, 21–24
  comparative, 34–38,
  current, 22, 114–115
  to call, 23, 107–108
  to maturity, 22–3, 114–115
  to worst, 23, 114–115
Yield curve, 26, 33–34, 110, 141
  inverted, 26, 110, 141

Zero-coupon bonds, 25, 82, 84, 87,
  94–95, 180